BRANDING & TRADE MARKS HANDBOOK

FOR CHARITABLE AND NOT-FOR-PROFIT ORGANIZATIONS

Terrance S. Carter

U. Shen Goh

Imagine Canada

Give. Volunteer. Engage
Donner. S'engager. Agir

LexisNexis®
Butterworths

Branding & Trade Marks Handbook For Charitable and Not-For-Profit Organizations
© LexisNexis Canada Inc. 2006
July 2006

Members of the LexisNexis Group worldwide

Canada	LexisNexis Canada Inc, 123 Commerce Valley Dr. E. Suite 700, MARKHAM, Ontario
Argentina	Abeledo Perrot, Jurisprudencia Argentina and Depalma, BUENOS AIRES
Australia	Butterworths, a Division of Reed International Books Australia Pty Ltd, CHATSWOOD, New South Wales
Austria	ARD Betriebsdienst and Verlag Orac, VIENNA
Chile	Publitecsa and Conosur Ltda, SANTIAGO DE CHILE
Czech Republic	Orac, sro, PRAGUE
France	Éditions du Juris-Classeur SA, PARIS
Hong Kong	Butterworths Asia (Hong Kong), HONG KONG
Hungary	Hvg Orac, BUDAPEST
India	Butterworths India, NEW DELHI
Ireland	Butterworths (Ireland) Ltd, DUBLIN
Italy	Giuffré, MILAN
Malaysia	Malayan Law Journal Sdn Bhd, KUALA LUMPUR
New Zealand	Butterworths of New Zealand, WELLINGTON
Poland	Wydawnictwa Prawnicze PWN, WARSAW
Singapore	Butterworths Asia, SINGAPORE
South Africa	Butterworth Publishers (Pty) Ltd, DURBAN
Switzerland	Stämpfli Verlag AG, BERNE
United Kingdom	Butterworths Tolley, a Division of Reed Elsevier (UK), LONDON, WC2A
USA	LexisNexis, DAYTON, Ohio

Library and Archives Canada Cataloguing in Publication

Carter, Terrance S.
    Branding & trade marks handbook for charitable and not-for-profit organizations / Terrance S. Carter, U. Shen Goh.

Includes index.
ISBN 0-433-45146-7

    1. Trademarks—Law and legislation—Canada. 2. Charity laws and legislation—Canada. 3. Nonprofit organizations—Law and legislation—Canada. I. Goh, U. Shen. II. Title. III. Title: Branding and trade-marks handbook for charitable and not-for-profit organizations.

KE2988.C37 2006   346.7104'88   C2006-901088-9
KF3180.C37 2006

Printed and bound in Canada.

ABOUT THE AUTHORS

Terrance Carter is the Managing Partner of Carters Professional Corporation, and practises in the area of charity and not-for-profit law. *Lexpert* and *The Best Lawyers in Canada* have recognized Mr. Carter as one of the leading experts in the area of charity, trust and not-for-profit law in Canada. Mr. Carter is also a registered Trade-mark Agent and a member of the Intellectual Property Institute of Canada and acts as legal counsel to the Toronto office of the national law firm Fasken Martineau DuMoulin LLP on charitable matters.

Mr. Carter is a member of Canada Revenue Agency's (CRA) Charity Advisory Committee, and the Technical Issues Committee of CRA's Charities Directorate representing the Canadian Bar Association (CBA), a past member of the Uniform Law Conference of Canada Task Force on Uniform Fundraising Legislation, Past Chair of the Charity and Not-for-Profit Law Sections of both the CBA and Ontario Bar Association (OBA), a member of the Government Relations Committee of the Canadian Association of Gift Planners (CAGP), a past director and founding member of the Christian Legal Fellowship and was the 2002 recipient of the AMS — John Hodgson Award of the OBA. He is also a member of the Association of Fundraising Professionals, and the American Bar Association Tax Exempt Section. He has participated in consultations with the Public Guardian and Trustee of Ontario, the Charities Directorate of CRA, and was a member of the Anti-terrorism Committee of the CBA in its submission to Parliament.

Mr. Carter has written numerous articles and been a frequent speaker on legal issues involving charities and not-for-profit organizations for the Law Society of Upper Canada, the CBA, the OBA, the Association of Fund Raising Professionals, the American Bar Association, the CAGP, the Canadian Tax Foundation, The Institute of Chartered Accountants, the Canadian Society of Association Executives, the New York University School of Law and the University of Waterloo Master of Tax program. He is a co-editor of *Charities Legislation & Commentary, 2006 Edition* (LexisNexis Butterworths), a contributing author to the *Primer for Directors of Not-for-Profit Corporations* (Industry Canada), and to *The Management of Charitable and Not-for-Profit Organizations in Canada* (LexisNexis Butterworths). Mr. Carter is also the editor of, and a contributor to, *Charity Law Bulletin*, and *Anti-Terrorism and Charity Law Alert*, and the websites <http://www.charitylaw.ca>, <http://www.churchlaw.ca>,

<http://www.carters.ca>, and <http://www.antiterrorismlaw.ca>, as well as Chair of the annual *Church & Charity Law* Seminar.

U. Shen Goh practises law with Carters Professional Corporation. Ms. Goh is also a registered Trade-mark Agent, whose practice focuses primarily on intellectual property and privacy law, as well as human rights and employment litigation. After graduating from Osgoode Hall Law School in 2001, Ms. Goh went on to obtain her LL.M. in 2003 from the School of Law at the University of San Diego, where her research focus was on the international protection of well-known trade-marks, and where she received the School of Law Merit Scholarship, as well as the Honorable Lillian Y. Lim Scholarship. Ms. Goh's experience prior to joining Carters includes being a Law Lecturer on international trade regulation, legal research and writing, and other fundamental courses in law for Ph.D. students and government officials at the Southwest University of Political Science & Law in China, as well as interning at the City of Toronto, the City of San Diego, and Parkdale Community Legal Services in Toronto.

Ms. Goh is a member of the Intellectual Property Institute of Canada, as well as the Privacy, Intellectual Property and Employment Sections of the Ontario Bar Association, and she has written articles for *The Lawyers Weekly*, the *Canadian Association eZine*, and Carters' *Charity Law Bulletin*.

ACKNOWLEDGMENTS

We wish to thank Elizabeth Gouthro, B.A., a registered trademark agent and senior Associate with Fasken Martineau DuMoulin LLP, for lending her extensive experience and knowledge in reviewing this handbook.

We would also like to thank Nancy E. Claridge, B.A., M.A., LL.B., our articling student, for the extensive amount of time and effort she spent researching and editing the book.

TABLE OF CONTENTS

INTRODUCTION

Trade mark law is perhaps one of the oldest, most pervasive and complex areas of intellectual property law, elements of which can be traced back to the ancient Egyptians. Trade marks can be found at common law as well as in statutes and treaties, and can be found in both the national and international contexts. Perhaps because trade marks are generally associated with commerce — most public trade mark disputes are over high-profile commercial brands — charitable and not-for-profit organizations generally do not recognize the importance of trade marks in their non-commercial world. Consider, for example, the growing trend of trade marks to not just identify the source of products, but to create new commodities in which the trade mark becomes part of the product.[1] Instead of the discreet mark to identify the source, the mark is prominently displayed on clothing and accessories. Examples would be ROOTS, GAP and NIKE. In many instances the product is less important than the trade mark, as the trade mark denotes status, loyalty, belonging or admiration. Accordingly, trade marks in their own right have been valuable assets for sports teams and movies, bringing into question the traditional theory that one of the benefits of trade marks was in reducing consumer search costs by requiring the producer of the trade marked good to "maintain a consistent quality over time and across consumers".[2]

But the traditional economic analysis of trade marks law or the newer concept of trade marks as valuable commodities may have little resonance for organizations that traditionally depend on the philanthropic nature of individuals in order to support their good works. Yet, in recent years, trade mark issues have taken on a greater significance for charitable and not-for-profit organizations and, as a result, are requiring these organizations to become more familiar with the issues surrounding one of their most valuable assets.

---

[1] Alex Kozinski, "Trademarks Unplugged" (1993) 68 N.Y.U.L. Rev. 960.
[2] William M. Landes & Richard A. Posner, "Trademark Law: An Economic Perspective" (1987) 30 J.L. & Econ. 265 at 269.

DEFINING CHARITABLE AND NOT-FOR-PROFIT ORGANIZATIONS[3]

It is important to recognize that while all charities are not-for-profit organizations, not all not-for-profit organizations are charities. As such, care should be taken when referring to such organizations. Additionally, despite the growth in the number and size of charitable and not-for-profit organizations in Canada,[4] the legal framework from both the federal and provincial governments has not kept pace, relying heavily upon concepts developed in the seventeenth and nineteenth centuries, thereby leaving the distinction between the various types of charities and not-for-profit organizations in a somewhat confused state. This is particularly so for members of the public, who often use the terms interchangeably.

Charitable and not-for-profit organizations operate on a not-for-profit basis, in that both must devote all of their resources to their activities and neither may distribute any income to members, officers, directors, or trustees. Both are exempt from tax on their income (with some exception for not-for-profit organizations), and both will often have similar governance structures. Charitable and not-for-profit organizations are, however, two distinct types of legal entities with different legal obligations and rights. An organization which has charitable objects is much more limited in the types of activities it can engage in, but in return, receives substantial advantages in carrying out its objects by being able to issue charitable receipts for income tax purposes in response to donations that are received.

At law, charity has a specific meaning that often eludes the popular conception. For an organization to be considered charitable at law, its objects or purposes must be undertaken to achieve a charitable purpose. Presently, only four categories or heads of charity are recognized in Canadian law. In the seminal decision of *Special Commissioners of Income*

---

[3] This section is reprinted in part by permission of LexisNexis Canada Inc. from Terrance S. Carter & Karen J. Cooper, "The Legal Context of Not-for-Profit Management" in Vic Murray, ed., *The Management of Charitable and Not-for-Profit Organizations in Canada* (Toronto: LexisNexis Canada) [forthcoming]. For detailed commentary on the law of charitable and not-for-profit organizations, see Donald J. Burgeois, *The Law of Charitable and Not-for-Profit Organizations*, 3d ed. (Markham, Ont.: Butterworths, 2002).

[4] For example, Statistics Canada released the results of its survey of charitable and not-for-profit organizations in 2004, which indicated that there were approximately 161,000 such organizations in Canada in 2003. These organizations had revenues totalling $112 billion ($8 billion of which came from individual donations), and they drew upon two billion volunteer hours and 139 million memberships. See Michael H. Hall *et al.*, *Cornerstones of the Community: Highlights of the National Survey of Nonprofit and Voluntary Organizations* (Ottawa: Statistics Canada, 2004) at 7, 9 and 10.

Tax v. Pemsel,[5] Lord MacNaghten identified four heads of charity: relief of poverty, advancement of education, advancement of religion, and other purposes beneficial to the community not falling under any of the preceding heads. This definition is mirrored in Ontario's *Charities Accounting Act*[6] (the "CAA"), and although the federal *Income Tax Act*[7] (the "ITA") does not make specific reference to these categories, both the Charities Directorate of Canada Revenue Agency ("CRA") and the courts rely on the same categories in regulating the sector. The Supreme Court of Canada, in *Vancouver Society of Immigrant and Visible Minority Women v. Canada (Minister of National Revenue)*,[8] clarified the Canadian approach to recognizing charities, noting that while the ITA focuses on the character of the activity undertaken by the organization, thereby linking them to the categories established in *Pemsel*, the focus should be on the purpose in furtherance of which an activity is carried out in order to determine whether charitable status should be granted. An organization with objects and activities that fall into one of these four categories will qualify as a registered charity for the purposes of the ITA. A registered charity may take one of three legal forms, depending upon the types of activities undertaken and the relationship between the organization and its main source of funds: (1) a charitable organization; (2) a public foundation; or (3) a private foundation.

Under the ITA, a non-profit organization is defined as a

> ... club, society or association that ... was not a charity ... and that was organized and operated exclusively for social welfare, civic improvement, pleasure or recreation or for any other purpose except profit, no part of the income of which was payable to, or was otherwise available for the personal benefit of, any proprietor, member or shareholder ... .[9]

The ITA clearly establishes that, for its purposes, non-profit organizations and charities are two mutually exclusive categories of organizations, and expressly provides that a non-profit organization is not a charity. As such, any organization whose objects and activities fall exclusively within the four heads of charity discussed above is not a non-profit organization and should seek registration as a charity under the ITA in order to avoid being taxed on its income. Although a non-profit organization, like a charity, has tax exempt status and does not pay tax on income or capital gains (except

---

[5] [1891] A.C. 531 (H.L.) [hereinafter "*Pemsel*"].
[6] R.S.O. 1990, c. C.10.
[7] R.S.C. 1985 (5th Supp.), c. 1.
[8] [1999] S.C.J. No. 5, [1999] 1 S.C.R. 10 [hereinafter "*Vancouver Society*"].
[9] *Income Tax Act*, R.S.C. 1985 (5th Supp.), c. 1, s. 149(1)(l).

income from property of an organization whose main purpose is to provide dining, recreation, or sporting facilities), it is not able to issue charitable receipts for income tax purposes. However, it is not required to disburse a specified percentage of its earnings.

TRADE MARKS AND CHARITABLE AND NOT-FOR-PROFIT ORGANIZATIONS

Regardless of a charitable organization's status under the ITA, both statute and the common law place a heavy burden upon its directors to ensure that all assets of an organization are properly identified, protected and applied in fulfilment of the organization's objects, particularly if it is a charity. The assets of an organization in this regard include the organization's intellectual property. This follows from the fiduciary obligation placed upon directors of a charity (as opposed to a not-for-profit organization) to act as trustee-like stewards of the charitable property entrusted to them and to take appropriate steps to protect those charitable assets. As such, familiarity with trade mark issues is especially important for today's charities. Yet the protection of an organization's trade marks should be just as important to a not-for-profit organization, as the trade marks of both charitable and not-for-profit organizations may be the most valuable asset the organization owns, and failure to protect this asset could have serious and, in some situations, even disastrous consequences for both the organization and its directors.

Of course, directors of these organizations cannot take steps to protect the trade marks of a charitable or not-for-profit organization if they do not know anything about trade marks or how vulnerable the intellectual property rights are that are associated with trade marks. As a result, directors need to take the initiative to learn about trade marks, the nature of the intellectual property rights in trade marks, the risks to trade mark rights, and the steps required to protect trade mark rights.

Consequently, some general familiarity with trade mark issues should be a practical necessity for lawyers who advise the more than 161,000 charitable and not-for-profit organizations that currently are in operation in Canada,[10] as it is often the general practitioner and not the trade mark agent who is in the best position to bring trade mark matters to a client's attention. This is particularly so for charitable and not-for-profit organizations which seldom, if ever, contact a trade mark agent, partly as a result of the perceived

---

[10]   Michael H. Hall, *et al.*, *Cornerstones of the Community: Highlights of the National Survey of Nonprofit and Voluntary Organizations* (Ottawa: Statistics Canada, 2004) at 4.

expense involved and partly because of a general lack of understanding of trade mark issues.

More often than not, it is only after a problem develops that charitable or not-for-profit organizations become aware of trade marks issues, learning with surprise or dismay that it is too late to do anything to reverse the damage that has been done. As can be expected, there is little point in the lawyer explaining trade mark issues to the organization's directors after the fact. Instead, what is needed is proactive legal risk management advice concerning trade mark issues. Therefore, it is increasingly important that lawyers who are advising charitable and not-for-profit organizations become familiar with trade mark issues affecting their clients.

Unfortunately, while there are a number of resources available on trade marks in general, the focus tends to be on for-profit business, and there are few resource materials available for the charitable or not-for-profit organization. This book is an attempt to fill this void by providing an overview of some of the key trade mark concepts for charitable or not-for-profit organizations and the lawyers who advise them. Although this book focuses on trade mark issues that are unique to charitable and not-for-profit clients, the comments and observations contained herein may have equal application for for-profit clients as well.

CHAPTER 1

BRANDING AND ITS IMPORTANCE TO CHARITABLE AND NOT-FOR-PROFIT ORGANIZATIONS

1. What is Branding?
2. Why Bother Branding?
    (a) Identify the owner
    (b) Distinguish the ware or service
    (c) Increase market share
    (d) Create equity
3. Importance of Branding to Charitable and Not-For-Profit Organizations
    (a) Identify the charitable or not-for-profit organization
    (b) Distinguish the charitable or not-for-profit organization
    (c) Increase market share
    (d) Create equity
4. Branding, Marketing and Trade Marks
5. How Trade Marks Become Wasting Assets for Charitable or Not-For-Profit Organizations
    (a) Failing to conduct searches
    (b) Failing to stop unauthorized uses
    (c) Failing to regulate authorized uses
    (d) Failing to use
    (e) Failing to register
Summary

Statistics Canada indicates that there are more than 161,000 charitable and not-for-profit organizations currently operating in Canada.[1] This includes hospitals, universities, private schools, food banks, environmental groups, day-care centres, sports clubs, places of worship, social justice groups, groups that raise funds and awareness for various diseases, *etc.* Collectively, the 161,000 charitable and not-for-profit organizations have revenues totaling $112 billion,[2] $8 billion of which come from individual donations.[3] These organizations also draw upon two billion volunteer hours and 139 million memberships.[4] Certainly, these numbers are impressive.

Yet, an important issue for all of the 161,000 charitable and not-for-profit organizations to consider is: what makes an organization stand out from all the others? How can an organization ensure that it attracts not only the funding required to finance its operations, but the necessary people to carry out its operations and the constituency that it is intended to serve? How can one ensure that an organization does not lose donors and constituents to fraudulent or opportunistic individuals or organizations?

While there is not a single answer to those questions, one of the most effective means of protecting an organization, and in turn its donors and constituents, is by effectively branding the organization. As such, this chapter provides a brief introduction to the importance of branding for the charitable and not-for-profit organization, as well as the importance in avoiding the organization's trade marks from becoming a wasting asset.

1.   WHAT IS BRANDING?

Branding is the marking of wares or services for the purpose of identification.[5] It is an ancient process originating from the Egyptians, who burned marks into the hides of their livestock or made impressions in their pottery in order to identify themselves as the owner of the livestock or pottery. Throughout history, archaeological evidence suggests that marks have been used to identify the makers of everything from bricks, tiles, jars, tools, pottery and water pipes to even loaves of bread! In 1365, the City of London even went so far as to pass an ordinance requiring every smith to mark the swords, knives and other weapons they made, "so that every

---

[1]   Michael H. Hall, *et al.*, *Cornerstones of the Community: Highlights of the National Survey of Nonprofit and Voluntary Organizations* (Ottawa: Statistics Canada, 2004) at 7.
[2]   *Ibid.* at 10.
[3]   *Ibid.* at 9.
[4]   *Ibid.*
[5]   *Black's Law Dictionary*, 6th ed., *s.v.* "brand".

man's work might be known by his mark".[6] In modern days, the concept of branding is more complex, as it no longer serves merely to identify the owner of a ware or service, but also to distinguish the wares or services of a business from those of its competitors, which can lead to an increase in market share and can even create equity in the goodwill associated with the brand.

Naturally, this leads one to wonder what can be used to mark one's wares or services. In other words, what is a brand? A brand is any word, mark, symbol, design, term or a combination of these used for the purpose of identifying some ware or service.[7] In the past, one could put whatever mark one wished on the livestock or pottery as the identifying mark of ownership. Nowadays, one cannot compose his or her own brand as freely. One reason for this is that in present commercial terms, a brand is much more than just a word, mark, a symbol, design, term or combination of these. Another reason stems from the proliferation of brands already on the market and the concerns with regard to the registrability of certain brands as trade marks, which will be addressed later in this book.

2.   WHY BOTHER BRANDING?

Most organizations do not operate in an insular world, where there is only one grocer, one baker, one church and one university. Rather, we live in an environment where there is constant competition, even in the charitable and not-for-profit sector. With competition, it is important that the organization brand itself so that the public can easily identify the owner of the brand and distinguish the ware or service from the organization's competitor. In turn, the organization can increase its market share and create equity.

(a) Identify the owner

The original purpose of branding was to identify the owner. Owners burned marks into the hide of their livestock or made impressions in their pottery so that if an animal strayed or if a piece of pottery was stolen, its lawful owner could be identified easily through the brand.

---

[6]   Gordon Sustrik & Emery Jamieson, *Trade mark Transactions: Assignments, Licences and Security Interests* (Sponsored by the Patent and Trademark Institute of Canada, 1999) at 4.

[7]   *Black's Law Dictionary*, 6th ed., *s.v.* "brand".

(b) Distinguish the ware or service

Farmers and craftspeople selling their livestock and pottery realized a second purpose for branding: to distinguish the ware or service of a farmer or craftsperson from those of his or her competitors. This also enabled the buyer to predetermine the quality of the ware by identifying the seller through the brand. For example, whether buying a cow directly from Farmer Bob at his farm or indirectly from the county fair, the brand on the cow confirmed that the cow was from Farmer Bob's herd and allowed the buyer to make certain prejudgments about the quality of the livestock through his or her knowledge of Farmer Bob's farming practices or previous purchases of Farmer Bob's livestock.

The same principle applies today. Branding can protect buyers by identifying a ware or its source, thereby distinguishing the ware from its competition. By relying on the brand, today's buyer of various wares and services can be assured that the ware or service purchased is indeed what it claims to be; for example, an authentic MONOPOLY game as opposed to a cheap rip-off. In the same way, today's buyer ordering an ANGUS BEEF steak is reassured about the quality of the steak by the knowledge that the steak is certified to be ANGUS BEEF steak, and by familiarity with the strict requirements for a steak to receive the ANGUS BEEF certification. As such, branding has evolved from simply protecting the owner to also protecting the buyer.

(c) Increase market share

This has led to a third purpose of using branding as a means to increase market share.

First, businesses use branding to market their wares and services to members of the public who have never bought their wares or used their services before. This is difficult to do in today's society, where buyers often no longer have personal knowledge of the wares they are purchasing or personal relationships with the manufacturers of the wares. For example, today's buyer cannot walk down the street to share a coffee with his neighbour Sven while Sven takes a break from building the buyer's new chair in the workshop. However, today's buyer can drive to the IKEA store to buy a chair and know what to expect of the chair's quality, even though he has never bought an IKEA chair before and does not know who designed the chair, who built the parts, who assembled the parts, who packaged the chair or who delivered the chair. Branding tells the buyer what the ware is, who manufactured it, what the values of the manufacturer are and what to expect of the ware's quality.

Second, businesses use branding to make their wares and services so desirable to the public that the public will not settle for a substitute, even if the substitute is cheaper. Effective branding can imbue a ware with a certain prestige factor related to a perception of the quality of the ware or the type of person who would own a certain ware or brand. For example, Jaguar Cars Limited, the manufacturer of JAGUAR automobiles, markets itself as not only selling a car, but also selling "premium luxury" and "the Jaguar lifestyle". This prestige factor has permitted the company to claim a premium for its cars because people wanting to be associated with a certain lifestyle or with the perceived quality of the car are willing to spend more for the Jaguar brand. As such, branding has evolved from simply identifying the owner to a powerful tool by which businesses can increase the market share of their wares and services.

(d) Create equity

The fourth purpose of branding is to create equity in the goodwill associated with the brand. In today's society, brands play a vital role in helping a business grow and become profitable. They create goodwill by promoting a positive image of the business, thereby increasing the value of the business. Accordingly, brands can now be recognized as an asset of the business and can also be included in calculating the equity of a business. In fact, a brand may become the most valuable asset of a business or may be even more valuable than all the physical assets of the business. For example, someone looking to purchase the local furniture shop may pay mostly for the physical inventory owned by the business and may not pay much, if anything at all, for the name of the local furniture shop. However, someone looking to purchase the IKEA corporation may pay more for the business than the value of the physical inventory. Why? This is because the value of the IKEA brand drives up the purchase price. As such, branding has evolved from simply identifying the owner to a powerful tool by which a business can increase its equity.

Given the proliferation of competing brands on the market, however, some people argue that brands have outlived their usefulness. A brief search on the Internet reveals an animated discussion about the demise of branding.[8] Traditional brands, it would seem, have lost their power to attract the public or retain public loyalty as new brands are introduced to the marketplace and the public becomes more savvy and less willing to pay a premium for a ware simply because of the name on the label.

The proliferation of brands in the commercial sphere has levelled the playing field and taken the premium out of a brand. In doing so, it has arguably taken the prestige factor out of brands and returned the focus to the protection of the public by providing clarity and knowledge. For example, NOKIA ranked sixth among the world's most valuable brands in 2002, valued at $30 billion; however, Nokia's sales fell in 2003 when it failed to produce the clamshell-design cell phones that its competitors were producing, resulting in a $6 billion decrease in its equity.[9] In a sense then, contrary to the view that the apparent importance of branding underscores its demise, it would seem rather that the apparent demise of branding actually affirms its importance. Rather than being a platform for a certain prestige associated with the use of a particular brand, the brand can once again become a tool to guide the buyer through the bewildering array of choices in the market.

3.   IMPORTANCE OF BRANDING TO CHARITABLE AND NOT-FOR-PROFIT ORGANIZATIONS

The role of branding in an increasingly competitive marketplace is fairly obvious. But what does this mean for the non-commercial world of charities and not-for-profit organizations? Does the concept of branding apply to these types of organizations? How can they benefit from branding? Why is it important for a charitable or not-for-profit organization to protect its trade marks?

(a) Identify the charitable or not-for-profit organization

The importance of branding to a charitable or not-for-profit organization must be looked at from two viewpoints: that of the donor or user, and that of the charitable or not-for-profit organization. With respect to the potential donor or user, the original purpose of branding — to identify the owner — appears at first blush to be inapplicable to charitable and not-for-profit

---

[8]   Cory Doctorow, "Brands aren't worth as much as we thought" (6 November 2004), online: Boing Boing: A Directory of Wonderful Things <http://boingboing.net/2004/11/06/brands_arent_worth_a.html>.
[9]   *Ibid.*

organizations, since they are not established to sell products or provide services on a for-profit basis. In the commercial world, the buyer who purchases a ware or service receives a concrete object or a benefit in one form or another from the transaction, whether or not the ware or service has a brand. A brand simply helps to identify some desirable characteristic of the ware or service, such as quality, style, or prestige. Charitable or not-for-profit organizations, on the other hand, do not usually offer a tangible benefit to the donor or user. Rather, they offer the donor an intangible benefit of a sense of well-being: the knowledge that the donor has done something good by contributing to a person or to society (in the case of a charity) or using a service or purchasing an item on a non-for-profit basis (in the case of a not-for-profit organization).

By way of examples involving charities, consider the parishioner who regularly donates offerings to his or her church; the trucker who gives a donation to a medical research organization to pursue research into cures for breast cancer; or the philanthropist who gives to the town's operatic association. The parishioner receives the return of knowing that the church will be able to continue providing the opportunity for people to worship in accordance with that church's creed, but the donor himself or herself may never set foot in the church or may only attend the celebration of certain rites. The trucker who donates to breast cancer research may be a man whose wife or mother has suffered from breast cancer, but he could equally have no connection with the disease and therefore receives no direct or indirect benefit from his donation other than the knowledge that he has contributed to a worthy cause. The philanthropist may dislike opera but feel that the arts in general need support in order to provide future generations with the opportunity to benefit from them.

These examples illustrate that most people will assist others in need or donate to civic causes as long as doing so gives them a sense of satisfaction from having done something worthwhile. However, potential donors often do not have direct contact with people in need or cannot, by themselves, make any appreciable impact on the need. Most donors do not have the ability to assess needs or determine the impact of their gift. Absent these abilities, many will not give, as they cannot ascertain that their donation has actually accomplished something worthwhile.

In this respect, charitable and not-for-profit organizations can be said to function as financial intermediaries of sorts. They are in the business of matching donors and users with needs, thus providing a necessary service. They are connected. They make it their business to be aware of society's needs and to seek out the most efficient ways of meeting those needs. Because it is their business, they are also in a position to do an appropriate follow-up in order to measure the effectiveness of the aid. Thus, when a donor gives to a trusted charitable or not-for-profit organization that has a significant track record, she can be reasonably confident that she is, in fact, getting the service which she is purchasing — her donation will go to help the needy in the way the donor intends. This point has been demonstrated consistently in the surveys by the global public relations firm Edelman International, which shows that the not-for-profit organization GREENPEACE has bigger and better brand recognition in Europe than such for-profit organizations like MCDONALD'S.[10] Effectively developing the brand for such organizations like Greenpeace has meant developing the "trust factor", which is seen as a key factor to soliciting donations. As one expert academic on marketing and brands has stated: "Giving to Unicef means you trust your money will be spent helping people thousands of miles away who need it".[11]

In the same way, branding can be essential for clients and users to identify which charitable or not-for-profit organization to turn to for assistance. Without an identifiable brand, there may be confusion as to what services the organization can provide. Such a problem was one of the reasons behind the recent name change for PLANNED PARENTHOOD CANADA to the CANADIAN FEDERATION FOR SEXUAL HEALTH.[12] The advocacy group services about 310,000 clients a year, but focus-group research revealed that the organization's branding lead to a lot of misinformation among younger members of the public who were unaware of the organization's historic achievements in the area of birth control in the 1960s. As the executive director explained: "A lot of young people thought they would only turn to us if they were ready to start having children. They didn't see that we had a much broader focus and broader range of services".[13]

However, there remains dissention in the ranks, with three Ontario affiliates breaking with the national parent group over the decision to change the name. As one affiliate explained, the group rejected the new name because it was too broad, which would lead to a shift in the advocacy group's original principles. Although the group conceded that the Planned Parenthood brand tended to have a certain stigma in some

---

[10] Diane Francis "In marketing, choice raises consumption" *National Post* (29 October 2005) FP2.

[11] *Ibid.*

[12] Jered Stuffco "This name change is one mother of a battle" *The Globe and Mail* (27 October 2005) A3.

[13] *Ibid.*

communities, their preference would be to work to shift the public's conceptions.

(b) Distinguish the charitable or not-for-profit organization

The second purpose of branding — to distinguish the wares or services of a charitable or not-for-profit organization from those of its competitors — has recently become more of a necessity. Although charities do not generally set out to compete against one another (since they are non-profit and share the common goal of attempting to better society), instances of predatory practices have come to light in recent years that show the vulnerability of charitable and not-for-profit organizations when the goodwill of an organization is intentionally misappropriated by another organization. For example, in November 2002, an organization calling itself the CANADIAN ASSOCIATION OF THE BLIND had its charitable registration revoked after it was reported to have collected donations in the amount of $1.5 million over a period of three years, yet only $10,912, or less than one cent on the dollar, made its way to the association's purported charitable purposes, while the remainder was directed to certain fundraising companies.[14] The CANADIAN NATIONAL INSTITUTE FOR THE BLIND, the long-standing, highly respected charity that assists the visually impaired, complained that the similarity between the two organizations' names worked in the Canadian Association of the Blind's favour and accused the organization of trading on the Canadian National Institute for the Blind's reputation.

Abuses, like the case discussed above, have inspired scepticism in the public. As such, donors are more demanding and less easily satisfied that their donation has achieved the purpose for which it was given, sometimes resulting in a less-than-charitable attitude toward giving. As a result, the pursuit of donor funds by charities has become increasingly competitive. While the aforementioned example was a registered charity status case and not directly a trade mark case, it highlights the importance of organizations maintaining vigilance over their names and marks, and the potential pitfalls of not paying the necessary attention to this area. Under these circumstances, how can a charitable or not-for-profit organization get its

---

[14] K. Donovan "Bad boys of charity are wasting your money" *The Toronto Star* (13 November 2002) A1; K. Donovan "Charity ends fight to retain its status" *The Toronto Star* (12 December 2002) A3; and Canada Customs and Revenue Agency, News Release 2002-12-21, "CCRA revokes registered-charity status of Canadian Association of the Blind" (21 December 2002).

message across to potential donors and distinguish itself from the pack? How can a charitable or not-for-profit organization ensure that its reputation does not get tainted, and ultimately its donor base shrunken, by association with unscrupulous operators taking advantage of the privileges granted to charities or even by association with an innocent but simply inept charitable or not-for-profit organization?

The charitable and not-for-profit sector functions very differently from the commercial and for-profit sector. It includes a diverse array of interests from religious organizations (*e.g.*, churches), to cultural organizations (*e.g.*, operatic associations), as well as community organizations, ranging from abuse associations, service clubs, sport clubs and social clubs (*e.g.*, golf clubs). Nevertheless, the one unifying factor is that the charitable and not-for-profit sector cannot function without the financial participation of its members and donors. In a world of competition for limited funds, diminishing loyalties, and sometimes questionable ethics by the few involved in predatory fundraising, branding can be a critical tool to help charitable and not-for-profit organizations pursue their purposes. It can assist a charitable or not-for-profit organization in distinguishing its wares and services from those of others in the sector. Studies have shown that in emerging markets, the public is more interested in the brand name, as it is perceived to be subjected to higher standards than those of less famous brands. As one academic, John Quelch, notes: "When there is more choice, consumers need a trustworthy handrail [a brand name] to guide them through the complexity".[15] Branding can also protect the organization and donors from unscrupulous impostors and, by doing so, ensure that donors can trust that their donations are achieving the purposes for which they are intended.

(c) Increase market share

The third purpose of branding — to increase market share — is also applicable in the non-commercial world of charitable and not-for-profit organizations. This applies in relation to the wares and, more importantly, services offered by these organizations, not only from the perspective of the recipients and users but also from that of the donors. Homeless people seek out SALVATION ARMY shelters in the winter because they know they will receive a warm bed to sleep in, offered with a caring attitude. On the other hand, donors give to the Salvation Army because they recognize

---

[15] Diane Francis "In marketing, choice raises consumption" *National Post* (29 October 2005) FP2.

the work that the Salvation Army has done and continues to do in the community. They see volunteers dressed in the trade mark uniforms granting assistance to the needy, whether it is in the community or on promotional pieces on television, and they recognize the uniform when they see volunteers soliciting donations on the street. The uniform provides a channel for the donor's knowledge of the purposes to which the requested donation will be put. In this regard, branding is important in the context of both present and future fundraising: as a focal point for donations from regular supporters of a charity and estate gifts, enhancing the present reputation of a charity with current supporters, building potential for the charity to expand its charitable activities, and developing future sponsorship arrangements.

In addition, branding can increase market share by strengthening the common identity of multiple divisions or chapters of the same charitable or not-for-profit organization, both internally and externally (*i.e.*, in the public eye). For example, a donor from Ottawa visiting a mall in Vancouver during the pre-Christmas rush recognizes the same Salvation Army uniform that she sees at the foodbank down the street from her office in Ottawa. As she drops a donation in the plastic globe, she has the assurance that it will be used by the Vancouver Salvation Army for similar charitable needs as those pursued by the Ottawa Salvation Army and it will presumably be protected by the same measures of accountability. This is because the organization's branding tells the donor what the need is, who the organization is, what its values are, and what to expect of the organization's use of donations.

(d) Create equity

The fourth purpose of branding — to create equity in the goodwill associated with the brand — has also proved beneficial to charitable and not-for-profit organizations. In addition to securing the organization's reputation and donor base, branding has incidental value with regard to its activities, including related businesses, publicity, and specific fundraising events. Specifically, branding creates both present and future marketing value in relation to the sale of related items associated with the services of a charitable or not-for-profit organization, such as books, tapes, videos, and promotional materials, as well as in relation to facilitating access to the charitable or not-for-profit organization on the Internet or other forms of electronic communication. For example, the HEART AND STROKE FOUNDATION OF CANADA has been particularly successful in employing its brand to promote cookbooks and related services, making *The Lighthearted Cookbook* a bestseller.

Furthermore, branding can create equity by licensing the charitable or not-for-profit organization's trade mark to an associated organization located either in Canada or abroad, or to third parties for commercial or quasi-commercial purposes. In this respect, many businesses are prepared to pay a licensing fee for the right to be associated as an official sponsor of an event held in the name of a charitable or not-for-profit organization. Examples of branding creating equity are:

- Canadian Imperial Bank of Commerce ("CIBC") sponsoring CANADIAN BREAST CANCER FOUNDATION ("CBCF") in its "Run for the Cure" campaign. The annual one-day event is now in its 14th year, involving 40 communities across Canada, 170,000 runners, and raising approximately $21 million. CIBC works with the Canadian Breast Cancer Foundation to support the CBCF CIBC Run for the Cure by employee fundraising and corporate contributions for marketing, public relations, promotional materials and banking services;

- Enbridge sponsoring THE UNITED WAY in its "CN Tower Stair Climb" campaign. In 2004, over 10,500 people participated in the event, helping to raise $1.125 million for the United Way; and

- UL Canada Limited, the owner of BECEL margarine, sponsoring the HEART AND STROKE FOUNDATION OF CANADA in its "Ride for Heart" campaign. More than $1.9 million was raised in 2005 in an event that took place in Toronto, Calgary and Edmonton.

Licensing the charitable or not-for-profit organization's logo for use in the fundraising sale of commercial items is another way to take advantage of the equity in a trade mark through licensing. Examples of using a charitable or not-for-profit organization's brand to promote the manufacture and sale of commercial wares are:

- Danier Leather or Eddie Bauer emblazoning the WORLD WILDLIFE FUND's panda logo on its backpacks and day-timers;

- McDonald's featuring the INTERNATIONAL OLYMPIC COMMITTEE's Olympic logo on its cups and packaging;

- Hallmark supporting NATIONAL BREAST CANCER AWARE-NESS MONTH by manufacturing and selling wares in its breast cancer awareness gift collection; and

- ESSO promising to donate one cent for every litre of gas purchased on September 10, 2005 to THE UNITED WAY

An effective branding program for a charitable or not-for-profit organization requires a careful trade mark selection process and a deliberate and calculated program of trade mark management and promotion. Just like in the commercial world, trade marks form the basis of an effective branding and marketing strategy, providing a focal point for all the information that a charitable or not-for-profit organization wishes to communicate to the public about its work.

4.   BRANDING, MARKETING AND TRADE MARKS

Branding is an essential and interrelated element of marketing in today's commercial society. Whereas branding is the process of creating a ware identity that permits effective marketing, effective marketing is an essential part of a successful branding initiative. The key element of successful branding and marketing, however, is the judicious use of trade marks. Without the right trade mark to serve as the foundation for a strong brand, effective marketing cannot take place. The Canadian Intellectual Property Office sums it up as "your identity in the marketplace":

> Success in the business world depends largely on the message you convey and the image you project. This was the case 50 years ago and is even more true [*sic*] in the competitive global marketplace of today. You may have an excellent ware or service to offer, but if people can't pick you out easily in the crowd, you'll probably be overlooked in favour of a firm with a stronger presence.

> It's no coincidence that certain brand names that dominated the North American market in the 1920s still are leaders today. The public gravitates towards familiar names and symbols that have become associated with quality and reliability. That's why companies spend millions of dollars nurturing their corporate images. They may research, design, market and protect a name, logo or package design as much as the physical product itself.[16]

Trade marks are everywhere in our market-based society. LEVI'S, COCA-COLA, NIKE and SONY are all trade marks which have developed into household names through vastly successful branding and marketing campaigns. In and of themselves, however, these concepts have no inherent meaning or connection with the ware or company they embody. If you never drank a can of Coke or saw one of the various ads showing someone

---

[16] "A Guide to Trade marks: Introduction" (14 June 2004), online: Canadian Intellectual Property Office <http://strategis.gc.ca/sc_mrksv/cipo/tm/tm_gd_intro-e.html#section01>.

quenching their thirst with the drink, the terms COCA-COLA or COKE would mean nothing to you. The fact that these terms can be classified under the legal category of "trade mark" adds nothing further to an understanding of the connection between the trade mark and the ware; it simply indicates that a person or company wishes to protect the use of the term or logo. The legal status of a trade mark only tells the public a company wishes its business or a particular ware to be identified by the trade marked name, but it does not tell the public anything more about the business or ware.

Branding and marketing, however, fill this gap by explaining the business and ware to the public. Nevertheless, a trade mark is a critical part of the branding and marketing process. By limiting the use of a mark (a term, logo or other distinctive design), a trade mark enables the owner of the trade mark to determine the content or meaning of the mark. A well-chosen and properly used mark becomes a focal point for the owner's communication with the outside world. Through effective marketing, the owner can create an association between the trade mark and the ware or producer:

> Trade marks help consumers to select goods. By identifying the source of the goods, they convey valuable information to consumers at low costs. Easily identified trade marks reduce the costs consumers incur in searching for what they desire, and the lower the costs of search the more competitive the market. A trade mark also may induce the supplier of goods to make higher quality products and to adhere to a consistent level of quality. The trade mark is a valuable asset, part of the "goodwill" of a business. If the seller provides an inconsistent level of quality, or reduces quality below what consumers expect from earlier experience, that reduces the value of the trade mark. The value of a trade mark is in a sense a "hostage" of consumers; if the seller disappoints the consumers, they respond by devaluing the trade mark.[17]

In addition, the trade mark itself and how it is promoted can create certain associations with the mark. The NIKE logo, for example, a "swoosh" which looks like a stylized checkmark, symbolizing Nike, the Greek winged goddess of victory, immediately conjures up thoughts of something positive, forward-looking, active and triumphant. Effective marketing capitalizes on these connotations by connecting the attributes to the ware — high-powered sports equipment — reflecting, if not creating, a subculture in the process. Another example is CHIVAS REGAL, with its associations of sophistication and maturity. One well-known printed advertisement for this product did not even have the product name or logo accompany the product, only the cheeky line: "If

---

[17] *Scandia Down Corp. v. Euroquilt, Inc.*, 227 U.S.P.Q. 138 at 142 (C.A. 7 1985).

you don't recognize it, you're probably not ready for it".[18] This process of branding has become an enormous industry and a virtual necessity in today's highly competitive marketplace:

> Brand management is much more "scientific" than it once was. In some respects, the evolution of marketing is best expressed in the concept of "brand equity," coined in the mid-1980s. Impressed by the values assigned to trade marks in a series of high-profile corporate mergers, CEOs began to view brand names not merely as tactical programs to be delegated to an advertising manager, but as strategic assets to be built, protected and leveraged. Companies building brands and attempting empirically to measure their brand value are now challenged by the realization that brands encompass not only consumer awareness, but also perceived quality, customer loyalty and a rich set of associations. Furthermore, companies increasingly understand that trade marks can be the legal representative and source of protection for this complex constellation of associations and perceptions evolving over time.[19]

As the cases of Nike and Chivas Regal illustrate, in a successful branding campaign the trade mark will come to embody the owner's business, ethos and wares, collectively in one focal point. The trade mark is, in a sense, a gateway through which the trade mark owner and the public can communicate. However, it is only as useful as the owner's ability to control its use, a fact recognized by the courts:

> The protection of trade marks is the law's recognition of the psychological function of symbols. If it is true that we live by symbols, it is no less true that we purchase goods by them. A trade mark is a merchandising short-cut which induces a purchaser to select what he wants, or what he has been led to believe he wants. The owner of a mark exploits this human propensity by making every effort to impregnate the atmosphere of the market with the drawing power of a congenial symbol. Whatever the means employed, the aim is the same — to convey through the mark, in the minds of potential customers, the desirability of the commodity upon which it appears. Once this is attained, the trade mark owner has something of value. If another poaches upon the commercial magnetism of the symbol he has created, the owner can obtain legal redress.[20]

A recent article from the United States sets out the different benefits of trade marks from the perspectives of the public and the trade mark owners:

---

[18] Keith McArthur "Top Ad Guru Quits in Sexist Huff" *The Globe and Mail* (21 October 2005) A1.

[19] Jerre B. Swann, David A. Aaker & Matt Reback, "Trademarks and Marketing" (2002) 91 T.M.R. 787.

[20] *Mishawaka Rubber & Woolen Manufacturing Co. v. S.S. Kresge Co.*, 316 U.S. 203 (1942) at 205.

The publics' perspective:[21]

- Comprehend a product's otherwise unobservable characteristics;
- Avoid risks;
- Create an easy way to fulfil emotional and self-expressive needs (*e.g.*, to advertise themselves subtly or otherwise generate "favourable" impressions);
- Satisfy social needs (*e.g.*, to participate in a larger (or smaller) "sisterhood" or to reflect a "lifestyle"); and
- Create a greater variety of products and price points, due to increased competition in the marketplace.

Trade mark owners' perspective:[22]

- Allow access to the public's mind;
- Make advertising less expensive or more impactful (or both);
- Enable a manufacturer to communicate more directly with the public, cushioning any vagaries of distribution;
- Assist in attaining channel power;
- Provide a more efficient and credible means of extending into related goods, and give rise to licensing opportunities;
- Serve as certificates of "authenticity";
- Afford resilience; and
- Constitute an asset-brand equity, which is frequently a company's most valuable single property.

In addition, there are further benefits for the organization that recognizes and treats trade marks as business assets in that the organization can choose to do the following:[23]

- **Use** — a trade mark's value depends largely on its usefulness or effectiveness in selling the wares or services associated with it.
- **Sell** — a trade mark also has resell value, either alone or with the goodwill of the business associated with it.

---

[21] Jerre B. Swann, David A. Aaker & Matt Reback, "Trademarks and Marketing" (2002) 91 T.M.R. 787 at 798.

[22] *Ibid.* at 807.

[23] Gordon Sustrik & Emery Jamieson, *Trade mark Transactions: Assignments, Licences and Security Interests* (Sponsored by the Patent and Trademark Institute of Canada, 1999) at 7.

- **License** — a trade mark also has licensing value, as many organizations may prefer to pay to license a well-known trade mark instead of paying to create a brand new trade mark.
- **Finance** — a trade mark also has financing value, as it can serve as a security interest as collateral for debt financing.

For all of these reasons, a trade mark will normally be one of the most valuable assets of a charitable or not-for-profit organization. Trade marks, though, are fragile assets, the value of which can be lost or seriously eroded through error of commission and/or omission. Failure to properly identify and preserve trade mark rights could lead to the organization's eventual loss of the right to preclude others from using its trade marks. In this regard, it is essential that trade marks be used properly in order to enhance and protect their value instead of unintentionally diminishing their value.

5.   HOW TRADE MARKS BECOME WASTING ASSETS FOR CHARITABLE OR NOT-FOR-PROFIT ORGANIZATIONS

A "wasting asset" is an asset that has lost some of its value or has become a liability for its owner. Some assets, particularly tangible assets, such as real estate, hold their value well and do not easily become wasting assets. Intangible assets, such as trade marks, however, can become wasting assets quickly if their use is not appropriately managed.

Effective branding requires an active and deliberate agenda of marketing, ware development, and customer relations built around a program of trade mark management. A trade mark is relatively easy to obtain, but at the same time is also very easy to lose, taking with it the brand and all the careful work that has gone into developing the brand and the associated goodwill. This value can be lost as easily through inaction as through inept action.

From the beginning, a trade mark can be a wasting asset if the charitable or not-for-profit organization adopts a trade mark that is a liability. Once a trade mark is properly identified as a potential asset for the organization, the directors, along with the executive staff, must properly manage that asset in order to develop the value of the trade mark. This includes using the trade mark consistently and protecting the trade mark against unauthorized use.

There are a number of ways in which a charitable or not-for-profit organization's trade marks can become a wasting asset, including the following key points.

(a) Failing to conduct searches

Through a failure to conduct appropriate searches to disclose existing registered or unregistered trade marks of a similar or conflicting nature, the charitable or not-for-profit organization may unwittingly adopt a trade mark that may not have been an asset in the first place. As a result of failing to conduct the necessary searches, the charitable or not-for-profit organization may find its right to use the name it has chosen challenged by the owner of the pre-existing registered or unregistered trade mark. As such, the trade mark could actually be a liability from the outset, as the charitable or not-for-profit organization is, probably unwittingly, infringing a pre-existing trade mark. This result could be very expensive for the organization, which may have spent significant amounts of resources in developing brand identity around the trade mark, or worse yet, may have to pay damages or a settlement to the original owner along with legal fees to fight the challenge.

Another consideration is that the original owner of the trade mark may have used the trade mark in a way that is not compatible with the values of the charitable or not-for-profit organization. In this case, the organization could find it very difficult to build a brand identity around the pre-existing trade mark, since certain members of the public may still associate the trade mark with its prior use. Moreover, if the values of the charitable or not-for-profit organization clash with the values identified with the pre-existing brand, the publicity arising from a trade mark challenge could do irreparable harm to the charitable or not-for-profit organization's public image.

In order to protect the value of a trade mark as an asset for a charitable or not-for-profit organization, it is critically important for the organization to do its research and conduct the proper searches to ensure that the proposed trade mark will actually provide the organization with an asset and not a liability.

(b) Failing to stop unauthorized uses

In the event that a charitable or not-for-profit organization adopts a trade mark that is not previously owned by someone else, the trade mark will generally have value and therefore be an asset rather than a liability to the organization. However, if the charitable or not-for-profit organization fails to stop unauthorized uses of its trade mark, this asset can become a wasting asset, its value could decrease, its reputation could become sullied, or it could lose distinctiveness because it is used by multiple users and is no longer capable of distinguishing the original owner from other users in the marketplace.

A charitable or not-for-profit organization could find itself in the position of the original owner of the trade mark, as in the example above, faced with the sudden use of its pre-existing trade mark by an infringer, the potential consequences of which can be devastating. If the infringer is using the trade mark in a manner that is incompatible with the values or purposes of the charitable or not-for-profit organization, the damage done to the organization's reputation could be such that no amount of financial reparations could compensate for the harm.

For example, the U.S. organization, MAKE-A-WISH FOUNDATION,[24] faced the potential loss of goodwill due to the fraudulent acts of an Ohio car salesman who solicited funds on behalf of the organization without permission. The man claimed in advertisements, which used the charity's logo, that proceeds from donated vehicles would go to the Make-A-Wish Foundation, but he retained all of the proceeds. In a commercial context, a U.S. court found that a parody of Coca-Cola's trade mark ENJOY COCA-COLA violated Coca-Cola's trade mark rights.[25] The court recognized that the parody was an injury to its reputation and goodwill.

One of the more infamous examples is the dispute between the charity WORLD WILDLIFE FUND (World Wide Fund for Nature) and WORLD WRESTLING FEDERATION ENTERTAINMENT over the use of the initials "WWF". The World Wildlife Fund, established in 1961, is recognized as the largest private international nature organization, with a worldwide presence through its affiliated national organizations. It is easily identified by its panda logo and the initials WWF. The wrestling federation took on the name and initials in 1979. Although the two bodies do not appear to have a shared business (and most people are unlikely to confuse a wrestler with a panda bear), with globalization and market convergence, the two brands began to clash with increasing frequency. The wrestling federation's image was seen to be antithetical to that of the wildlife fund, and there were increasing concerns over any negative effects a series of legal troubles for the wrestling federation would have on the wildlife fund's 4.5 million individual contributors. Confusion of the two brands was not of significant concern; rather, the wildlife fund wanted to avoid any "insalubrious connotation when the initials WWF are used".[26]

---

[24] Arthur Drache, "Did You Ever Wonder?" (2005) 13 Canadian Not-For-Profit News 5.
[25] *Coca-Cola Co. v. Gemini Rising, Inc.*, 346 F. Supp. 1183 (E.D.N.Y. 1972).
[26] *World Wide Fund for Nature v. World Wrestling Federation Entertainment Inc.*, [2002] E.W.J. No. 4293 at para. 38, aff'd [2002] E.W.J. No. 830, [2002] EWCA Civ. 196.

In what has been described as "an inevitable result of sensible trade mark management",[27] the two bodies entered into an agreement in 1994 that restricted the wrestling federation's ability to use the WWF initials in its business activities. After adhering to the agreement for several years, the wrestling federation started ignoring its contractual obligations, culminating in the registration of the domain name "www.wwf.com" to promote its business. The wildlife fund sued for breach of contract, claiming damages and seeking an injunction to force the wrestling federation to abide by the terms of the 1994 agreement. In rejecting the wrestling federation's defence that the agreement was a restraint of trade, the court concluded that where parties have freely entered into a settlement of a dispute, they must abide by the bargain they made.[28] There will be a presumption that the agreed-upon restraints represent a reasonable division of their interests.[29] Reports at the time indicated the estimated costs associated with the wrestling federation's rebranding would be $50 million.[30] As one commentator put it, "courts have little sympathy with an organisation that realises, too late, that it has struck a bad bargain."[31]

Though not directly on point, the damage to the reputation of the CANADIAN RED CROSS in the mid- to late-1990s from the tainted blood scandal is also illustrative. The scandal caused a momentous loss of confidence in the Canadian blood supply and, by association, the Red Cross, such that after 50 years of handling the Canadian blood supply, the Red Cross was forced to relinquish this substantial part of its operations to the newly established CANADIAN BLOOD SERVICES AND HÉMA QUÉBEC. What was once an asset became a liability, and a new "brand" actually had to be created in order to provide the conditions that would restore Canadians' faith in the country's blood supply.

While the failure of a charitable or not-for-profit organization to stop the unauthorized use of its trade marks may not have as dramatic an impact as the tainted blood scandal did on the Red Cross, the possible damage should not be underestimated. One of the essential elements of a trade mark is distinctiveness, which can quickly be lost if the charitable

---

[27] Graeme Fearon, "Panda power KOs wrestlers over TM" *Brand Strategy* (5 October 2001) 6.

[28] *World Wide Fund for Nature v. World Wrestling Federation Entertainment Inc.*, [2001] E.W.J. No. 4293 at para. 45.

[29] S.J. Berwin & Edwin Coe, "Intellectual property settlements are made to be observed" *The Times (London)* (14 March 2002).

[30] *World Wide Fund for Nature v. World Wrestling Federation Entertainment Inc.*, [2002] E.W.J. No. 4293 at para. 38, aff'd [2002] E.W.J. No. 830, [2002] EWCA Civ. 196.

[31] *Ibid.*

or not-for-profit organization's trade mark or a confusingly similar mark is permitted to be used unchecked. Examples of such failure to stop unauthorized uses are:

- Not objecting to another organization using a similar corporate name;

- Not objecting to another organization adopting a similar charitable operating name;

- Not objecting to another organization developing a similar logo; or

- Not objecting to another organization adopting a domain name on the Internet that is the same as the trade mark of a charitable or not-for-profit organization.

Failure to restrain the unauthorized use of a trade mark at an early stage may result in a charitable or not-for-profit organization having its registered trade mark expunged from the trade mark register, or losing the right to assert control over the trade mark at common law. Where unauthorized use of a trade mark has occurred, it is essential that the charitable or not-for-profit organization take immediate steps to stop such unauthorized use, otherwise it may well lose the legal right to do so at a later time. The appropriate steps in this regard are discussed in more detail later in this book.

However, even if the charitable or not-for-profit organization does not lose its trade mark, the misuse of an organization's trade mark can have a significant impact on its image and reputation. A more immediate concern may be the loss of donations in favour of another organization as a result of the loss of distinctiveness. This could result in either the honest mistake of a donor or an opportunistic legal challenge to a bequest made in favour of the charitable or not-for-profit organization by another organization with the same or confusingly similar name. In either case, the court may grant a *cy-pres* order resulting in the charitable or not-for-profit organization receiving little, if any, of the gift the testator intended for the organization. The legal costs associated with fighting the challenge can be significant and divert precious resources from the charity's pursuit of its charitable objects, not to mention the possibility that the infringer might actually succeed in its challenge.

In order to protect the value of a trade mark as an asset, charitable or not-for-profit organizations should register for "watching services", which monitor for and alert them to similar and confusing trade marks. This would assist in stopping unauthorized uses of its trade mark so that the trade mark does not become a liability or become lost to another organization.

(c) Failing to regulate authorized uses

In addition to restraining the unauthorized use of a trade mark, a charitable or not-for-profit organization must also be very careful to regulate the authorized use of its trade marks. When a charitable or not-for-profit organization permits other parties (including its affiliates or associated charitable or not-for-profit organizations) to use its trade mark, it is essential to do so in accordance with a written license agreement. The organization's failure to protect its trade marks through proper licensing agreements and identification of the organization as the licensor may result in the loss of entitlement to the trade mark as a result of multiple use. A proper licensing agreement will also set out the standards that must be maintained in order for the licensee to retain its right to continued use of the mark. This will enable the charitable or not-for-profit organization to maintain control of how the authorized licensee projects the organization's image and reputation so that the licensee does not unintentionally harm the organization's image.

(d) Failing to use

A trade mark can be lost or considered abandoned through lack of use. This stems from the principle that the value of a trade mark resides in its ability to distinguish one's wares or services from those of a competitor. This purpose can only be accomplished if the trade mark is used, thereby creating a strong association between the trade mark and its owner or the owner's wares and services. On this same principle, a trade mark can be diluted and possibly lost altogether if the trade mark is used inconsistently by the trade mark owner or by unauthorized users.

Even if a charitable or not-for-profit organization has a registered trade mark, the failure to use the trade mark in association with the wares and services referred to in the trade mark registration could result in the charitable or not-for-profit organization being found to have abandoned its trade mark entitlement. In furtherance of this, the *Trade-marks Act* states that after the trade mark registration has been in existence for at least three years, a person may request at any time that the registered owner provide evidence of its use of the trade mark with respect to the wares and/or services for which the trade mark is registered during the preceding three-year period.[32]

Furthermore, the use of trade marks in association with specific wares and services that are not listed in the registration will not protect the trade mark registration against abandonment for lack of use. The *Trade-marks Act* only provides protection for trade marks in relation to the wares and services listed in the registration. Consequently, should a charitable or not-for-profit organization desire to use the trade mark in relation to a different set of wares or services, the registration would have to be amended in order to extend protection to the other wares or services.

(e) Failing to register

Registration of a trade mark is not necessary to provide rights to the trade mark. At common law, the first person to use a trade mark is deemed the owner of the trade mark, not the first person to register it. In this regard, the common law provides protection to the unregistered trade mark owner by enabling the owner to restrain other parties from passing off their wares and services under its trade mark.

However, a charitable or not-for-profit organization's common law trade mark rights may be prejudiced if the organization fails to register the trade mark. The *Trade-marks Act* provides that, after a period of five years from the date of registration, a registered trade mark cannot be contested on the basis of a claim of prior use, unless the owner of the registered trade mark was aware at the time of registration of the pre-existing unregistered trade mark.[33] As a result, if a charitable or not-for-profit organization owns a trade mark but another party subsequently registers the same trade mark, five years after the date of registration the organization can no longer challenge the registered trade mark on the basis of the organization's prior use of a similar mark unless it can show that the registered trade mark owner knew of the prior use at the time it obtained the registration. This could be very difficult to prove. Furthermore, the rights may be territorially restricted to only that area where use can be proven. Although a comprehensive trade mark search normally includes common law sources, such as magazines, trade directories and domain name registries, it may not find every unregistered trade mark, and it is conceivable that the owner of the registered trade mark may have never had notice of the

---

[32] *Trade-marks Act*, R.S.C. 1985, c. T-13, s. 45(1).
[33] *Trade-marks Act*, R.S.C. 1985, c. T-13, s. 17(2).

unregistered trade mark that had first been used by the charitable or not-for-profit organization.

The charitable or not-for-profit organization may also face a legal challenge from the owner of the registered trade mark to an expansion in use of its unregistered trade mark, even though the organization was the first to use the trade mark. As a result, failure by a charitable or not-for-profit organization to register a trade mark not only precludes the organization from the statutory protections provided by the *Trade-marks Act* for a registered trade mark, but it could also result in a restriction of the charitable or not-for-profit organization's common law rights it acquired over the years in the unregistered trade mark.

The remainder of the book will discuss what steps charitable and not-for-profit organizations should take to identify, protect, enforce and manage their trade marks so that the trade marks do not become wasting assets.

SUMMARY

Effective branding enables the public to immediately identify a charitable or not-for-profit organization, thereby protecting the organization, donors and users by distinguishing the organization from its competitors, and leading to an increased market share. An effectively controlled brand can create value for charitable and not-for-profit organizations by attracting corporate sponsors who want to be associated with the positive values the charitable or not-for-profit organization portrays.

Whereas branding is the process of creating a ware identity that permits effective marketing to take place, effective marketing is an essential part of a successful branding initiative. A well-chosen and properly used mark can become the focal point for the owner's communication with the outside world as part of marketing the brand. In a successful branding campaign, the trade mark will come to embody the owner's business, ethos, wares and services, collectively in one focal point.

Accordingly, an effective trade mark can become the charitable or not-for-profit organization's most valuable asset. Yet, without proper management of the trade mark, the trade mark may become a wasting asset for the organization. Proper management of a trade mark includes ensuring use and registration, and regulating its use by outside parties.

CHAPTER 2

TRADE MARK OVERVIEW FOR CHARITABLE AND NOT-FOR-PROFIT ORGANIZATIONS

1. What is a Trade Mark?
    (a) A trade mark can be a mark
    (b) A trade mark can be a certification mark
    (c) A trade mark can be a distinguishing guise
    (d) A trade mark can be a proposed trade mark
2. What is the Difference Between a Trade Mark and Other Types of Marks?
    (a) Prohibited marks
    (b) Official marks
3. What is the Difference Between a Trade Mark and Other Types of Intellectual Property?
    (a) Patents
    (b) Copyrights
    (c) Industrial designs
    (d) Integrated circuit topographies
    (e) Trade secrets
4. What is the Difference Between a Trade Mark and Other Types of Names?
    (a) Trade names
    (b) Business names
    (c) Corporate names

Summary

An essential element of effective branding of a charitable or not-for-profit organization is the proper management of the organization's trade marks. Although trade marks may comprise one of the most valuable assets of a charitable or not-for-profit organization, many officers and directors of these organizations do not have a good understanding of the fundamentals of trade marks and how they differ from other forms of intellectual property and branding of the organization. This chapter will provide an overview of these fundamentals.

1.   WHAT IS A TRADE MARK?

The *Trade-marks Act* defines a trade mark as:

(a)   a mark that is used by a person for the purpose of distinguishing or so as to distinguish wares and services manufactured, sold, leased, hired or performed by him from those manufactured, sold, leased, hired or performed by others,

(b)   a certification mark,

(c)   a distinguishing guise, or

(d)   a proposed trade mark.[1]

(a)   A trade mark can be a mark

The *Trade-marks Act* does not define the word "mark", therefore, we must turn to the courts for a common law definition of the word "mark". In *Insurance Corp. of British Columbia v. Canada (Registrar of Trade Marks)*,[2] the Federal Court of Canada determined that:

A certification mark, distinguishing guise and proposed trade mark are individually and specifically defined in the same section. The word "mark" is not and resort may therefore be had to dictionaries to ascertain the meaning of the word "mark" in its ordinary sense.

In various dictionaries, the word "mark" has been defined as:

the sign, writing, or ticket put upon manufactured goods to distinguish them from others;[3]

a sign affixed or impressed for distinction;[4]

---

[1]   *Trade-marks Act*, R.S.C. 1985, c. T-13, s. 2.
[2]   *Insurance Corp. of British Columbia v. Canada (Registrar of Trade Marks)* (1979), 44 C.P.R. (2d) 1 at 7–8 (F.C.T.D.).
[3]   *Black's Law Dictionary*, 7th ed./s.v. "mark".
[4]   *Wrights & Ropes Ltd. v. Broderick & Bascom Rope Co.*, [1931] Ex. C.R. 143 at 145 (Ex. Ct.), quoting the Oxford Dictionary.

or

an affixed, impressed or assumed distinguishing sign or token, as well as a character, device, label, brand, seal, or the like, put on an article to show the maker or owner, to certify quality, for identification.[5]

In practical terms, a mark may consist of any of the following:

- a single word — LEGO;[6]
- a combination of words — MISS CLAIROL;[7]
- a logo or symbol — the arched "M" for MCDONALD'S;[8]

Figure 1 — McDonald's trade mark

- a slogan — YOU DESERVE A BREAK TODAY;[9] or
- even a telephone number — the number "967-1111" for PIZZA PIZZA.[10]

While most charitable or not-for-profit organizations are not in the business of manufacturing or selling wares, they are generally involved in the performance of some sort of service, and as such would normally be able to fulfill the definition of a trade mark under the *Trade-marks Act*. The organization can also use marks to identify the source of wares and services associated with a particular mark and, in so doing, represent the goodwill of a charitable or not-for-profit organization. A mark used in conjunction with the operations of such an organization is usually any word, combination of words or logo that is used as the primary identifier of the operations of a charitable or not-for-profit organization. This could consist of any one of the following combinations:

---

[5] *Ibid.*, quoting Webster's New International Dictionary.
[6] Canadian Intellectual Property Office, Registration Number TMA106457.
[7] Canadian Intellectual Property Office, Registration Number TMA379249.
[8] Canadian Intellectual Property Office, Registration Number TMA632169.
[9] Canadian Intellectual Property Office, Registration Number TMA235886.
[10] Canadian Intellectual Property Office, Registration Number TMA428709.

- the full name of the charitable or not-for-profit organization — THE SALVATION ARMY;[11]

- a portion of the charitable or not-for-profit organization's full name — the phrase "Children's Wish" for THE CHILDREN'S WISH FOUNDATION OF CANADA;[12]

- a division of a charitable or not-for-profit organization — the division "World Vision Canada" for WORLD VISION INTERNATIONAL;[13]

- a logo — the "panda" design for WORLD WILDLIFE FUND;[14]

Figure 2 — World Wildlife Fund trade mark

- an emblem or crest — the "cross" design for the CANADIAN RED CROSS;[15] or

- a slogan — REACH FOR THE STARS for CAMP SPATIAL CANADA.[16]

It is also possible to have more than one mark used in combination, such as a word mark that is used in conjunction with a logo mark. For example, a university may use both its name and its school crest in close association of one another.

(b) A trade mark can be a certification mark

The *Trade-marks Act* defines a certification mark as:

a mark that is used for the purpose of distinguishing or so as to distinguish wares or services that are of a defined standard with respect to

---

[11] Canadian Intellectual Property Office, Registration Number TMA250536.
[12] Canadian Intellectual Property Office, Application Number 0909566.
[13] Canadian Intellectual Property Office, Registration Number TMA409154.
[14] Canadian Intellectual Property Office, Registration Number TMA196285.
[15] *Trade-marks Act*, R.S.C. 1985, c. T-13, s. 9(1)(f).
[16] Canadian Intellectual Property Office, Application Number 0907254.

(a) the character or quality of the wares or services,

(b) the working conditions under which the wares have been produced or the services performed,

(c) the class of persons by whom the wares have been produced or the services performed, or

(d) the area within which the wares have been produced or the services performed,

from wares or services that are not of that defined standard.[17]

Due to the definition and nature of certification marks, a certification mark may be adopted and registered only by a person who is not engaged in the manufacture, sale, leasing or hiring of wares or the performance of services, such as those in association with which the certification mark is used.[18]

Although the owner is prohibited from using the certification mark, the owner still has other rights with respect to the certification mark. For example:

- the owner of a certification mark may license others to use the mark in association with wares or services that meet the defined standard, and the use of the mark accordingly shall be deemed to be use thereof by the owner;[19]

- the owner of a registered certification mark may prevent its use by unlicensed persons or in association with any wares or services in respect of which the mark is registered, but to which the licence does not extend;[20]

- the owner of a registered certification mark has the exclusive right to control the use of the certification mark and to bring infringement proceedings against those not entitled to use the certification mark;[21] and

- the owner of a registered certification mark can oppose an application for the registration of any other trade mark, not just another certification mark.[22]

---

[17] *Trade-marks Act*, R.S.C. 1985, c. T-13, s. 2.

[18] *Ibid.*, s. 23(1).

[19] *Ibid.*, s. 23(2).

[20] *Ibid.*, s. 23(3).

[21] *Wool Bureau of Canada, Ltd. v. Queenswear (Canada) Ltd.* (1980), 47 C.P.R. (2d) 11 at 16 (F.C.T.D.) [hereinafter "*Wool Bureau of Canada*"]; *Trade-marks Act*, R.S.C. 1985, c. T-13, ss. 19 and 20.

[22] *Wool Bureau of Canada, ibid.*; *Trade-marks Act, ibid.*, s. 38(1).

However, any rights associated with a certification mark are only available if the certification mark is registered. Unlike an unregistered trade mark, an unregistered certification mark cannot form the basis for an infringement or passing-off action. In the case of *Life Underwriters Assn. of Canada v. Provincial Assn. of Quebec Life Underwriters*,[23] the national not-for-profit corporation sought an injunction to prevent the provincial corporation from conferring certain certification titles on members. In denying the injunction, the Court concluded:

> As a certification mark is not a creature of the common law or the civil law, but of the *Trade Marks Act*, if it is not registered in accordance with that Act it does not therefore deserve the same protection as other trade marks. Counsel submitted no precedents for or against this proposition. My research uncovered nothing on point. If the certification mark did not exist at common law and is the creature of a statute, it is limited by the provisions of that statute.[24]

The case reiterated the position that certification marks must apply to wares or services, and cannot apply to persons. As such, professional designations cannot be regarded as a certification mark.[25]

Some examples of certification marks are:

- WOOLMARK — The WOOLMARK certification mark is the world's best-known textile fibre brand and reassures consumers of quality, guaranteeing that the wares contain certain fibre content and meet quality specifications.[26]

Figure 3 — Woolmark certification mark

---

[23] [1988] F.C.J. No. 564, [1989] 1 F.C. 570 (T.D.), var'd on another ground by [1990] F.C.J. No. 572, [1990] 3 F.C. 500 (C.A.), rev'd [1992] S.C.J. No. 19, [1992] 1 S.C.R. 449.

[24] *Ibid.* at para. 39.

[25] *Ibid.* at para. 29.

[26] Canadian Intellectual Property Office, Registration Number TMA524754.

- FRUIT WINES OF CANADA — THE QUALITY CERTIFIED FRUIT WINES OF CANADA certification mark requires that all licensees must be members in good standing of Fruit Wines of Canada. In order for a product to bear the certification mark, the fruit wine must meet the definition and standards of the organization, including standards as to geographical indications and bottle size. The product must also be approved by a Tasting Panel established by Fruit Wines of Canada.[27]

Figure 4 — Fruit Wines of Canada certification mark

Although charitable and not-for-profit organizations are not-for-profit entities, they too can use certification marks for the purpose of establishing standards and encouraging activities in line with their mission. As such, a charitable or not-for-profit organization can also use certification marks to identify and recognize other entities which share the same values and abide by the same standards as the certifying organization, as the following examples illustrate:

- CANADIAN FAIR TRADE ASSOCIATION — The Canadian Fair Trade Association is a not-for-profit organization that works to improve the quality of life for coffee-growing families. By purchasing coffee that bears the certification mark, consumers can be assured the growers were paid fairly for their product. Producers who use the mark must meet strict standards set by the association.[28] There are similar organizations in other countries around the world.

---

[27]   Canadian Intellectual Property Office, Registration Number TMA572395.
[28]   Canadian Intellectual Property Office, Registration Number TMA605327.

Figure 5 — Canadian Fair Trade Association certification mark

- CCCC FINANCIAL ACCOUNTABILITY — The Canadian Council of Christian Charities uses its Financial Accountability certification mark to certify Christian charities that have voluntarily submitted to a standard of organizational integrity and accountability.[29]

**Figure 6 — Canadian Council of Christian Charities
certification mark**

(c) A trade mark can be a distinguishing guise

The *Trade-marks Act* defines a distinguishing guise as:

    (a) a shaping of wares or their containers, or

    (b) a mode of wrapping or packaging wares

the appearance of which is used by a person for the purpose of distinguishing or so as to distinguish wares or services manufactured, sold, leased, hired or performed by him from those manufactured, sold, leased, hired or performed by others.[30]

---

[29]   Canadian Intellectual Property Office, Registration Number TMA342921.

[30]   *Trade-marks Act*, R.S.C. 1985, c. T-13, s. 2.

Some examples of distinguishing guises are:

- the BACARDI bottle;[31]
- PEPPERIDGE goldfish crackers;[32]
- KRAFT lifesaver candy;[33]
- the BIC pen;[34]
- the CARTIER watch;[35]

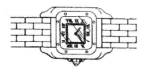

Figure 7 — Cartier Watch

- the BIC lighter;[36]

Figure 8 — BIC lighter

- the COCA-COLA bottle;[37] and

---

[31] Canadian Intellectual Property Office, Registration Number TMA630853.
[32] Canadian Intellectual Property Office, Registration Number TMA532558.
[33] Canadian Intellectual Property Office, Registration Number TMA562616.
[34] Canadian Intellectual Property Office, Registration Number TMA362414.
[35] Canadian Intellectual Property Office, Registration Number TMA459942.
[36] Canadian Intellectual Property Office, Registration Number TMA495518.
[37] Canadian Intellectual Property Office, Registration Number NFLD001423.

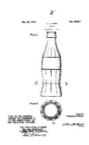

Figure 9 — Coca-Cola bottle

• the REALEMON lemon container.[38]

Figure 10 — ReaLemon container

Although charitable and not-for-profit organizations are generally not in the business of manufacturing or selling wares, they do sometimes use wares in the performance of their services and, as such, would also be able to use distinguishing guises. For example, UNICEF uses its orange collection boxes to identify the source of the services associated with its distinguishing guise and to differentiate its services from others. Doing all this also adds to the goodwill of UNICEF as a charity.[39]

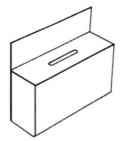

Figure 11 — UNICEF box

---

[38] Canadian Intellectual Property Office, Application Number 0275103 (abandoned).
[39] Canadian Intellectual Property Office, Registration Number TMA503410.

When considering applying for a distinguishing guise mark, charitable or not-for-profit organizations should be aware of the following difficulties or limitations posed by distinguishing guise marks:

- A distinguishing guise is not registrable in the same way as a trade mark, but may be registered only with proof that it has been used in Canada by the applicant or the applicant's predecessor in title so as to have become distinctive at the date of filing.[40] This is because the courts have traditionally held that any functional use or characteristic cannot be a trade mark.[41] As such, a distinguishing guise can only be registered if the distinguishing guise is secondary, in that it has no essential connection with the ware it embodies;[42]

- A distinguishing guise is not registrable if its registration will limit the development of any art or industry, or will hamper industry in its use of newly developed processes, materials or methods of merchandising;[43] and

- A distinguishing guise may not be registered as a certification mark.[44]

(d) A trade mark can be a proposed trade mark

The *Trade-marks Act* defines a proposed trade mark as:

a mark that is proposed to be used by a person for the purpose of distinguishing or so as to distinguish wares or services manufactured, sold, leased, hired or performed by him from those manufactured, sold, leased, hired or performed by others.[45]

Historically, there was no such thing as a proposed trade mark because a trade mark could not be registered without any prior use.[46] The *Trade-marks Act* changed that by specifically legislating that a proposed trade mark could

---

[40] *Intergold Ltd. v. Doherty* (2002), 27 C.P.R. (4th) 183 at 189 (T.M. Opp. Bd.); *Trade-marks Act*, R.S.C. 1985, c. T-13, s. 13(1)(a).

[41] *Parke, Davis & Co. v. Empire Laboratories Ltd.* (1964), 43 C.P.R. 1 (S.C.C.); *IVG v. Canada's Royal Gold Pinetree Manufacturing Co.* (1986), 9 C.P.R. (3d) 223 (F.C.A.); *Remington Rand Corp. v. Phillips Electronics N.V.*, [1995] F.C.J. No. 1660, 64 C.P.R. (3d) 467 [hereinafter "*Remington Rand*"].

[42] *Remington Rand*, ibid. at 475; *Pizza Pizza Ltd. v. Canada (Registrar of Trade Marks)*, [1989] F.C.J. No. 518, 26 C.P.R. (3d) 355 (F.C.A.).

[43] *Celliers du Monde Inc. c. Dumont Vins & Spiritueux Inc.* (2001), 15 C.P.R. (4th) 244 at 255 (F.C.T.D.); *Trade-marks Act*, R.S.C. 1985, c. T-13, s. 13(1)(b).

[44] *Canada (Registrar of Trade Marks) v. Brewers Assn. of Canada* (1982), 62 C.P.R. (2d) 145 (F.C.A.).

[45] *Trade-marks Act*, R.S.C. 1985, c. T-13, s. 2.

[46] *Standard Brands Ltd. v. Staley* (1946), 5 Fox Pat. C. 176 (Ex. Ct.).

be applied for before it has been used. However, the application cannot be finalized; *i.e.*, the trade mark cannot be registered until the trade mark is has been used and a Declaration of Use has been filed. As such, charitable or not-for-profit organizations planning to apply to register a proposed trade mark should be aware of the following:

- The proposed trade mark is not registrable if it is confusing with a trade mark that has previously been used in Canada or made known in Canada by any other person; a trade mark in respect of which an application for registration has previously been filed in Canada by any other person; or a trade name that has previously been used in Canada by any other person;[47]

- When applying, the applicant charitable or not-for-profit organization must file a statement that it, by itself or through a licensee, or by itself and through a licensee, intends to use the trade mark in Canada;[48] and

- A Declaration of Use must be filed with respect to all of the wares and services contained in the proposed use application prior to the registration issuing. If use has taken place with respect to only some of the wares and services in the application, the resultant registration will be limited to only those wares and services for which use can be claimed.

2.   WHAT IS THE DIFFERENCE BETWEEN A TRADE MARK AND OTHER TYPES OF MARKS?

As discussed earlier in this text, the *Trade-marks Act* defines a trade mark as:

(a) a mark that is used by a person for the purpose of distinguishing or so as to distinguish wares and services manufactured, sold, leased, hired or performed by him from those manufactured, sold, leased, hired or performed by others,

(b) a certification mark,

(c) a distinguishing guise, or

(d) a proposed trade mark.[49]

The terms "prohibited marks" and "official marks" are not mentioned in the definition as they are not trade marks. Instead, prohibited marks

---

[47] *Trade-marks Act*, R.S.C. 1985, c. T-13, s. 16(3).
[48] *Ibid.*, s. 30(e).
[49] *Ibid.*, s. 2.

and official marks are special marks governed by section 9 of the *Trade-marks Act* and are described below.

(a) Prohibited marks

Subsection 9(1) of the *Trade-marks Act* lists a series of marks that are prohibited marks, which receive special protection in that the Act specifically prohibits persons other than the owner from adopting the marks, or any mark consisting of or resembling the marks, in connection with a business. The list of prohibited marks is as follows:

(a)   the Royal Arms, Crest or Standard;

(b)   the arms or crest of any member of the Royal Family;

(c)   the standard, arms or crest of His Excellency the Governor General;

(d)   any word or symbol likely to lead to the belief that the wares or services in association with which it is used have received, or are produced, sold or performed under, royal, vice-regal or governmental patronage, approval or authority;

(e)   the arms, crest or flag adopted and used at any time by Canada or by any province or municipal corporation in Canada in respect of which the Registrar has, at the request of the Government of Canada or of the province or municipal corporation concerned, given public notice of its adoption and use;

(f)   the emblem of the Red Cross on a white ground, formed by reversing the federal colours of Switzerland and retained by the Geneva Convention for the Protection of War Victims of 1949 as the emblem and distinctive sign of the Medical Service of armed forces and used by the Canadian Red Cross Society, or the expression "Red Cross" or "Geneva Cross";

(g)   the emblem of the Red Crescent on a white ground adopted for the same purpose as specified in paragraph (f) by a number of Moslem countries;

(h)   the equivalent sign of the Red Lion and Sun used by Iran for the same purpose as specified in paragraph (f);

(h.1)   the international distinctive sign of civil defence (equilateral blue triangle on an orange ground) referred to in Article 66, paragraph 4 of Schedule V to the *Geneva Conventions Act*;

(i)   any territorial or civic flag or any national, territorial or civic arms, crest or emblem, of a country of the Union, if the flag, arms, crest or emblem is on a list communicated under article 6ter of the Convention or pursuant to the obligations under the Agreement on Trade-related Aspects of Intellectual Property Rights set out in Annex 1C to the WTO Agreement stemming from that article, and the Registrar gives public notice of the communication;

(i.1)   any official sign or hallmark indicating control or warranty adopted by a country of the Union, if the sign or hallmark is on a list communicated under article 6ter of the Convention or pursuant to the obligations under the Agreement on Trade-related Aspects of Intellectual Property Rights set out in Annex 1C to the WTO Agreement stemming from that article, and the Registrar gives public notice of the communication;

(i.2)   any national flag of a country of the Union;

(i.3)   any armorial bearing, flag or other emblem, or any abbreviation of the name, of an international intergovernmental organization, if the armorial bearing, flag, emblem or abbreviation is on a list communicated under article 6ter of the Convention or pursuant to the obligations under the Agreement on Trade-related Aspects of Intellectual Property Rights set out in Annex 1C to the WTO Agreement stemming from that article, and the Registrar gives public notice of the communication;

(j)   any scandalous, obscene or immoral word or device;

(k)   any matter that may falsely suggest a connection with any living individual;

(l)   the portrait or signature of any individual who is living or has died within the preceding thirty years;

(m)   the words "United Nations" or the official seal or emblem of the United Nations;

(n)   any badge, crest, emblem or mark

   (i)   adopted or used by any of Her Majesty's Forces as defined in the *National Defence Act,*

   (ii)   of any university, or

   (iii)   adopted and used by any public authority, in Canada as an official mark for wares or services,

   in respect of which the Registrar has, at the request of Her Majesty or of the university or public authority, as the case may be, given public notice of its adoption and use;

(n.1)   any armorial bearings granted, recorded or approved for use by a recipient pursuant to the prerogative powers of Her Majesty as exercised by the Governor General in respect of the granting of armorial bearings, if the Registrar has, at the request of the Governor General, given public notice of the grant, recording or approval; or

(o)   the name "Royal Canadian Mounted Police" or "R.C.M.P." or any other combination of letters relating to the Royal Canadian Mounted Police, or any pictorial representation of a uniformed member thereof.

(b) Official marks

The list of prohibited marks provided under subsection 9(1) of the *Trademarks Act* also includes a set of marks which are official marks. According to subsection 9(1)(n), official marks are any badge, crest, emblem or mark:

   (i)   adopted or used by any of Her Majesty's Forces as defined in the *National Defence Act,*

   (ii)   of any university, or

   (iii)   adopted and used by any public authority, in Canada as an Official Mark for wares or services,

   in respect of which the Registrar has, at the request of Her Majesty or of the university or public authority, as the case may be, given public notice of its adoption and use.

Some examples of charities and organizations that have official marks include the following:

- Alzheimer Society of Canada — FORGET ME NOT;[50]
- Canadian Baptist Ministries — CANADIAN BAPTIST FEDERATION;[51]
- Anne of Green Gables Licensing Authority Inc. — ANNE SHIRLEY;[52]
- Heart and Stroke Foundation of Canada — "www.heartandstroke.ca";[53]
- Canadian Cancer Society — CANADIAN CANCER SOCIETY;[54] and
- The Canadian Canoe Museum — "canoe design".[55]

Figure 12 — The canoe design is the official mark of the Canadian Canoe Museum

These organizations have sought out official marks because of the following advantages:

- The test of confusion for official marks — "so nearly resembling as to likely be mistaken for" — does not necessitate a comparison of wares and services as is required with the test of confusion for regular trade marks — "actual likelihood of confusion". The test under section 9 for official marks, although narrowly applied, involves only a comparison of the official mark with that of the mark used by another. If the mark on its face is obviously confusing with the prohibited official mark, even if it is being used in conjunction with different wares or services than that of the owner of the official mark, then section 9 may result in the other party being prohibited from using the mark in question. In contrast, the test for confusion under section 6 for regular trade marks, although more broadly applied, takes into consideration not only

---

[50] Canadian Intellectual Property Office, Application Number 0910593.
[51] Canadian Intellectual Property Office, Application Number 0907519.
[52] Canadian Intellectual Property Office, Application Number 0909023.
[53] Canadian Intellectual Property Office, Application Number 0911126.
[54] Canadian Intellectual Property Office, Application Number 0905027.
[55] Canadian Intellectual Property Office, Application Number 0908955.

whether the mark on its face is confusing, but also the nature of the wares or services and the circumstances of adopting the mark.

- An official mark can be descriptive but can be confused with another mark. For example, a public authority could secure an official mark that is descriptive of the wares and services that it provides, such as THE CAMERA STORE. This mark would not be available to a regular trade mark applicant, as the trade mark proposed for registration would be primarily descriptive of the applicant's wares and services.

- The comprehensive prohibition of an official mark means that a charitable or not-for-profit organization can totally "occupy the field" and ensure that the official mark cannot be used by anyone else for any application whatsoever. This is particularly important where a charitable or not-for-profit organization wants to ensure other organizations or businesses do not use a trade mark to embarrass the organization in an application that would otherwise fall outside the wares and services in a regular trade mark registration.

  Accordingly, the impact of an official mark has a very broad application and extends to the barring of an impending trade mark application by another person from proceeding to registration if it is found to be confusing. Although common law trade mark rights and existing trade mark registrations persist, arguably the owners of the common law trade mark would have no right to extend the use of that trade mark to other wares and services. However, the remedies associated with an official mark publication is limited to obtaining an order prohibiting the unauthorized use of the official mark but does not extend to a claim for damages.

- Although the filing fee for an official mark is significantly more than it is for a regular trade mark application, the legal fees for an official mark are considerably less than those associated with a regular trade mark registration, in part because there are no prosecution or opposition proceedings associated with an official mark application. In comparison to a regular trade mark, it is easier to obtain an official mark, provided the applicant qualifies as a "public authority", which, as discussed in more detail below, has become more difficult in recent years. In an application for a regular trade mark, the applicant must have an official search and examination performed by the Canadian Intellectual Property Office ("CIPO"). However, an official mark only requires CIPO to be satisfied the applicant is a "public authority", and the applicant has adopted the mark for wares and services.

- An official mark does not have to be renewed. Regular trade marks, on the other hand, must be renewed every 15 years with the payment of regular renewal fees. This is because official marks are not registered like regular trade marks on the Canadian trade mark database; they are merely advertised to the public.

- In addition, there is no statutory procedure to expunge the official mark once public notice has been given. As the law stands today, it is difficult for an official mark to be revoked except by an action through the courts. There is nothing in the *Trade-marks Act* outlining the procedure for an interested third party to challenge the public notice of an official mark, or providing for revocation of an official mark once public notice of the mark has been given. The only recourse a third party has is to challenge CIPO's decision by way of a judicial review pursuant to subsection 18.1(1) of the *Federal Courts Act*.[56]

- Regular trade marks are vulnerable to expungement for either abandonment or non-use. The only grounds upon which an official mark will be vulnerable is if the notice were to be challenged in the Federal Court on the basis it had been adopted by a body that was not a public authority. If true, it is likely the notice of the official mark would be void *ab initio*, although the underlining trade mark rights would still be in existence.

Charitable or not-for-profit organizations wishing to apply for an official mark as a public authority under subsection 9(1)(n)(iii) of the *Trade-marks Act* should be aware of recent court decisions from the Federal Court; namely, *Ontario Assn. of Architects v. Assn. of Architectural Technologists of Ontario*[57] and *Canadian Jewish Congress v. Chosen People Ministries,*

---

[56] R.S.C. 1985, c. F-7. See also *Canadian Jewish Congress v. Chosen People Ministries, Inc.*, [2002] F.C.J. No. 792, 219 F.T.R. 122, 214 D.L.R. (4th) 553, 19 C.P.R. (4th) 186, [2003] 1 F.C. 29 (T.D.), aff'd [2003] F.C.J. No. 980, 242 F.T.R. 160, 231 D.L.R. (4th) 309, 27 C.P.R. (4th) 193 (C.A.).

[57] [2002] F.C.J. No. 813, [2003] 1 F.C. 331, 2002 FCA 218, 215 D.L.R. (4th) 550, 19 C.P.R. (4th) 417, 226 F.T.R. 210 (C.A.), rev'g [2000] F.C.J. No. 1743, 196 F.T.R. 208, 9 C.P.R. (4th) 496, [2001] 1 F.C. 577 (T.D.) [hereinafter *"Architects"*].

Inc.,[58] which significantly restricted the continual availability of official marks for charitable and not-for-profit organizations.

One of the primary issues before the Federal Court in *Chosen People* was whether the organization could be considered a public authority under the *Trade-marks Act*. As the Court noted, there is no definition of a "public authority" in the *Trade-marks Act*, so a plain and ordinary interpretation was to be construed. The Court stated that a three-prong test must be applied to determine whether an entity is a public authority. The entity claiming to be a public authority must: (1) establish that it is a body under a duty to the public; (2) be subject to a significant degree of governmental control; and (3) be required to dedicate any profit earned for the benefit of the public and not for private benefit. The Court went on to conclude that Chosen People Ministries was not a public authority and, as a result, was not entitled to receive an official mark for its logo.

In reaching this conclusion, the Court made the following statements:

¶55   The fact that CPM [Chosen People Ministries] was incorporated as a not-for-profit corporation with charitable objects, had obtained tax-exempt status, the ability to issue charitable receipts to donors, and also the fact that as a foreign charity operating in Ontario, CPM could be asked to provide its accounts, financial and corporate information to the Public Guardian and Trustee of Ontario was not sufficient to determine CPM is a public authority. All charitable organizations have to comply with regulations in the United States and Ontario and, as soon as they comply with the regulations in place, the charitable organizations are not subject to "significant" government control.

· · · · ·

¶57   CPM is not subject to any similar or analogous government control [to cases previously cited, omitted here]. CPM's property is not to be disposed of at the direction of the government. The CPM is not funded by the Government of Canada or the United States and [CPM] is in no way subject to monitoring by the government in any shape or form.

¶58   To the contrary, as suggested by the CJC [Canadian Jewish Congress] counsel, the Government of Canada cannot intervene in any way with churches or charitable organizations like CPM [in how they] conduct their affairs.

On appeal to the Federal Court of Appeal,[59] the Court affirmed the decision that Chosen People Ministries was not a public authority. Writing for the Court, Justice Sexton said:

---

[58] [2002] F.C.J. No. 792, 219 F.T.R. 122, 214 D.L.R. (4th) 553, 19 C.P.R. (4th) 186, [2003] 1 F.C. 29, [2001] 1 F.C. 577 (T.D.), aff'd [2003] F.C.J. No. 980, 242 F.T.R. 160, 231 D.L.R. (4th) 309, 27 C.P.R. (4th) 193 (C.A.) [hereinafter "*Chosen People*"].

[59] *Ibid.*

We are of the view that there is no government control over the carrying out of CPM's activities in pursuit of these objects or in the way they conduct their affairs in pursuit of these objects. The fact that CPM, as a charity, is obliged to comply, as are all other charities, with the law generally relating to charities, including the *Income Tax Act* does not, in our view, give rise to sufficient government control to qualify CPM as a public authority.[60]

On the same day as the trial decision in *Chosen People*, the Federal Court of Appeal released its ruling in *Architects*.

The Association of Architectural Technologists of Ontario ("AATO"), an Ontario not-for-profit corporation without share capital, applied and received official marks for ARCHITECTURAL TECHNICIAN, ARCHITECTE-TECHNICIENT, ARCHITECTURAL TECHNOLOGIST, and ARCHITECTE-TECHNOLOGUE. The Ontario Association of Architects ("OAA") challenged the official marks on the ground that AATO is not a public authority. At the trial level, the Court held that the Registrar had not erred in concluding that AATO was a public authority because AATO was created by the Legislature and is controlled by legislation, which is capable of being amended at any time.[61]

In allowing the appeal, the Court pulled in the reins to a significant degree on official marks. The Court rejected the line of English cases adopting the three-prong test, as was applied in *Chosen People*, saying the public duty test was inappropriate for the purpose of official marks adopted and used by public authorities. Instead, the Court favoured a two-prong test requiring that an entity establish it is subject to: (1) a significant degree of governmental control exercised by the appropriate governmental authority; and (2) the activities of the body must benefit the public. However, the Court of Appeal did add that in applying the public benefit test, a court could consider the entity's objects, duties, and powers, and within this context, a duty to do something that is of benefit to the public was to be considered as a relevant element of the public benefit test.

In analyzing the test of government control, the Court provided some useful guidance, saying that it called for some ongoing supervision of the activities of the entity claiming to be a public authority. However, the fact that the legislature retained the power to change AATO's enabling statute was considered insufficient to satisfy the governmental control test because

---

[60] *Ibid.* at para. 4.
[61] [2000] F.C.J. No. 1743, 196 F.T.R. 208, 9 C.P.R. (4th) 496, [2001] 1 F.C. 577 at para. 18 (T.D.).

it is not a power that enables the government, directly or through its nominees, to exercise a degree of ongoing influence in the body's governance and decision-making similar to that often found in legislation dealing with statutory bodies that regulate the practice of a profession in which only those whom they license may engage, such as architecture and the law.[62]

Applying the two-prong test, the court concluded that AATO was not a public authority and, therefore, it was not entitled to an official mark registration. In reaching this conclusion, the Court held AATO's statutory origin was in itself not sufficient to make it a public authority. In other words, AATO was not subject to governmental control simply because it is a "statutory body with no delegated power to alter its corporate powers, objects or functions without an amendment to its statute".[63] The Court stated that governmental control required some ongoing government supervision of the activities of the body claiming to be a public authority.

It should be noted that AATO did satisfy the public benefit requirement of the test. The Court held that while not regulating a profession in the sense of controlling professional activities in which only its members may lawfully engage, by setting and enforcing standards of professional competence and ethical conduct of its members, AATO did regulate part of the practice of the profession. Its regulatory activities were also found to benefit the public.

As a result of *Architects* and *Chosen People*, there is now uncertainty concerning the availability of official marks to charities and not-for-profit organizations. Some legal commentators have interpreted the decisions as judicial authority for the proposition that charitable entities do not meet the test for public authority and, therefore, are not entitled to official marks. This proposition stems from the Court's decision that the mere fact that charities are obliged to comply with the law, including the *Income Tax Act*,[64] that does not in itself constitute sufficient government control to qualify the charity as a public authority.[65] The recent decisions have done away with the "public duty" requirement, but narrowed the definition of "government control" and, in so doing, significantly raised

---

[62] [2002] F.C.J. No. 813, [2003] 1 F.C. 331, 2002 FCA 218, 215 D.L.R. (4th) 550, 19 C.P.R. (4th) 417, 226 F.T.R. 210 at para. 62 (C.A.).
[63] *Ibid.* at para. 57.
[64] R.S.C. 1985 (5th Supp.), c. 1.
[65] *Canadian Jewish Congress v. Chosen People Ministries, Inc.,* [2002] F.C.J. No. 792, 219 F.T.R. 122, 214 D.L.R. (4th) 553, 19 C.P.R. (4th) 186, [2003] 1 F.C. 29 (T.D.), aff'd [2003] F.C.J. No. 980, 242 F.T.R. 160, 231 D.L.R. (4th) 309, 27 C.P.R. (4th) 193 (C.A.).

the bar for charities to be able to obtain official marks.[66] It appears the only charities capable of meeting the bar might be those receiving considerable government funding and ongoing government monitoring, such as public universities and hospitals. Not only do the decisions raise the possibility that charitable and not-for-profit organizations will no longer be able to obtain official marks, but more importantly, the decisions raise the possibility that those organizations might possibly lose the official marks they currently hold if they are challenged.

In response to these two decisions, CIPO published a new Practice Notice[67] for deciding whether a particular entity qualifies as a public authority. In deciding whether or not a body is a public authority, CIPO will now use the two-prong test affirmed in *Architects*. CIPO must find that:

1. A significant degree of control must be exercised by the appropriate government over the activities of the body; and

2. The activities of the body must benefit the public.[68]

In determining the existence of a significant degree of governmental control, CIPO looks for evidence of ongoing government supervision of the organization's activities, and that the government is enabled, directly or through its nominees, to exercise a degree of ongoing influence in the organization's governance and decision-making. Reference should be made to the Practice Notice for a full description of the consideration. Charitable and not-for-profit organizations should also note that the Federal Court of Canada further clarified in *Canada Post Corp. v. United States Postal Service*[69] (decided November 30, 2005) that the term "public authority" refers only to Canadian public authorities recognized by and subject to the control of the government of Canada. As such, public authorities in other countries are not relevant for the purpose of determining entitlement to official marks.

The second prong of the test requires the body to demonstrate that its activities benefit the public. The Practice Notice adopted by CIPO will consider the objects, duties and powers, including the distribution of the bodies' assets.

---

[66] See *e.g.* Teresa Scassa, "Nickled and Dimed: The Dispute over Intellectual Property Rights in Bluenose II" (2004) 27 Dal. L.J. 293 at 306; and Juda Strawczynski, "Note: Is Canada Ready for the Vancouver Winter Games?: An Examination of Canada's Olympic Intellectual Property Protection" (2004) 62 U.T. Fac. L. Rev. 213 at 219.

[67] Practice Notice: "Public Authority Status under Sub-paragraph 9(1)(n)(iii)" (2 October 2002).

[68] *Ibid.*

[69] *Canada Post Corp. v. United States Postal Service*, [2005] F.C.J. No. 2004.

The effect of the rulings in *Chosen People* and *Architects*, in conjunction with the new Practice Notice, is that the bar has been considerably heightened for charitable and not-for-profit organizations to obtain official marks, thereby making it more difficult for charitable and not-for-profit organizations to qualify as a public authority in the future. However, it will depend upon the specific circumstance of each charity whether CIPO will find that the charity can meet the two-prong test in *Architects*.

As a result of the recent changes, charities currently holding official marks should ensure they have registered parallel regular trade marks for all official marks they currently hold, since there are distinctive benefits available through regular trade marks not necessarily associated with official marks.

3.   WHAT IS THE DIFFERENCE BETWEEN A TRADE MARK AND OTHER TYPES OF INTELLECTUAL PROPERTY?

To better understand what a trade mark is, it is also important to understand how a trade mark is different from other types of intellectual property. In this regard, the following is given as a brief summary of the characteristics of the different types of intellectual property other than trade marks.

(a) Patents

Patents are regulated under the *Patent Act*.[70] A patent is a statutory protection given to an inventor to make, use and sell to others the invention he or she has made. An invention is defined under the *Patent Act* as any new and useful art, process, machine, manufacture or composition of matter, or any new and useful improvement in any art, process, machine, manufacture or composition of matter.[71]

Under patent law in Canada, there is a principle referred to as the "modified absolute novelty requirement", which means that the public disclosure by the inventor of an invention for more than 12 months prior to the date of application will bar the ability of the inventor to obtain a valid patent.

If a patent application was filed on or after October 1, 1989, the patent has a term of 20 years from the filing date. However, patent applications

---

[70]   R.S.C. 1985, c. P-4.
[71]   *Ibid.*, s. 2.

filed before October 1, 1989, will receive a limited protection of only 17 years from the date the patent was issued.

(b) Copyrights

Copyrights are regulated by the *Copyright Act.*[72] Copyright is the sole right to reproduce original works of art, music, drama, literature, photographs, manuscripts and computer programs. It is not necessary to register a copyright, although under certain circumstances it may be advisable so that an official record that the author created the work has been established.

Copyright protection is limited by the notion of "fair dealing", as demonstrated by the Supreme Court of Canada decision in *CCH Canadian Ltd. v. Law Society of Upper Canada.*[73] In that landmark decision, the Court held that one can photocopy copyrighted material for research purposes pursuant to the fair dealing exception without paying a licensing fee to the author of the copyrighted work. Furthermore, the Court held that the act of providing self-service photocopiers alone did not constitute authorization of copyright infringement.

Generally, a copyright exists for the life of the author plus 50 years thereafter. A copyright and a trade mark can coexist in the same subject matter, such as when a work of art also constitutes the trade mark for the owner. A classic example of where this occurred is with the character of MICKEY MOUSE, which in its creative context is a work of art but in a business context constitutes a primary trade mark for the Disney corporation.

(c) Industrial designs

Industrial designs are regulated by the *Industrial Design Act.*[74] This Act provides the registrant with exclusive rights to apply an ornamental design to an article of manufacture, such as the shape of a bottle. However, the rights are limited to the ornamental appearance only of the article of manufacture.

Unless the industrial design is registered, there can be no legal claim to ownership and no legal protection or defence available. Registration gives exclusive rights in Canada for up to 10 years. However, it should

---

[72] R.S.C. 1985, c. C-42.
[73] [2004] S.C.J. No. 12, var'g [2002] F.C.J. No. 690 (C.A.), var'g [1999] F.C.J. No. 1647 (T.D.).
[74] R.S.C. 1985, c. I-9.

be noted that a distinguishing guise trade mark can often be applied for upon the demise of industrial design rights, assuming that the design has become well-known in the marketplace and is used to distinguish the wares of one owner from another; for example, perfume bottles.

(d) Integrated circuit topographies

Integrated circuit topographies are regulated by the *Integrated Circuit Topography Act*.[75] They provide exclusive rights to the owner to reproduce and manufacture the topography of integrated circuits; *i.e.*, a three-dimensional configuration. An example of this is the highly technical integrated circuit of a computer chip; *e.g.*, a microchip. There are no rights, though, unless the topography is registered. An application must be filed within two years of first commercial exploitation of the topography.[76]

(e) Trade secrets

Trade secrets are not regulated by any statutes and only receive protection through common law. A trade secret is a secret known only to the owner. The secret is protected only to the extent that it is kept secret. As a result, it is essential that the owners of a trade secret ensure the matter is never disclosed and is maintained as a secret. An example of a trade secret is the formula for COCA-COLA, which continues to have protection as a trade secret because the company has taken extraordinary steps to ensure the formula is always kept a secret.

4. WHAT IS THE DIFFERENCE BETWEEN A TRADE MARK AND OTHER TYPES OF NAMES?

The public often assumes that a trade mark and a trade name, and a business name and a corporate name are the same thing. This confusion is in part due to the fact that a trade name, business name or corporate name could be registered as a trade mark if it meets the statutory requirements, as discussed in more detail below. This confusion often misleads charitable and not-for-profit organizations into concluding that their trade name, business name or corporate name is valid under Canadian trade mark law.

---

[75] S.C. 1990, c. 37.
[76] *Ibid.*, s. 4(1)(b).

(a) Trade names

The *Trade-marks Act* defines trade name as the name under which any business is carried on, whether or not it is the name of a corporation, a partnership or an individual.[77] As such, trade names only identify and distinguish corporations, partnerships or individuals, and not the wares or services produced by those corporations, partnerships or individuals. This means that trade names generally cannot be registered under the *Trade-marks Act*. However, a trade name or parts of a trade name can be registered as a trade mark if it fulfills the requirements for a trade mark. An example of this would be the corporation operating under the trade name "The Coca-Cola Company", which has registered the word COCA-COLA as a trade mark.[78]

Although the trade names that cannot be registered as a trade mark are not statutorily protected under the *Trade-marks Act*, they still have other forms of protection:

- The owner of a trade name can receive common law protection from the courts under the passing-off doctrine. The passing-off doctrine enables a corporation, partnership, or individual that has established a reputation or goodwill under a trade name to stop others from using the exact trade name, or a similar trade name, to pass off their business as being the same as that of the corporation, partnership or individual;

- The owner of a trade name can also seek common law protection from the courts to stop others from using an unregistered trade mark that is the same as or similar to the trade name;

- The owner of a trade name can still use the *Trade-marks Act*, even though the trade name is not registered as a trade mark under the *Trade-marks Act*, to oppose an application for registration or a registration of a trade mark that is the same as or similar to the trade name;[79] and

- The owner of a trade name can also use the *Trade-marks Act*, even though the trade name is not registered as a trade mark under the Act, to bring an application to expunge a registered trade mark that is the same as or similar to the pre-existing trade name, provided

---

[77] R.S.C. 1985, c. T-13, s. 2.
[78] Canadian Intellectual Property Office, Registration Number NFLD001429.
[79] *Trade-marks Act*, R.S.C. 1985, c. T-13, s. 38.

the expungement application is brought within five years of the trade mark's registration.[80]

(b) Business names

A business name is the name under which a corporation, a partnership or an individual uses to carry on business or make itself known to the public. The term "business name" means the same as and is interchangeable with the term "trade name". As such, the earlier discussion on trade names and their protection are equally applicable to business names.

Some jurisdictions have legislation stating that no corporation shall carry on business or identify itself to the public under a name other than its corporate name unless the name is registered by that corporation, and that no individual shall carry on business or identify his or her business to the public under a name other than his or her own name unless the name is registered by that individual.[81]

Charitable and not-for-profit organizations should be aware that registering a business name is only for public information purposes. Registration places the business name on the public record maintained by the government, allowing consumers and business people to find the owners or the principals behind a business name. This sort of information is especially important to people trying to settle disputes. As such, registering a business name is not the same thing as registering a trade mark; it does not permit exclusive use of the business name and does not give any trade mark protection for the business name. Any protection for a business name would have to come from its use as a trade mark and an action for passing off.

Organizations should also be aware that governmental approval of a business name does not mean the business name is not in violation of any trade marks. Generally, the onus is on the applicant to ensure the proposed business name complies with the law and that there is no risk of confusion with an existing corporate name, business name or trade mark. As such, the government authority responsible for registering business names will not check whether a business name is infringing on a trade mark before approving it. As a result, a charitable or not-for-profit organization which has received approval to operate under the business name of RED CROSS AID FOR CHILDREN may be shocked to receive letters from the RED CROSS stating the charity owns the trade mark and

---

[80]   *Ibid.*, s. 17.
[81]   *Business Names Act*, R.S.O. 1990, c. B.17, s. 2.

has the exclusive right to use the trade mark, and demanding that Red Cross Aid for Children stop using the term "Red Cross".

(c) Corporate names

A corporate name is the name under which the corporation is incorporated. Charities, being non-share capital corporations, can be incorporated either under provincial legislation, such as Ontario's *Corporations Act*,[82] or under federal legislation, such as the *Canada Corporations Act*.[83]

Similar to business names, charities should be aware that incorporating and registering the corporate name is only for public information purposes. Registration does not give any trade mark protection. In order to receive any sort of protection for the corporate name, charities must use the corporate name in carrying out their business and in making themselves known to the public.

If the corporation decides to use the corporate name to carry on business, then the corporate name would also be the corporation's business name or trade name. However, if the corporation decides not to use the corporate name to carry on business, then the corporate name will differ from the corporation's business name or trade name. Why would a corporation decide to do such a thing? One reason may be that the owners wanted to incorporate as soon as possible, but had not yet thought of a name under which they would like to carry on business or make themselves known to the public. In such a situation, the best solution would be to incorporate as a numbered company, such as 12345 Ontario Inc., and then carry on business or become known to the public as BOB'S MEATS.

Similar to business names, charitable and not-for-profitation organizations should also be aware that governmental approval of a corporate name does not mean that the corporate name is not in violation of pre-existing trade marks. Once again, the onus is on the applicant to ensure the proposed corporate name complies with the law and that there is no risk of confusion with another corporate name, business name or trade mark. As a result, a church which has received approval to operate under the corporate name of UNITED CHURCH OF TIMBUKTU may be surprised to receive letters from the UNITED CHURCH OF CANADA stating that the charity owns the trade mark and has the exclusive right to use the trade mark, and demanding that the United Church of Timbuktu stop using the term "United Church".

---

[82] R.S.O. 1990, c. C.38.
[83] R.S.O. 1970, c. C-32.

SUMMARY

As this chapter has demonstrated, trade marks, as well as other intellectual property, will play an important role in the success of a charitable or not-for-profit organization. As such, it is important for directors and officers of such organizations to have a clear understanding of the fundamentals of trade marks and how they differ from other forms of intellectual property and branding of the organization.

With a proper understanding of trade marks, the charitable or not-for-profit organization can choose the appropriate form of trade mark. The *Trade-marks Act* recognizes four types of trade marks: (1) a mark to distinguish wares or services; (2) a certification mark; (3) a distinguishing guise; and (4) a proposed trade mark. These are distinguished from prohibited marks and official marks by their characteristics and requirements for attaining such marks. If a charitable or not-for-profit organization is able to obtain an official mark, the protection for the mark is much broader than that of a trade mark, as an official mark enables the owner to occupy the field. But recent jurisprudence significantly restricted the continual availability of official marks for charitable and not-for-profit organizations, and as such, it is prudent to register official marks as trade marks to ensure protection.

It is important to remember that trade marks do not include patents, copyright, industrial designs, integrated circuit topographies or trade secrets. A trade name, corporate name or business name is not necessarily acceptable in terms of trade mark requirements, but such names may receive limited protection under the common law. Similarly, registering a business name pursuant to provincial legislation does not provide protection in the same manner as a trade mark, as the purpose behind the legislation is consumer protection, not business protection.

With this knowledge of the fundamentals of trade marks, it is important to then consider what form of protection the charitable or not-for-profit organization should seek for its trade marks: common law protection or the protection of registration under the *Trade-marks Act*. These issues will be discussed in the following chapters.

CHAPTER 3

TRADE MARK PROTECTION UNDER THE COMMON LAW SYSTEM

A charitable or not-for-profit organization's trade marks have two possible levels of protection: (1) the common law; or (2) statutory protection through registration, which is discussed in greater detail in Chapter 4. The common law provides protection by restraining a competitor from "passing off" its goods or services as that of the trade mark owner's, a benefit that is reserved in Canada for the first person or organization to use the trade mark. However, it is not enough to claim a trade mark in Canada. An organization claiming rights to a trade mark must meet basic requirements before the courts will afford any protection. Charitable and not-for-profit organizations must also be aware of the limitations of relying on the common law system for protecting trade mark rights in Canada.

1. WHAT IS THE COMMON LAW SYSTEM?

The common law refers to judge-made law, as opposed to laws made by statute through the federal, provincial or municipal governments. As such, common law rights are rights that are recognized by the courts, even though they are not granted by a specific piece of legislation enacted by the municipal, provincial or federal levels of government in Canada.

Canada's trade mark system is based upon a first-to-use system instead of a first-to-file system as in some other countries. Therefore, the first user of a trade mark in Canada is deemed the owner of the trade mark in Canada, even if the user does not register the trade mark. Although registering the trade mark would confirm and enhance the trade mark rights that have already been acquired under the common law, it is not necessary to register a trade mark in order to enforce the common law rights acquired in the trade mark.

2. HOW ARE TRADE MARK RIGHTS ACQUIRED UNDER THE COMMON LAW SYSTEM?

Trade mark rights can be acquired under the common law simply through use. There is no minimum length of time a trade mark must be used, provided the use is continuous and has not been abandoned. As such, the moment a charitable or not-for-profit organization uses a mark for the purpose of distinguishing their wares or services from those of others, that organization acquires common law rights in the trade mark used.

It is important to keep in mind, however, that only certain types of uses are acceptable when it comes to acquiring trade mark rights under the common law.

(a) Use must be visual

The common law only recognizes use that is visual.[1] Although a person could distinguish his or her wares or services from those of others through use of other senses (*i.e.*, the sound, smell, touch, weight or flavour of the ware), the courts in Canada have made it clear that such uses are not recognized because they are not visual. Canada differs from the United States in this aspect because Canada focuses on the concept of "use", whereas the underlying principle of trade mark rights in the U.S. is the

---

[1] *Playboy Enterprises Inc. v. Germain*, [1987] F.C.J. No. 616, 16 C.P.R. (3d) 517 (T.D.); *Phillips (Re)*, [1997] T.M.O.B. No. 19.

concept of "distinctiveness", allowing any use that is distinctive because a mark serves the purpose of distinguishing wares and services, as illustrated below.

- **Sound** — The U.S. has permitted the registration of sounds such as the NBC chimes, the TARZAN yell, the SWEET GEORGIA BROWN melody and MGM's lion roar.[2]

- **Perfume** — The U.S. has permitted the registration of "a high impact, fresh, floral fragrance reminiscent of Plumeria blossoms" applied to sewing thread and embroidery yarn.[3]

- **Texture** — The U.S. could conceivably permit the registration of a particular texture on a ware or its packaging.

- **Weight** — The U.S. could conceivably permit the registration of a unique weighting of a package of wares.

- **Flavour** — The U.S. could conceivably permit the registration of a bubble gum or a mouthwash flavour.

(b) Use must be lawful

It is not enough that the trade mark use is not criminal. In addition to ensuring the use is not violating criminal law, charitable and not-for-profit organizations must also ensure the use is not in violation of other general laws. For example, the use cannot be in violation of tort law (*e.g.*, breach of fiduciary duty) or contract law (*e.g.*, breach of contract).

(c) Use must be for the purpose of distinguishing

A person is not considered to be using a mark for the purpose of distinguishing his or her wares or services from those of others if the use was not primarily for the purpose of identifying the source of those wares or services. Examples of unacceptable uses are:

- **Identify the nature of the wares or services** — Where the use of the SKI-DOO mark with a statement that the mark belonged to another corporation, the Court found that SKI-DOO was not

---

[2]   United States Patent and Trademark Office, Registration Numbers 916522, 2210506, 1700895 and 1395550.
[3]   *Re Clarke*, 17 U.S.P.Q. 2d 1238 (T.T.A.B. 1990).

being used as a mark to distinguish the motor oil from other motor oils;[4]

- **Functional use** — Where "coloured bands" around certain pharmaceutical capsules served the function of sealing the two halves of the pharmaceutical capsules, the Court found that the "coloured bands" were not being used as a mark to distinguish the source of the pharmaceutical capsules;[5]

- **Descriptive use** — Where the VOLCANO mark was being used to identify the level of spiciness of a certain hot pepper sauce, the Court found that "Volcano" was not being used as a mark to distinguish the hot pepper sauce from other hot pepper sauces;[6] and

- **Ornamental use** — Where a "corn flower" design was applied to cut glass tableware as a pattern, the Court found that the "corn flower" design was not being used as a mark to distinguish the source of the cut glass tableware.[7]

(d) Use with wares

The *Trade-marks Act*[8] provides a long and complicated description of when a trademark is deemed to be used with wares. Subsection 4(1) states:

> A trade mark is deemed to be used in association with wares if, at the time of the transfer of the property in or possession of the wares, in the normal course of trade, it is marked on the wares themselves or on the packages in which they are distributed or it is in any other manner so associated with the wares that notice of the association is then given to the person to whom the property or possession is transferred.

A number of these elements require explanation:

- "time of transfer of property or possession" — This phrase requires the wares to be actually transferred; therefore, placing an order for the wares is not sufficient to constitute use.[9] Or, alternatively, this phrase requires the wares to be in the actual possession of a

---

[4]   *Bombardier Ltd. v. British Petroleum Co. Ltd.* (1973), 10 C.P.R. (2d) 21 (F.C.A.).
[5]   *Parke, Davis & Co. v. Empire Laboratories Ltd.* (1964), 43 C.P.R. 1 (S.C.C.).
[6]   *Pepper King Ltd. v. Sunfresh Ltd.*, [2000] F.C.J. No. 1455, 8 C.P.R. (4th) 485 (T.D.).
[7]   *W.J. Hughes & Sons "Corn Flower" Ltd. v. Morawiec* (1970), 62 C.P.R. 21 (Ex. Ct.).
[8]   *Trade-marks Act*, R.S.C. 1985, c. T-13.
[9]   *Sassy Lassy, Inc. (Re)*, [2001] T.M.O.B. No. 32, (*sub nom. Gowling, Strathy & Henderson v. Sassy Lassy, Inc.*), 11 C.P.R. (4th) 549.

purchaser in Canada; therefore, constructive possession is not sufficient to constitute use.[10]

- "normal course of trade" — This phrase requires the wares to be transferred for the purpose of acquiring goodwill and profits. Although it is not necessary for there to be a monetary exchange for the transfer of wares,[11] charitable and not-for-profit organizations should be aware that the transfer of wares must still be for the purpose of acquiring goodwill and profits; therefore, donating wares for charitable purposes is not sufficient to constitute use, even if the purpose of the donation was to increase goodwill and encourage future sales.[12]

- "associated with the wares" — This phrase requires the wares or their packaging to be marked so that the mark is clearly associated with the wares or packaging. This requirement raises an interesting issue for charitable and not-for-profit organizations, which may display multiple trade marks from multiple sponsors on a single ware. Although the *Trade-marks Act* is silent on the issue of displaying a group of trade marks together on a ware, the common law does provide examples of multiple trade marks being used on a single ware as still satisfying this requirement. One example is the use of KRAFT and MIRACLE WHIP on the same mayonnaise jar.

(e) Use with services

A trade mark is deemed to be used in association with services if it is used or displayed in the performance or advertising of those services.[13] Organizations that operate on an international basis should be aware that the mere advertising of services is not sufficient to constitute use. In order to show use with services, the organization must be able to follow up on the advertising and be willing and able to perform the services in

---

[10] *Manhattan Industries Inc. v. Princeton Manufacturing Ltd.* (1970), 4 C.P.R. (2d) 6 (F.C.T.D.).

[11] *Bradale Distribution Enterprises Inc. v. Safety First Inc.*, [1978] A.Q. no 702, 18 C.I.P.R. 71 (Sup. Ct.).

[12] *Ports International Ltd. v. Canada (Registrar of Trade Marks)* (1983), 79 C.P.R. (2d) 191 (F.C.T.D.).

[13] *Trade-marks Act,* R.S.C. 1985, c. T-13, s. 4(2).

Canada.[14] It is important to note that the use with services is not required to be in the normal course of trade, as in the case of use with wares; therefore, the use need not be with for-profit services and, as such, charitable services are sufficient to constitute use.[15]

3. ADVANTAGES OF THE COMMON LAW SYSTEM

As explained earlier, Canada's trade mark system is based upon a first-to-use system instead of a first-to-file system as in some other countries; therefore, the first user of a trade mark in Canada generally is deemed the owner of the trade mark in Canada, even if the user does not register the trade mark pursuant to the *Trade-marks Act*.

For most charitable and not-for-profit organizations, which are unfamiliar with the trade mark registration system or which lack the financial resources to register their trade marks, Canada's system is advantageous because they can obtain common law rights for their unregistered trade marks. Not only will the common law generally recognize the first user of the trade mark as the owner of the trade mark, it will also allow the first user to restrain others from passing off their wares or services under the first user's unregistered trade mark.

4. DISADVANTAGES OF THE COMMON LAW SYSTEM

A disadvantage of common law rights is its limitation to the local geographic area in which the unregistered trade mark is known. This means a charitable or not-for-profit organziation that has been using an unregistered trade mark in solely Toronto can only restrain others from using the unregistered trade mark in association with the same wares and services in the local geographic area of Toronto. As such, the organization cannot restrain others from using the unregistered trade mark, even if it is in association with the same wares and services, in other geographic areas such as Vancouver or Calgary.

Another disadvantage of common law rights is that the onus is on the owner to prove such rights. In order to restrain others from passing off

---

[14] *Cornerstone Securities Canda Inc. v. Canada (Registrar of Trade Marks)*, [1994] F.C.J. No. 1713, 58 C.P.R. (3d) 417 (T.D.); *Clark O'Neill Inc. v. PharmaCommunications Group Inc.*, [2004] F.C.J. No. 147, 30 C.P.R. (4th) 499 (T.D.).

[15] *War Amputations of Canada v. Faber-Castell Canada Inc.*, [1992] T.M.O.B. No. 6, 41 C.P.R. (3d) 557.

their wares or services under its unregistered trade mark, a charitable or not-for-profit organization must prove three things:[16]

1. There must be goodwill or reputation attached to the wares or services used in association with the unregistered trade mark;

2. The defendant's misrepresentation, whether intentional or not, leads or is likely to lead the public to believe that the defendant's wares or services are those of the organization; and

3. The organization has or is likely to have suffered damage to goodwill as a result of the misrepresentation.

From a review of the three requirements set out above, it is evident that winning a passing-off action to protect an unregistered trade mark under common law system is difficult. It is easier to win an "infringement" action to protect a registered trade mark under the *Trade-marks Act*. That is why it is highly recommended that charitable and not-for-profit organizations register their trade marks in order to confirm and enhance the trade mark rights they may have already acquired under the common law system.

The following chapters of this book will discuss how these organizations can register their trade marks to receive the maximum statutory protection available.

SUMMARY

Canada's trade mark system is based on a first-to-use system, so a charitable or not-for-profit organization can obtain ownership rights in a trade mark without registration. Such unregistered trade marks can be protected under the common law (judge-made law), while registered trade marks are protected under the *Trade-marks Act*. Charitable and not-for-profit organizations should be aware that what is registrable in a foreign country like the United States or the European Community may not necessarily be registrable in Canada, and thus should review any proposed mark to see if it will fit within the Canadian trade mark regime.

In order to acquire common law rights in Canada, the trade mark must be visual, lawful, for the purpose of distinguishing wares or services, and used with wares or services. There are geographical limitations to

---

[16] *Ciba – Geigy Canada Ltd. v. Apotex Inc.*, [1992] S.C.J. No. 83, 44 C.P.R. (3d) 289 at 296–99.

common law trade mark rights in that the protection is limited to the local area in which the trade mark is used.

There are three elements to a common law passing-off action: (1) goodwill and reputation; (2) misrepresentation; and (3) damage to the goodwill attached to a trade mark. As it is difficult for any organization to demonstrate these three elements of passing-off, it is generally considered to be easier and more prudent to claim an infringement under the *Trademarks Act* rather than pursuing a common law passing-off action.

CHAPTER 4

TRADE MARK PROTECTION UNDER THE REGISTRATION SYSTEM

As was discussed in Chapter 3, trade mark rights can exist regardless of whether the mark is registered, with the trade mark owner initiating a common law passing-off action. However, should a charitable or not-for-profit organization register their trade marks under the *Trade-marks Act*,[1] the rights are easier to enforce and have numerous other advantages that are not present in the common law system. These advantages include *prima facie* evidence of ownership, a presumption of validity, enforcement on a national geographic scale and facilitation of registration in Convention countries. Although the cost to register a trade mark may seem like a luxury to charitable and not-for-profit organizations with meagre budgets, should such an organization be forced to enforce their rights through judicial action, most of the difficult evidentiary issues could have been avoided through registration.

1.   WHAT IS THE REGISTRATION SYSTEM?

The trade mark registration system in Canada is managed by the Government of Canada through the Canadian Intellectual Property Office ("CIPO"). If a trade mark application meets with CIPO's approval and passes through the examination and opposition stages, CIPO then enters the trade mark, giving notice to the public that the trade mark is registered and protected.

2.   HOW ARE TRADE MARK RIGHTS ACQUIRED UNDER THE REGISTRATION SYSTEM?

Trade mark rights can be acquired under the registration system by making an application to register the trade mark on four possible grounds:

1.   Actual use in Canada

2.   Making known in Canada

3.   Registration and use in a foreign country

4.   Proposed use in Canada

(a) Actual use in Canada

A trade mark application based upon the ground of actual use in Canada must set out the date of first use for each of the applicable wares and

---

[1]   R.S.C. 1985, c. T-13.

services. If the first use is relatively recent, then the date of first use should be shown as the date, month and year (*e.g.*, January 1, 2006). If, on the other hand, the first use is many years earlier, then the date of first use should be shown as either a month and a year or just a year (*e.g.*, January 1943, or just 1943). However, when only a month and a year or just a year is shown, the date of first use is presumed to be the last date of the calendar unit shown (*e.g.*, January 31, 1943, or just December 31, 1943).

(b) Making known in Canada

Canada is a signatory to the *Paris Convention for the Protection of Industrial Property* ("Convention").[2] As a result, a trade mark application can be based on the ground that the trade mark has been made known in Canada, even though it is not actually used in Canada, provided it is used in a Convention country. An example of this would be the NFL, which was made known in Canada before it was actually used in association with football memorabilia sold in the country, as a result of the publications and broadcasts from the United States.[3] Trade mark applications are seldom based on this ground because it is difficult to establish that a trade mark has been made known in Canada when it has not actually been used in Canada. A trade mark will be considered to have been made known in Canada if the wares are distributed in association with the trade mark in Canada, or if the wares or services are advertised in association with the trade mark through either printed publications circulated in Canada or broadcasts received in Canada.

(c) Registration and use in a foreign country

Canada's participation in the Convention also enables a trade mark application to be based on the ground of application or registration in a Convention country and use abroad. If a trade mark has been applied for or registered in a Convention country, then the trade mark may also be registered in Canada as long as it was used abroad. It is important to point out that many foreign countries use the international classification system, which allows the foreign application or registration to list all wares or services in a class. It will be necessary to list the particular wares or services in the Canadian application for which use can be shown. This

---

[2]   Adopted in Paris on 20 March 1883, last revised by the Paris Union on 28 September 1979, 828 U.N.T.S. 305, 21 U.S.T. 1583.

[3]   Canadian Intellectual Property Office, Registration Number TMA256830.

may effectively limit the Canadian application to fewer wares and services than in the original application or registration.

(d) Proposed use in Canada

A trade mark application based on the ground of proposed use in Canada must set out a statement that the applicant, either on his or her own or through a licensee or both, intends to use the trade mark in Canada. The applicant must then make actual use of the trade mark in Canada and provide proof of actual use, by filing a declaration of use, before CIPO will actually register the trade mark.

This ground is especially useful for charitable or not-for-profit organizations that are planning a future fundraiser or campaign. Such organizations may spend funds on advertising and publications, only to find out later that the trade mark has been registered by another organization during the time they were putting it into use. Now, a charitable or not-for-profit organization can reserve the trade mark associated with the fundraiser or campaign before any use has actually taken place, and then spend the funds on advertising and publications.

A trade mark application is not limited to only one ground for the application; instead, a trade mark application can be based on more than one ground. For example, a foreign charitable or not-for-profit organization can base its trade mark application on the combined grounds of use and registration in a Convention country as well as a proposed use in Canada.

Additionally, if an applicant applies for trade mark registration in Canada within six months of the date of filing in another Convention country, then the priority filing date in Canada would be deemed to be the priority filing date in the other jurisdiction. Obtaining an earlier priority date can be of great importance where a foreign charitable or not-for-profit organization is intending to expand operations into Canada and would like to obtain as early a priority filing date for its proposed use trade mark registration in Canada as possible.

3.   ADVANTAGES OF THE REGISTRATION SYSTEM

Charitable and not-for-profit organizations will understandably want to comprehend the advantages associated with proceeding with trade mark registration before deciding to commit to the time and expense involved. The key advantages of the registration system are summarized under the following 10 points.

(a) Presumption of validity

A trade mark registration establishes legal title to a trade mark, similar to the registration of a deed for real property. This means a court will presume the trade mark in question is a validly registered trade mark owned by the registered owner. In contrast, at common law the validity of a trade mark must be established before a court will be able to enforce a common law action for passing-off, and even at that, the common law action for passing-off is a lengthy, expensive and difficult remedy to pursue.

(b) Effective throughout Canada

A trade mark registration is effective throughout Canada, even if the trade mark is used only in one geographic area of the country. This differs from the common law, where an unregistered trade mark can only be enforced within the local geographic area in which the trade mark is known. This means a charitable or not-for-profit organization that carries on operations in Ontario will be able to restrain unauthorized use of the registered trade mark by others in another province, even though the organization has no presence in the other province nor any plans to do so.

(c) Enforcement throughout Canada

Registration of a trade mark provides the owner with potentially three causes of action, without the geographical limitation that is associated with an unregistered trade mark. Under the *Trade-marks Act*, the owner of a registered mark may bring a passing-off action pursuant to section 7 and the common law, which prohibits the passing off of any wares or services.[4] The owner may also bring an action for infringement under section 20.[5] The only defence to an infringement action is that of a *bona fide* use that is not likely to have the effect of depreciating the goodwill attached to the mark. Finally, section 22 provides a cause of action for depreciating the goodwill attached to a mark.[6]

Actions may be brought in the Federal Court of Canada, and any decision may be enforced in any province in Canada. This differs from the common law action for passing-off, which must be brought within the provincial

---

[4] *Trade-marks Act*, R.S.C. 1985, c. T-13, s. 7.

[5] *Ibid.*, s. 20.

[6] *Ibid.*, s. 22.

Superior Court where the trade mark has been used and cannot, as a matter of right, be enforced throughout the country.

(d) Exclusive right to use

Trade mark registration remains in effect for a period of 15 years subject to renewal,[7] and gives the owner the exclusive right to use the trade mark throughout Canada in respect of the wares and services for which the trade mark has been registered.[8] At the end of the 15-year period, CIPO will send a notice to the trade mark owner and to the trade mark owner's representative, if applicable. Trade mark owners are cautioned that failure to pay the prescribed renewal fee within the six-month period specified in the notice will lead to the expungement of the trade mark from the register.

The full implication of "exclusive right" has been highlighted recently in the 2002 case of *Molson Canada v. Oland Breweries Ltd./Les Brasseries Oland Ltée,*[9] in which it was established that a registered trade mark can now serve as a complete answer against an action for passing-off. Unless the validity of the registration itself is contested, a trade mark owner's exclusive right to use the mark is unassailable, and any unregistered trade mark owner who complains of confusion from a registered trade mark would himself or herself be infringing on the registered trade mark upon establishing the confusion. As such, the owner of a registered trade mark has the exclusive right to use the trade mark for the wares and services for which it has been registered to the exclusion of anyone else.

(e) Gives public notice

One of the more important advantages of a registered trade mark is that the trade mark will be listed in the registered trade mark index maintained by CIPO, and will appear in subsequent trade mark searches conducted by trade mark agents and by CIPO itself. This helps to ensure no confusing trade marks are subsequently registered in Canada.

In addition, the NUANS (Newly Upgraded Automated Name Search) Corporate Name Search system, maintained by Industry Canada, will also include the registered trade mark in its search of similar names, thereby warning businesses that may be considering adopting a trade name or

---

[7] *Ibid.*, s. 46(1).
[8] *Ibid.*, s. 19 as am. by S.C. 1993, c. 15.
[9] [2002] O.J. No. 2029 (C.A.), aff'g [2001] O.J. No. 431 (Sup. Ct.).

unregistered trade mark similar to that of the trade mark. Since unregistered trade marks do not show up in the NUANS system, a corporation may unwittingly register a corporate or business name that is confusing.

(f) Incontestable in some situations

A registered trade mark generally cannot be contested after five years from its date of registration on the basis of a claim of prior use, subject to limited exceptions, even if an unregistered trade mark has an earlier date of first use.[10] However, a registered trade mark can be contested after the five years if the person who registered the trade mark did so with knowledge of the previous use or making known. No such similar benefit extends to an unregistered trade mark at common law.

(g) Failure to register may limit rights

Since a registered trade mark becomes incontestable for a claim of prior use or making known of a similar trade mark after a period of five years, the owner of an unregistered trade mark who failed to take the initiative and register the trade mark may be confronted by a legal challenge from the owner of a subsequent registered trade mark that is the same or similar to the unregistered trade mark. If the five-year period passes and the unregistered owner does not contest the registered trade mark, the owner of the registered trade mark may object to an expansion in use of the unregistered trade mark by the prior owner and thereby restrict the unregistered owner's rights. An unregistered owner can only overcome this barrier if he or she can prove that the person who adopted the trade mark did so with the knowledge of the prior use or making known in Canada. Evidence of such knowledge is virtually impossible to find.

(h) Protect domain names

As will be explained in Chapter 9, a trade mark registration can greatly assist in protecting a key domain name on the Internet. Pursuant to the Uniform Domain Name Dispute Resolution Policy ("UDRP") that came into effect on October 24, 1999, as well as Canada's own Canadian Internet Registration Authority's Domain Name Dispute Resolution Policy ("CIRA's Policy") that came into effect in 2003, in order to successfully

---

[10] *Trade-marks Act*, R.S.C. 1985, c. T-13, s. 17.

challenge a domain name, a complainant needs to prove the domain name owner has no rights or legitimate interest in the domain name. One way of proving the domain name owner's lack of legitimate interest is to show that the domain name does not correspond to any trade marks owned by the domain name owner. Therefore, a trade mark registration can assist in defending against a domain name challenge by serving as *prima facie* evidence the domain name owner has a legitimate interest in the domain name.

Charitable or not-for-profit organizations that have an Internet domain name must remember that official marks are unique to Canada and are not the equivalent of regular trade marks required by the UDRP and, as such, cannot be relied upon to substantiate an Internet domain name from possible challenges. Instead, a regular trade mark must be registered to obtain the required protection in this regard. However, with respect to .ca domain names, official marks are recognized by CIRA's policy, and as such, can be relied upon to show legitimate interest in a domain name.

(i)   Facilitates registration in Convention countries

The *Trade-marks Act* permits the filing date for a trade mark application in Canada to be the same filing date used for a trade mark application filed in another Convention country, provided the application in the Convention country is filed within six months of the filing date in Canada.[11] This entitlement can provide a significant advantage to a charitable or not-for-profit organization wishing to establish a priority claim to a trade mark in another country based upon the earlier date of filing in Canada.

4.   DISADVANTAGES OF THE REGISTRATION SYSTEM

As explained earlier, registration is not mandatory but is advantageous. Usually, the only disadvantage of registration is the expense. Charitable and not-for-profit organizations, which may be unfamiliar with the trade mark registration system or which may lack the financial resources to register their trade marks, may mistakenly perceive the process of registration as not worth the effort or expense required. A common error for charitable and not-for-profit organizations is to not respond in a timely

---

[11]   *Ibid.*, s. 34.

manner to correspondence from their trade mark agents. Such a failure commonly leads to additional expenses that could have been avoided.

SUMMARY

In order to obtain protection under the *Trade-marks Act*, an application must be made to CIPO. Trade mark rights under the Act can be acquired based on four grounds: (1) actual use in Canada; (2) making known in Canada; (3) registration in a foreign country; or (4) proposed use in Canada. Although the common law confers certain rights to the unregistered trade mark owner, registration significantly expands those rights, most importantly eliminating the geographical limitation on the rights, as well as conferring exclusive rights across Canada. Registration assists in avoiding the possibility of confusing trade marks being registered by other organizations, as the trade mark will show up in subsequent trade mark searches by trade mark agents and CIPO.

Trade mark registration can also greatly assist in protecting a key domain name on the Internet, as it assists in proving the cybersquatter has no rights or legitimate interest in the domain name. It also facilitates registration in Convention countries, enabling the trade mark owner to establish an earlier filing date. Registration may seem like a luxury in the short-term, but may prove to be a smart choice in the long-term.

Five years after registration, a registered trade mark is virtually uncontestable, even if there is prior use by another person. The bar is set high for an unregistered owner to contest the registration, requiring the unregistered owner to prove the registered owner adopted the trade mark with knowledge of the prior use or making known in Canada.

A registered trade mark owner has potentially three causes of action: (1) a common law passing-off action; (2) a trade mark infringement action; or (3) an action for the depreciation of the value of the goodwill attached to the registered trade mark.

With the numerous advantages under the trade mark registration system, charitable and not-for-profit organizations should give serious consideration to obtaining protection for their trade marks as discussed above. In subsequent chapters, we will discuss the importance of also obtaining registration in foreign jurisdictions, which is another important consideration for all organizations.

CHAPTER 5

REGISTERING A TRADE MARK IN CANADA

(f)   Registration

Summary

As the previous chapters have explained, a trade mark may be registered in Canada under the federal *Trade-marks Act*.[1] By so doing, the charitable or not-for-profit organization obtains the exclusive right to use the registered trade mark throughout the country, as well as having access to certain protection measures that are easier to enforce than through an unregistered trade mark. This chapter will discuss the various elements of a trade mark application and the process the applicant will encounter with the Canadian Intellectual Property Office ("CIPO").

1.   WHEN TO FILE AN APPLICATION

Conventional wisdom suggests that a charitable or not-for-profit organization should file a trade mark application as soon as a decision is made to obtain the protection of registration under the *Trade-marks Act*. This advice should not be considered lightly. Organizations considering applying for registration of a trade mark should be aware of the two situations where the importance of quickly filing a trade mark registration should not be underestimated.

First, where a charitable or not-for-profit organization intends to use a trade mark for particular wares or services in the future but would like protection for it as soon as possible, an application based on proposed use in Canada should be filed. Such an application will enable the earlier filing date to become the priority date instead of the subsequent date of actual usage. The ability to use the earlier filing date as the priority date is important in situations where another organization subsequently begins using the same or a confusingly similar trade mark. By obtaining the earlier filing date as the priority date, the charitable or not-for-profit organization is able to use the date which is earlier than when they actually began to use the trade mark in Canada. Obtaining registration on proposed use in Canada can lead to a significant cost savings, as it enables the organization to coordinate marketing plans that include the trade mark without concerns that they may be infringing upon another trade mark, which would necessitate going back to the drawing board for the organization's marketing plans.

---

[1]   R.S.C. 1985, c. T-13.

Second, where a charitable or not-for-profit organization has, in the past six months, registered a trade mark in a foreign country that is a signatory to the *Paris Convention for the Protection of Industrial Property*[2] ("Convention"), the *Trade-marks Act* enables the organization to file a trade mark application in Canada within the same six-month period and obtain the benefit of the earlier foreign filing date as it becomes the priority date instead of the subsequent date of actual filing in Canada.

2. WHAT TO COVER IN THE APPLICATION

Although the actual preparation of a trade mark application is the responsibility of the trade mark agent, the next section of this book discusses some of the basic information that should be covered in the trade mark application, so that charitable and not-for-profit organizations will have a better idea of what information to provide to their trade mark agent.

(a) Applicant

The organization or individual listed as the applicant on the trade mark application will be the organization or individual that will hold the rights to the trade mark once it is registered. Only the registered trade mark owner will have the ability to enforce rights to the trade mark. As such, a preliminary decision for the charitable or not-for-profit organization will be the name of the organization or individual who will be listed as the applicant. Once that decision is made, the trade mark application must provide the name and address of the applicant by making a statement similar to the following:[3]

> *The applicant, _____, the full post office address of whose principal office or place of business is _____ applies for the registration, in accordance with the provisions of the* Trade-marks Act, *of the trade mark identified below.*

In the case of a corporation, the full legal name should be provided in the trade mark application, whereas in the case of an individual, the surname and at least one given name should be specified. If the individual trades under a name other than the individual's own name, the individual's name should be followed by the words "trading as" and the trading name used by

---

[2] Adopted in Paris on 20 March 1883, last revised by the Paris Union on 28 September 1979, 828 U.N.T.S. 305, 21 U.S.T. 1583.

[3] *Trade-marks Act*, R.S.C. 1985, c. T-13, s. 30(g).

the individual. In the case of a partnership, the trade mark application should provide the name under which the partnership trades.

Any organization seeking to register a trade mark should be cautioned of the importance of providing the correct legal name to the trade mark agent, as it is difficult to amend the trade mark registration at a later time. If the charitable or not-for-profit organization has only recently become incorporated or has changed its name, it will be important for the trade mark application to reflect the name of the predecessor in title that established earlier use of the trade mark.

Where a charitable or not-for-profit organization does not have a principal office or place of business in Canada, as may be the case with an international organization, the organization must provide its address in the foreign jurisdiction and the name and address in Canada of a person or firm who will receive any documentation relating to the application or registration.[4]

(b) Trade mark

The trade mark application must make a statement identifying what is the trade mark:[5]

The trade mark is _____.

If the trade mark is a word or words, or a word or words alone featuring French or English accents or punctuation, the trade mark application must set out the word or words in capital letters; *i.e.*, MR. CHRISTIE[6] or YAHOO!.[7] If the word or words are in a special form or type (*e.g.*, in upper and lower case letters or in italicized type), the trade mark will be treated as a design.

If the trade mark is a design, the trade mark application should insert the phrase "shown in the accompanying drawing", and annex the drawing to the application form. Generally, drawings should be submitted to CIPO in black and white only and it is not necessary to claim colour as a feature of a trade mark simply because the trade mark appears in colour. However, if the colour is important, the organization can include a claim to a specific colour or colours. For accuracy purposes, the application should make the claim to a colour by claiming the colour's corresponding number from a

---

4   *Ibid.*, ss. 30(g) and 42.
5   *Ibid.*, s. 30(g).
6   Canadian Intellectual Property Office, Registration Number TMA290982.
7   Canadian Intellectual Property Office, Registration Number TMA571707.

chart in the PANTONE[8] Matching System. The PANTONE Matching System is an international colour language that provides an accurate method for selecting, reproducing and matching a colour. For example, if an application claims PANTONE 201, trade mark offices and printers worldwide will know this refers to a specific shade of burgundy.

Should the charitable or not-for-profit organization wish to register more than one trade mark, a separate application would need to be filed for each trade mark, since Canada only allows one trade mark claim per trade mark application.

Charitable and not-for-profit organizations that have operations in Quebec should be aware of provincial legislation requiring the use of the French language in Quebec. Since the *Charter of the French Language*[9] requires that "public signs and posters and commercial advertising must be in French",[10] it is generally accepted that English trade marks being used in Quebec must be translated into French. However, charitable and not-for-profit organizations may fall under the exception found in section 59 of the *Charter of the French Language*, which provides that "section 58 does not apply to ... messages of a religious, political, ideological or humanitarian nature if not for a profit motive". Still, charitable and not-for-profit organizations operating in Quebec should consider filing one application for the English trade mark and a separate application for the French trade mark. This will allow the most flexibility in mixing and matching trade marks; *i.e.*, the organization can choose to use the English trade mark only in certain provinces, use the French trade mark only in Quebec, or use the English and French trade marks together in other provinces.

(c) Disclaimer

Many trade marks will inevitably include words for which the applicant cannot reasonably make a legal claim to exclusive use and are consequently unregistrable. However, that does not mean that the word cannot form a part of the trade mark. In order to include such a term, the trade mark application must include a disclaimer to the following effect:[11]

> *The applicant disclaims the right to the exclusive use of _____ apart from the trade mark.*

---

[8] Canadian Intellectual Property Office, Registration Number TMA210636.
[9] R.S.Q. c. C-11.
[10] *Ibid.*, s. 58.
[11] *Trade-marks Act*, R.S.C. 1985, c. T-13, s. 35.

A disclaimer is necessary only where some word that is part of the trade mark is not independently registrable; *i.e.*, the trade mark HOME HARDWARE BUILDING CENTRE includes a disclaimer which states: "The right to the exclusive use of the words HARDWARE and BUILDING CENTRE is disclaimed apart from the trade mark".[12] This will be discussed later in more detail with the concept of registrability. A word would usually be considered unregistrable according to subsection 12(1) of the *Trade-marks Act* if the word is:

    (a)   a word that is primarily merely the name or the surname of an individual who is living or has died within the preceding thirty years;

    (b)   whether depicted, written or sounded, either clearly descriptive or deceptively misdescriptive in the English or French language of the character or quality of the wares or services in association with which it is used or proposed to be used or of the conditions of or the persons employed in their production or of their place of origin;

    (c)   the name in any language of any of the wares or services in connection with which it is used or proposed to be used;

    (d)   confusing with a registered trade mark;

    (e)   a mark of which the adoption is prohibited by section 9 or 10;

    (f)   a denomination the adoption of which is prohibited by section 10.1;

    (g)   in whole or in part a protected geographical indication, where the trade mark is to be registered in association with a wine not originating in a territory indicated by the geographical indication; and

    (h)   in whole or in part a protected geographical indication, where the trade mark is to be registered in association with a spirit not originating in a territory indicated by the geographical indication.

A disclaimer means that the applicant gives up the right to exclusive use of the word apart from the trade mark. Section 35 of the *Trade-marks Act* provides that disclaimers will not prejudice nor affect the rights then existing or thereafter arising in the disclaimed matter, nor will the disclaimer prejudice or affect the right to registration later if the disclaimed matter then becomes distinctive.

The owner of a registered trade mark containing disclaimed matter still has the right to challenge use by an unauthorized person of a confusing trade mark, including the disclaimed matter. When determining if two trade marks are confusing, the disclaimed matter will be taken into account because the trade marks in question must be considered in their totalities. However, if the only similarity between the two trade marks is the disclaimed matter, the challenge will not succeed because the purpose of

---

[12]   Canadian Intellectual Property Office, Registration Number TMA638451.

the disclaimer is to permit other persons to use such independently non-registerable matter.

(d) Wares and/or services

The trade mark application must identify the wares and/or services with which the trade mark is to be associated.[13] What kind of statements should be made to this effect will be discussed in the next section.

Since Canada does not use the international classification system, one application can cover both wares and services in Canada. In addition, there is no limit to the number of wares and services that can be included in one application in Canada, which is different from other countries using the international classification system,[14] set out in the table below, which requires a separate filing fee for each separate class.

Class	International Classification of Goods & Services
1	Chemical substances
2	Paints, varnishes and lacquers
3	Bleaching, cleaning, polishing, scouring and abrasive preparations; cosmetics
4	Industrial oils and greases; lubricants; fuels
5	Pharmaceutical, veterinary and sanitary products
6	Common metals and their alloys; ores
7	Machines and machine tools
8	Hand tools and implements
9	Scientific and electric apparatus and instruments
10	Medical apparatus and instruments
11	Environmental control apparatus
12	Vehicles
13	Firearms; explosives

---

[13] *Trade-marks Act*, R.S.C. 1985, c. T-13, s. 30(a).

[14] The *International (Nice) Classification of Goods and Services for the Purposes of the Registration of Marks* was established by the Nice Agreement concluded at the Nice Diplomatic Conference, on June 15, 1957, and was revised at Stockholm, in 1967, and at Geneva, in 1977. World Intellectual Property Organization, "Nice Classification", online: <http://www.wipo.int/classifications/fulltext/nice8/ennpre.htm>.

14	Precious metal and their alloys; jewelry; time-keeping instruments
15	Musical instruments
16	Paper, cardboard and goods made form these materials
17	Rubber and plastic goods
18	Leather and imitations of leather
19	Non-metallic building materials
20	Furniture and decorative products
21	Household or kitchen utensils, containers and cleaning materials; glassware; porcelain; earthenware
22	Ropes; padding and stuffing materials; raw fibrous textile materials
23	Yarns and threads for textile use
24	Textiles and textile goods
25	Clothing; footwear; headgear
26	Fanciful or novelty items; sewing notions
27	Floor and wall coverings
28	Games; toys; sports equipment
29	Meats and prepared or preserved foods; dairy products
30	Basic staples
31	Agricultural products; live animals
32	Beers; non-alcoholic drinks and beverages
33	Alcoholic beverages
34	Tobacco; smokers-articles
35	Advertising; business
36	Insurance; financial affairs
37	Building; repairs
38	Telecommunications
39	Transport, packaging and storing
40	Treatment of materials
41	Education; entertainment

42	Various services and/or scientific and technological services and research and design relating thereto; industrial analysis and research services; design and development of computer hardware and software; legal services
43	Services for providing food and drink; temporary accommodation
44	Medical services; veterinary services; hygienic and beauty care for human beings or animals; agriculture, horticulture and forestry services
45	Personal and social services rendered by others to meet the needs of individuals; security services for the protection of property and individuals

For example, a food bank could file one application and pay one filing fee in Canada for the wares "meats and processed foods, staple foods and natural agricultural products" and for the services "charitable social services relating to the provision and distribution of food and drink to the less fortunate". Compare this to the same food bank's application in the United States, where it would have to pay multiple filing fees because "meats and processed meats" fall under class 29, "staple foods" fall under class 30, "natural agricultural products" fall under class 31, and "charitable social services relating to the provision and distribution of food and drink to the less fortunate" fall under class 42. As such, an application covering the same range of wares and services is normally less expensive to file and prosecute in Canada than in the United States, which uses the international classification system.

Section 30 of the *Trade-marks Act* requires the application for a trade mark to describe the wares and/or services in "ordinary commercial terms". The *Trade-marks Act* does not define the phrase, but CIPO does provide a Wares and Services Manual, which provides a list of terms it considers as ordinary commercial terms. The Wares and Services Manual will change over time as what is considered "ordinary commercial terms" changes. For example, computer software was a very narrow term when first adopted and was considered an ordinary commercial term. However, over time, computer software became an extremely broad term and must now be specific as to the area of use and function of the computer software. If there are no ordinary commercial terms to describe the wares and/or services, then CIPO will accept a description of the composition and function of the wares and/or services.

Applicants are cautioned to ensure the wares and/or services listed are as broad as possible, because an application can be amended to limit the wares and/or services but cannot be amended to extend the wares and/or services.[15]

(e) Basis

The trade mark application must state whether the application is based on the grounds of "actual use in Canada", "making known in Canada", "foreign country application or registration and use abroad", "proposed use in Canada", or a combination of these four grounds.[16]

(i) Actual use in Canada

Where the trade mark application is based on the ground of actual use in Canada, the application must state that use of the trade mark has occurred and provide the date of first use.[17] For example:

> The trade mark has been used in Canada by the applicant (or his predecessor(s) in title _____) in association with all the specific wares and/or services listed hereafter, and the applicant requests registration in respect of such wares and/or services. The trade mark has been so used in Canada in association with the general class of wares comprising the following specific ware and/or services _____ since _____ and in association with the general class of wares and/or services comprising the following specific wares and/or service _____ since _____.

A predecessor in title is necessary if the charitable or not-for-profit organization incorporates after first use of the trade mark, or if the organization used to operate under a different name after first use of the trade mark; that is, the application should identify the individual or organization who or which first began to use the trade mark in association with the wares and/or services listed in the application, as well as any intervening predecessor(s) down to the applicant.

The date can be specific (e.g., September 1, 2002) or general (e.g., September 2002 or simply 2002). If the date provided is general, the presumed date will be the last day of that time period (e.g., if the date provided on the application is September 2002, the CIPO will presume the date of first use to be September 30, 2002, while 2002 will be presumed to be December 31, 2002). Using general dates on a trade mark application may not be permissible if the general date is in the same month or the same year as the application is filed. For example, if the general date is in the same year as the application is filed, then a month must also be

---

[15] *Trade marks Regulations (1996)*, S.O.R./96-195, s. 31(e).
[16] *Trade-marks Act*, R.S.C. 1985, c. T-13, s. 30(b)–(d).
[17] *Ibid.*, s. 30(b).

listed. However, if the general date is in the same month and year as the application is filed, then a specific date must be given.

(ii)   *Making known in Canada*

Where the application is based on the ground of making known in Canada, the trade mark application must state that the trade mark was used in a foreign jurisdiction and has been made known in Canada, as well as specify how and when the trade mark first became known in Canada.[18] The application would include a statement such as the following:

> The applicant (and his predecessor(s) in title _____) has (have) made the trade mark known in Canada in association with all the specific wares and/or services listed hereafter by reason of having used the trade mark in association with such wares and/or services in _____ and by reason of _____. By reason of such distribution and/or advertising the trade mark has become well-known in Canada. The trade mark has been so made known in Canada in association with the general class of wares and/or services comprising the following specific wares and/or services _____ since _____. The applicant requests registration of the trade mark in respect of the specific wares and/or services aforesaid.

With respect to the phrase "use abroad", the trade mark must have been used in a foreign country recognized by the *Trade-marks Act*. With respect to the phrase "been made known in Canada", the trade mark must have been made known by the distribution of wares in Canada or by the advertising of wares and/or services in Canada through printed publication or radio broadcasts. Due to the difficulty in establishing that a trade mark has been made known in Canada when it has not actually been used in Canada, trade mark applications are seldom based on this basis.

(iii)   *Foreign country application or registration and use abroad*

Where the application is based on the ground of foreign country application or registration and use abroad, the application must state that the trade mark has been applied for or registered in a foreign country and used abroad.[19] The applicant must also provide the date of the application or registration in the foreign country, by stating something to the following effect:

> The trade mark has been duly registered by the applicant (or the applicant's predecessor in title named in such registration) in or for _____ the country of origin of the applicant (or the said predecessor). The registration was made in _____ under No. _____ in association with _____. The applicant (or the applicant's said predecessor) has used the trade mark in association with _____,

---

[18] *Ibid.*, s. 30(c).
[19] *Ibid.*, s. 30(d).

in _____, and the applicant requests registration of the trade mark in respect of the wares and/or services in association with which it has been registered and used as aforesaid.

Or

An application to register the trade mark has been filed by the applicant (or the applicant's predecessor in title named in the said application) in or for _____, the country of origin of the applicant (or the said predecessor). The application was filed in _____ on _____ under No. _____ in association with _____. The applicant (or the applicant's said predecessor) has used the trade mark in association with _____, in _____, and the applicant requests registration of the trade mark, upon its registration in the country of origin, in respect of the wares and/or services in association with which the trade mark has been used as aforesaid and which are covered by such registration in the country of origin.

If the trade mark is already registered in the foreign country, then a statement should be made in accordance to the first sample paragraph. If the trade mark has not been registered and an application is pending, then a statement should be made in accordance with the second sample paragraph.

This basis of application is available if the applicant has applied for or registered the trade mark in a foreign country recognized by the *Trade-marks Act*; *i.e.*, a Convention country. In addition, the trade mark must have been used abroad. Once again, "use abroad" means the trade mark must have been used in a foreign country that is recognized by the *Trade-marks Act*.

(iv)   Proposed use in Canada

Where the application is based on the ground of proposed use in Canada, the trade mark application must state that either the applicant or its licensee, or both, intend to use the trade mark in Canada:[20]

The applicant by itself or through a licensee, or by itself and through a licensee, intends to use the trade mark in Canada in association with _____ and requests registration of the trade mark in respect of such wares and/or services.

Once an application based on the ground of proposed use in Canada is allowed, subsection 40(3) of the *Trade-marks Act* requires a Declaration of Use be filed, before the later of six months from the date of the Notice of Allowance or three years from the date of filing the application in Canada, in order for CIPO to register the trade mark.

---

[20]   *Ibid.*, s. 30(e).

(f) Priority claim

Where a trade mark application is filed in a Convention country, an application for the same trade mark can be made in Canada within six months and claim the earlier foreign filing date as the priority date instead of the subsequent date of actual filing in Canada.[21] A priority claim should state something to the following effect:

> The applicant claims priority under section 34 of the Act on the ground that an application for registration of the same or substantially the same trade mark was filed in or for _____ by the applicant (or the applicant's predecessor in title named in the said application). The application was filed in _____ on _____ under No. _____ and such application was the earliest application filed in any country of the Union other than Canada by the applicant or any predecessor in title of the applicant for the registration of the same or substantially the same trade mark for use in association with the same kind of wares (or services) as those set out above. At the date of such application the applicant (or the predecessor in the title aforesaid) _____ the country aforesaid.

The six-month period is strictly observed and cannot be extended.[22] As such, charitable and not-for-profit organizations should be proactive in coordinating their trade marks to ensure they get the full benefit of the earliest filing date.

(g) Registrability claim

The trade mark application can also include a registrability claim where the trade mark would otherwise be unregistrable. One way for a trade mark that is otherwise unregistrable to still be registered is to claim that the trade mark has become distinctive as of the date of filing the application.[23] The concepts of unregistrability and distinctiveness are discussed in more detail in Chapter 7. Another way to register an otherwise unregistrable trade mark is to claim that the trade mark is registered in the applicant's country of origin.[24] The trade mark being applied for in Canada must be the same or substantially the same as the trade mark registered in the applicant's country of origin. In addition, the trade mark must meet a number of other conditions imposed by the *Trade-marks Act*:

- The trade mark cannot be confusing with a registered trade mark;[25]

---

[21]   *Ibid.*, s. 34.
[22]   *Ibid.*, s. 34(a).
[23]   *Ibid.*, s. 12(2).
[24]   *Ibid.*, s. 14(1).
[25]   *Ibid.*, s. 14(1)(a).

- The trade mark cannot be without distinctive character, having regard to all the circumstances of the case including the length of time during which it has been used in any country;[26]
- The trade mark cannot be contrary to morality or public order or of such a nature as to deceive the public;[27] and
- The trade mark cannot be a trade mark prohibited by sections 9 or 10 of the *Trade-marks Act*.[28]

(h) Agent and/or representative

The trade mark application can also include an appointment of representative for service. The agent or representative would be responsible for receiving notices or communications from CIPO on behalf of the charitable or not-for-profit organization. The agent or representative can be appointed by making the following statement in the trade mark application:

> The applicant appoints _____, whose full post office address in Canada is _____ as the person (or firm) to whom any notice in respect of the application or registration may be sent, and upon whom service of any proceedings in respect of the application or registration may be given or served with the same effect as if they had been given to or served upon the applicant or registrant.

An agent or representative is particularly useful for charitable or not-for-profit organizations who do not have a principal office or place of business in Canada, or simply as a matter of effectively managing the documentation with respect to the organization's trade marks when the person who fulfils the responsible position in the organization may frequently change. Further, as previously mentioned, the *Trade-marks Act* requires that a charitable or not-for-profit organization that does not have a principal office or place of business in Canada must provide its address abroad, and the name and address in Canada of a person or firm who will receive any documentation relating to the application or registration.[29]

(i) Entitlement

Subsection 30(i) of the *Trade-marks Act* requires that the trade mark application must provide a statement of entitlement to registration, such as:

---

[26]   *Ibid.*, s. 14(1)(b).
[27]   *Ibid.*, s. 14(1)(c).
[28]   *Ibid.*, s. 14(1)(d).
[29]   *Ibid.*, ss. 30(g) and 42.

The applicant is satisfied that it is entitled to use the trade mark in Canada in association with the wares and/or services described above.

This statement of entitlement is deemed to be a statement made in good faith. Although bad faith, in and of itself, is not a ground for opposition to the registration of the trade mark, an opponent could claim that the applicant is not the person entitled to registration of the trade mark and bad faith could be used to support this ground of opposition.

(j) Fee

The trade mark application can be filed with CIPO, along with a fee payable to the Receiver General of Canada.[30] Only one fee is required for a single trade mark application to register a single trade mark, regardless of the number of wares and/or services covered and regardless of the number of bases relied upon. At the time of writing, the following are the published fees:

- If the application is filed online, the filing fee is $250 and can be paid by using American Express, MasterCard, VISA or the CIPO Deposit Account.

- If the application is filed by mail, the filing fee is $300 and can be paid by cheque.

3. HOW TO AMEND THE APPLICATION

Section 31 of the *Trade marks Regulations (1996)*[31] is a good reminder for charitable and not-for-profit organizations to ensure careful thought is put into their application for registration of a trade mark, and that their trade mark agents are provided with as accurate and complete information as possible because it can be very costly and difficult to amend the application after it is filed. The Regulations state that no amendments to the application may be made where the amendment would change the following:

(a) the identity of the applicant, except after recognition of a transfer by the Registrar [CIPO];

(b) the trade mark, except in respects that do not alter its distinctive character or affect its identity;

(c) the date of first use or making known in Canada of the trade mark to an earlier date, except where the evidence proves that the change is justified by the facts;

---

[30] *Trade marks Regulations (1996)*, S.O.R./96-195, Sch., Part I.
[31] *Trade marks Regulations (1996)*, S.O.R./96-195.

(d)   the application from one not alleging use or making known of the trade mark in Canada before the filing of the application to one alleging such use or making known; or

(e)   the statement of wares or services so as to be broader than the statement of wares or services contained in the application at the time the application was filed pursuant to section 30 of the Act.[32]

4.   OVERVIEW OF THE APPLICATION PROCESS

The actual preparation, filing and prosecution of a trade mark application is the responsibility of the trade mark agent. However, some basic information about the process would be useful for the charitable or not-for-profit organization going through the application process. What follows is intended to be only a very brief overview of what a normal examination process would involve.

(a) Formalities

If the trade mark application is complete and includes the filing fee, CIPO will issue a filing notice within two or three weeks if the application was filed by mail, or within 24 hours if the application was filed electronically. The filing notice will show all the information about the application and should be reviewed carefully. Should any errors or omissions be discovered, CIPO should be advised immediately. The filing notice will also state the filing date and an application number.

(b) Examination

CIPO will then examine the application to see if the trade mark can be registered. First, it will review its records to see whether there are any prior registrations or pending applications that are confusingly similar to the application. Second, it will review the trade mark in the application to see if the trade mark is registrable, in addition to determining if the applicant is the person entitled to registration. Third, the application will be reviewed to see if it meets the formalities requirement.

A response to the trade mark application will then be sent by CIPO, approving the application, requiring amendments to the application or rejecting the application.[33] An adverse ruling may be the result of the

---

[32]   *Ibid.*, s. 31.
[33]   *Trade-marks Act*, R.S.C. 1985, c. T-13, s. 37.

applicant not being the person entitled to registration of the trade mark; the trade mark is not being registrable according to section 12 of the *Trade-marks Act*; or the application not conforming to the requirements of section 30 of the *Trade-marks Act.*

In response to CIPO's requirement that an application be amended, a charitable or not-for-profit organization can abandon the application, amend the application or submit arguments against making the amendments. If CIPO refuses the submitted arguments and subsequently rejects the application, an appeal can be made to the courts. Failing to respond to CIPO may result in automatic abandonment status.

If the application is approved, CIPO will issue a notice of approval. The notice of approval should be received in about six to eight months if the application was received correctly and approved without amendments.

(c) Advertisement

After all concerns and objections raised by CIPO have been dealt with to its satisfaction, CIPO will approve the application and publish the application in the weekly *Trade marks Journal.*[34] The application should appear in the *Trade marks Journal* about five weeks after it is approved. Once published, anybody can file an opposition to the registration of a trade mark within two months. Should this occur, the application will then be removed from the normal processing cycle until the opposition has been resolved. The trade mark agent will need to defend it on behalf of the applicant and, if necessary, have the matter dealt with pursuant to the trade mark opposition proceedings described below.

(d) Opposition

If the application is opposed after being published in the *Trade marks Journal*, CIPO will forward a copy of the statement of opposition to the applicant. An opposition is a complex adversarial proceeding. Most proceedings are settled during the course of the opposition, but a complete opposition may last more than three or four years. Once the statement of opposition is received, the applicant will then have one month to file a counter statement. Both parties will then have an opportunity to file affidavit evidence and written arguments, as well as to make submissions at an oral

---

[34] *Trade marks Regulations (1996)*, S.O.R./96-195, s. 17.

hearing. If the opposition is withdrawn or is unsuccessful, the application will proceed to allowance.

(e) Allowance

A notice of allowance does not mean the trade mark is registered, only that the application has been approved for the trade mark to be registered. If the application was not opposed, the notice of allowance should be received approximately three months after the application appeared in the *Trade marks Journal*. It is at the allowance stage that the applicant submits the required registration fee for the trade mark to be registered. If the trade mark application was based on the ground of proposed use in Canada, a Declaration of Use must also be submitted before the trade mark will be registered. CIPO will then issue a certificate of registration for the trade mark.

(f) Registration

After receiving the registration fee, and the Declaration of Use, if applicable, CIPO will issue a certificate of registration within three or four weeks. The trade mark registration, once issued, is valid for 15 years and can be renewed every 15 years thereafter.

How long it will take to register a trade mark can vary. If the application is submitted correctly, approved without changes, and is not opposed, it can be approved for registration in about 20 months. If the application is submitted incorrectly, not approved on the first examination, or is opposed, it will take longer. A charitable or not-for-profit organization can assist its trade mark agent in expediting the process by responding quickly to notices from CIPO.

SUMMARY

Registering a trade mark in Canada necessitates some careful consideration by the charitable or not-for-profit organization prior to submitting the application. The first consideration for the organization is when to file an application. There are many advantages to coordinating an organization's application process, whether it be obtaining the benefit of an earlier filing date in a Convention country, or ensuring the security of the organization's marketing plans by obtaining registration prior to actual use in Canada. After determining when the application will be filed, the organization must turn its mind to the details of the application so as to ensure the application is accurate and complete when it is filed, as it is costly and difficult to amend an application once it is filed. Once an application is filed, the organization must be prepared for a long application process; however, the organization can expedite matters by promptly responding to any correspondence from the trade mark agent or CIPO.

CHAPTER 6

REGISTERING A TRADE MARK INTERNATIONALLY

As discussed in earlier chapters, for most charitable or not-for-profit organizations, the goodwill associated with their name as a trade mark is their most important asset. The value of the organization's name is reflected in its ability to attract donations through either *inter vivos* or testamentary gifts. In the context of a national governing body, its name as a trade mark and associated logo constitute the basis by which the public will identify the organization and the activities that it carries on. As such, the national governing association will need to be diligent in ensuring that the goodwill associated with its trade marks is not compromised. The same is true of the charitable or not-for-profit organization that operates in an international context. While the majority of charitable and not-for-profit organizations tend to focus on local issues, globalization has affected this sector as well as the commercial sector. Increasingly, a global response to an issue is the only effective measure and, within this context, it is necessary for an organization that desires to operate on an international basis to consider seeking protection for their trade marks in foreign jurisdictions.

Although a trade mark agent in a foreign jurisdiction will perform the actual work related to filing such an application, it is useful for the charitable or not-for-profit organization to understand the process. As such, although there are many foreign jurisdictions in which a charitable or not-for-profit organization may wish to register trade marks, this book will focus on the two main destinations for Canadian organizations: the United States and Europe.

1.   WHEN ARE FOREIGN REGISTRATIONS RELEVANT?

Often a charitable or not-for-profit organization will be involved in operations in more than one country. When this occurs, the organization should give serious consideration to obtaining a trade mark registration in each country in which it operates. The organization may think that because it has trade mark registration in one country, it is automatically protected in other countries, but this is not the case. Trade marks are national in scope and only receive protection for the country in which they are registered.

Just as a trade mark application can be filed in Canada within six months of filing an application in a foreign country that is a signatory to the *Paris*

Convention for the Protection of Industrial Property,[1] a trade mark application can be similarly filed in a Convention country within six months of filing the application in Canada. This is an important advantage to a charitable or not-for-profit organization that wants to expand its operations into another country, such as the United States, but has not yet been able to establish use or apply for trade mark registration in the foreign jurisdiction. In this regard, the organization must make a decision concerning foreign trade mark registration prior to the expiry of six months from the date of the trade mark application being filed in Canada. Otherwise, the ability to claim the earlier filing date established in Canada will be lost. This is particularly important in relation to filing a trade mark application in the United States, since there is obviously a great deal more competition for trade marks in that country where the population is 10 times that of Canada.

2. THE U.S. REGISTRATION SYSTEM

Due to Canada's proximity to the U.S., trade mark registration in the U.S. is often an important consideration, as many charitable or not-for-profit organizations will either have operations in or plan to expand to the U.S. When considering trade mark registration in the U.S., it is important to remember that something which is unregistrable in Canada may be perfectly acceptable in the U.S. For example, Canada requires that use be visual, whereas the U.S. allows use to be both visual and non-visual. Therefore, a trade mark application in Canada can only be for a mark, guise, sign, impression, token, character, device, label, brand, seal or the like that can be seen. However, a trade mark application in the U.S. can also be for a sound (the NBC chimes) or a gesture (the Pillsbury Doughboy being poked in the belly). This difference arises from the fact that Canada's trade mark theory emphasizes consumer protection, whereas the U.S. emphasizes business reputation in its trade mark theory. While Canada sees the purpose of a trade mark as being to inform the public that the wares or services bearing the trade mark came from a particular source, the U.S. sees the purpose of a trade mark as being to represent the goodwill of a business. As such, Canada holds to a strict concept of use (*i.e.*, use must be visual), whereas the U.S. holds to the theory of distinctiveness (*i.e.*, affording trade mark protection for anything that makes a business distinct from its competitors).

---

[1] Adopted in Paris on 20 March 1883, last revised by the Paris Union on 28 September 1979, 828 U.N.T.S. 305, 21 U.S.T. 1583.

(a) Formalities

A trade mark application must contain a number of elements before the United States Patent and Trademark Office (the "USPTO") will accept it, including the following:

- **Name of the applicant** — The applicant must be the owner of the trade mark. Just as is the case with a trade marks application in Canada, the owner of the trade mark is the person or entity controlling the nature and quality of the goods and/or the services used in association the trade mark. The owner is also the only person who can institute infringement proceedings. The owner may be an individual, corporation, partnership or other type of legal entity.

- **Name and address for correspondence** — The name and address given for correspondence will be where the USPTO sends communications concerning the application. If a charitable or not-for-profit organization decides not to represent itself but hires a lawyer instead, the name and address given for correspondence should be for the organization's lawyer, and the USPTO will correspond only with the lawyer. Unlike Canada, the U.S. does not have trade mark agents; only lawyers prosecute a trade mark application. An organization located outside the U.S. may list a domestic representative; that is, the name and address of any person residing in the U.S. with whom the USPTO may send correspondence concerning the application.

- **Drawing of the trade mark** — Every application must include a clear drawing of the mark. It is important to ensure the accuracy of this drawing, as it will be registered in the U.S. trade marks database, published in the *Official Gazette* and be used for the registration certificate.

  The drawing can be a standard character drawing if all letters and words in the trade mark are depicted in Latin characters; all numerals in the trade mark are depicted in Roman or Arabic numerals; the trade mark includes only common punctuation or diacritical marks; and the trade mark does not include a design element. In addition, the application must include a statement that the trade mark is presented in standard character format without claim to any particular font style, size or colour.

  The drawing must be a specialized or special form drawing if the particular style of lettering is important or the trade mark includes colour or a design or logo. The drawing page should show a black and white image of the trade mark, unless colour is claimed as a feature of the mark. The specialized or special form drawing must be a substantially exact representation of the trade mark.

- **Description of goods and/or services** — The goods and/or services must be specified in clear, concise terms; *i.e.*, common commercial names and language that the general public easily understands. Although the U.S. follows the international classification system, the terms used to classify the goods and/or services are broad and are not sufficient to specify the goods and/or services in an application. It is important to ensure the accuracy of the description of wares and/or services, as the description cannot be expanded or broadened after filing the application.

- **Basis for filing** — Canada recognizes four bases as grounds to apply for a trade mark application: (1) actual use in Canada; (2) making known in Canada; (3) foreign country application or registration and use abroad; and (4) proposed use in Canada. The U.S., on the other hand, does not recognize "making known" as a ground for a trade mark application because the goods and/or services must actually be offered on U.S. soil in order to count as use. Instead, the U.S. recognizes the following bases as grounds to apply for a trade mark application: actual use, intent to use and foreign registration.

  If the trade mark is already in use, a trade mark application can be filed based on that use. A use-based application must include a sworn statement that the trade mark is in use and list the date of first use. In addition, the charitable or not-for-profit organization must submit a specimen of the trade mark in use. If the trade mark has not been used but will be in the near future, a trade mark application can be filed based on a good faith intention to use the trade mark. An intent-to-use-based application must include a sworn statement that there is intent to use the trade mark. Once the application is allowed, the charitable or not-for-profit organization must file a Statement of Use and submit a specimen of that use before the trade mark can be registered.

  If there is a foreign registration for the trade mark, a trade mark application can be filed with a statement that the applicant has a good faith intention to use the trade mark. It is important to note that the foreign registration must be valid and in good standing at the time of the U.S. application. Where there is a foreign application for the trade mark, a trade mark application can also be filed with the statement that the applicant has a good faith intention to use the trade mark. However, it is important to understand that it is the expected foreign registration, and not the foreign application itself, that is the basis for the application. In either case, no specimen is required in order to obtain its registration.

- **Specimen** — Where a specimen is required, the applicant must submit actual examples of how the trade mark was used. Unlike the U.S., Canada does not require specimens. A proper specimen or acceptable evidence of use with respect to goods would be anything showing the trade mark on the actual goods or packaging for the goods (*e.g.*, a tag or label for the goods); a container for the goods; a display associated with the goods; or a photograph of the goods that shows use of the trade mark on the goods. An improper specimen or unacceptable evidence of use would be an invoice, announcement, order form, bill of lading, leaflet, brochure, publicity release, letterhead or business card. In addition, the USPTO will not accept actual products.

  A proper specimen or acceptable evidence of use with respect to services would be anything showing the trade mark used in the sale or advertising for the services (*e.g.*, a sign or a brochure about the services); an advertisement for the services; stationery or a business card displaying the trade mark in connection with the services; or a photograph displaying the trade mark as used in rendering or advertising the services. An improper specimen or unacceptable evidence of use would be blank letterheads, business cards or invoices that merely display the trade mark without any reference to the type of services rendered.

- **Application filing fee** — As discussed in Chapter 5, (which reviewed registering a trade mark domestically), Canada does not follow the international classification system and requires only one filing fee, regardless of how many wares and services are listed in the trade mark application. The U.S., however, does use the international classification system, and therefore requires a separate filing fee for each class of goods and/or services listed in the application.

- **Signature** — The applicant, or a person authorized to sign on behalf of the applicant, must sign the application.

(b) Examination

If the trade mark application meets the above requirements, the USPTO will then examine the application to see if the trade mark can be registered. This includes performing its own search of the U.S. trade mark database to see if the applicant's mark is confusingly similar to any trade mark registrations or pending trade mark applications. An interesting point to consider is that a trade mark that is thought at first to be confusingly similar to another trade mark can still be registered in the U.S. if the two trade mark owners sign a coexistence agreement stating that they believe the trade marks are not confusingly similar. While Canada does not recognize coexistence agreements because its trade mark theory emphasizes consumer protection, the U.S. will accept coexistence agreements because its trade mark theory emphasizes business reputation. As a result of this trade mark theory, the USPTO feels that the trade mark owners themselves would be in a better position to protect the goodwill of the business.

If the USPTO decides that the trade mark cannot be registered, it will issue a letter explaining any substantive reasons for refusal, and any technical or procedural deficiencies in the application. The applicant will then have six months to respond to the letter. Unlike Canada, which allows extensions, the U.S. requires a response within the six-month period or the application will be considered abandoned.

(c) Publication

If the USPTO has no objections, or after all concerns and objections raised by the USPTO have been dealt with to its satisfaction, the USPTO will approve the application and publish the trade mark in the weekly *Official Gazette*. Once the trade mark is published, any member of the public can file an opposition to the registration of a trade mark. Unlike Canada, which allows two months, the U.S. gives only 30 days from the date of publication to file an opposition or a request to extend time to oppose.

(d) Opposition

Generally, it is the owner of another registered trade mark who will file an opposition, alleging that the proposed mark is likely to cause confusion for the public. Once an opposition is filed within the 30-day period after publication in the *Official Gazette*, the trade mark applicant is given 30 days to file an answer. If the applicant fails to file an answer, the trade mark application is dismissed.

The opposition hearing process is likened to the civil litigation process, as it involves a discovery process that includes depositions, interrogatories, production of records and request for admissions. The actual proceeding is held before the Trademark Trial and Appeal Board, which is a USPTO administrative tribunal. Unlike civil litigation, the hearing before the Trademark Trial and Appeal Board is all based on written record.

The applicant and the opponent can come to an agreement with respect to the use of the trade mark, such as the aforementioned coexistence agreement. Should this occur, the opposition will be dismissed. Otherwise, the Trademark Trial and Appeal Board will determine whether the application will proceed to allowance.

As such, if there is no opposition, or if the opposition is withdrawn or is unsuccessful, the application will proceed to allowance.

(e) Allowance

If the trade mark application was based upon intent to use, the USPTO will issue a notice of allowance about 12 weeks after the date the trade mark was published. If no party files either an opposition or request to extend the time to oppose, the applicant then has six months from the date of the notice of allowance to submit a Statement of Use.

If the trade mark application is based upon actual use or upon a foreign registration, the USPTO will normally register the trade mark and issue a registration certificate about 12 weeks after the date the trade mark was published.

(f) Registration

After receiving the registration fee, and the Statement of Use, if applicable, the USPTO will issue a certificate of registration. Unlike Canada, where registration is valid for 15 years, a registration in the U.S. is valid only for 10 years and can only be renewed every 10 years thereafter. There is an exception to this rule for registrations or renewals issued before November 16, 1989, which carried terms of 20 years.

Unlike Canada, which does not require any evidence of continual use, the U.S. requires filing of further specimens evidencing continued use of the registered trade mark. If the owner of the registered trade mark does not file the necessary post-registration requirements between the fifth and sixth anniversary of the registration date, the USPTO will cancel the registration. If owner of the registered trade mark does file the necessary post-registration requirements and fulfil certain other conditions, the USPTO will deem the registration "incontestable", provided that there has been no final decision adverse to the registrant's claim of ownership of the mark for the goods and services and that there is no proceeding involving the registrant's rights pending with the USPTO or in court.

Unlike Canada, which does not address the issue of marking under the *Trade-marks Act*,[2] the U.S. specifically prohibits the use of the symbol ® unless the trade mark is registered. Before registration, only the symbol ™ can be used to give public notice of the trade mark claim of ownership. In addition, the U.S. requires the owner of a registered trade mark to give actual notice of the registration (*e.g.*, use of the symbol ®, in order to recover profits or damages in an infringement action).

3.   THE EUROPEAN COMMUNITY TRADE MARK REGISTRATION SYSTEM

In Europe, a charitable or not-for-profit organization need only file a single registration with the European Community Trade Mark Office to receive trade mark protection throughout all 25 members of the European Community: Austria, Belgium, Cyprus, the Czech Republic, Denmark, Estonia, Finland, France, Germany, Greece, Hungary, Ireland, Italy, Latvia, Lithuania, Luxembourg, Malta, Poland, Portugal, Slovakia, Slovenia, Spain, Sweden, the Netherlands and the United Kingdom. Although the application fee of   975 (about $1,400 Cdn) and the registration fees of   1,100 (about $1,620 Cdn) seem prohibitive, and the application process appears difficult, it is still cheaper and more efficient than pursuing individual trade mark registrations in each European Community country.

(a) Formalities

A European Community Trade Mark ("CTM") application should, at a minimum, contain the following:

---

[2]   R.S.C. 1985, c. T-13.

- **A request for registration** — Unlike Canada and the U.S., which are based on a "first to use" system, the CTM registration system is based on a "first to file" system. This means that there are no common law rights to a trade mark based on use and, as such, there are no trade mark rights unless the trade mark is registered.

- **Information regarding the applicant** — If the applicant is not from a European Community country (*e.g.*, a Canadian charitable or not-for-profit organization), it must appoint a professional representative from the European Community.

- **A description of goods and/or services** — Unlike Canada, the CTM Office classifies goods and/or services according to the international classification system. Also, the CTM Office charges different filing fees for different classes of goods and/or services listed in the application.

- **A drawing of the mark.**

(b) Examination

If the trade mark application meets the required formalities, the CTM Office will then examine it for registrability. This includes conducting a search of the CTM records to see if the trade mark application is confusingly similar to any registrations or pending applications. Unlike Canada and the U.S., the CTM Office will not refuse to register a trade mark application that is confusingly similar. Instead, the CTM Office will notify both the trade mark applicant and the owner of the registration or pending application and leave it to the parties to resolve the confusion themselves.

(c) Publication

If a trade mark application passes the examination stage, it will then be published in the *Gazette of the Community Trademarks Office*. Interested parties can then object to the trade mark application by either filing an observation or an opposition. The CTM Office also allows third parties without trade mark rights to observe deficiencies with an application. For example, a third party who has no personal right to assert trade mark rights can simply file an observation that the trade mark is not distinctive.

(d) Opposition

A CTM application is very much an all-or-nothing application. In order to succeed, the application must satisfy oppositions from each of the 25 national trade mark offices. If the applicant has difficulty overcoming a difficult opposition from one national trade mark office (*e.g.*, Germany), the applicant can convert the CTM application into national applications. Although each national application will have to restart the process from the beginning, as well as pay each of the national application fees, the national applications can maintain the CTM filing date.

(e) Allowance

If no opposition is filed, or if the trade mark application passes the opposition stage, the trade mark will be registered once the registration fee is paid.

(f) Registration

Unlike Canada, the CTM registration is valid for 10 years and can be renewed every 10 years thereafter, and, unlike Canada and the U.S., actual use or intent to use is not required to register the trade mark, nor is it required to renew the trade mark. However, the CTM Office will cancel a registration if the trade mark has not been used for five years in at least one of the European Community countries.

Since the CTM registration system does not require use, there have been instances of individuals registering U.S. or Canadian trade marks and selling them to the U.S. or Canadian trade mark owners. As such, it is imperative that Canadian charitable or not-for-profit organizations immediately register their trade marks not only in Canada and the U.S., but also in the European Community for two reasons. First, when the Canadian organization decides to have operations in or expand into the European Community, it may find that someone has already registered the organization's trade mark, which can prevent it from operating in the European Community. The charitable or not-for-profit organization will then be forced to purchase the CTM registration at a high price. Second, when the Canadian organization is negotiating to license its trade marks to potential affiliates in the European Community, it may find that the potential affiliate has already registered the organization's trade mark and has the upper hand in the negotiations. The charitable or not-for-profit organization will then be forced to negotiate with the potential affiliate for what should have been its trade mark.

4.   PROACTIVE MEANS TO FOREIGN TRADE MARK PROTECTION

Charitable or not-for-profit organizations with international operations, multiple affiliates and foreign trade marks may be naturally confused as to how best to manage their trade marks portfolio. Generally, all trade marks should be owned by the charitable or not-for-profit organization's central office for the following reasons:

- It is easier to assess what trade marks the central organization has, monitor the trade marks and plan future missions and activities in conjunction with the trade marks;

- The central organization can license the trade marks to its affiliates without complex licensing agreements;

- The central organization can claim priority filing under the Convention, whereas one affiliate cannot benefit from another affiliate's filing since they are different entities;

- The central organization can maintain the uniformity of the trade marks and prevent different affiliates from taking inconsistent or contradictory stands before different trade mark offices or courts;

- In the event of litigation, the central organization can make a stronger case for trade mark rights in a country if the organization can show uniform ownership of the trade marks throughout the rest of the world; and

- The central organization can set up a parallel intellectual property foundation, separate and distinct from the central organization, to hold the trade marks and protect them from litigants.

Charitable or not-for-profit organizations with international operations, multiple affiliates and foreign trade marks also have a formidable challenge in monitoring their trade mark rights on a worldwide basis. How should such an organization begin to watch for and spot infringement? One way is to sign up for "watching services" with a trade mark search company. For a modest fee, the company will monitor trade mark applications around the world and notify the organization of potentially confusing trade mark applications. Another way is to encourage employees to be vigilant.

Designate a point person and have employees document and report potential violations to that point person. A third way is to search the Internet periodically. Charitable or not-for-profit organizations that are operating on a tight budget can have in-house personnel conduct the searches instead of hiring a professional search company.

5.   ALTERNATIVE MEANS TO FOREIGN TRADE MARK PROTECTION

If the charitable or not-for-profit organization decides not to obtain a trade mark registration in each country in which it operates, the organization should review with its legal counsel alternative means of foreign trade mark protection, along with the strengths and weaknesses of those means. There are four major international agreements protecting trade marks abroad. Three of them, the *Paris Convention for the Protection of Industrial Property* (the "Convention"),[3] the *Madrid Agreement for the Repression of False or Deceptive Indications of Source on Goods*[4] and the *Trademark Law Treaty*,[5] are managed by the World Intellectual Property Organization, a specialized agency of the United Nations. The fourth international agreement, the *Agreement on Trade-Related Aspects of Intellectual Property Rights* ("TRIPs"),[6] is managed by the World Trade Organization. Since Canada signed only the Convention and TRIPs, these two will be the focus of the discussion on foreign trade mark protection through international agreements.

(a) Paris Convention for the Protection of Industrial Property

The first international agreement for trade mark protection that Canada signed was the Convention, which has a national treatment principle prohibiting the unequal treatment of a foreign trade mark owner and requiring foreign trade mark owners to be treated as a citizen of the country where the rights are asserted.[7] The limitation with the Convention is that it lacks enforcement provisions to back up its protection of trade marks.

---

[3]   Adopted in Paris on 20 March 1883, last revised by the Paris Union on 28 September 1979, 828 U.N.T.S. 305, 21 U.S.T. 1583.

[4]   Adopted in Madrid on 14 April 1891, last revised at Lisbon on 31 October, 1958.

[5]   Adopted in Geneva 27 October, 1994.

[6]   15 April 1994, Marrakesh Agreement establishing the World Trade Agreement, Annex 1C, Legal Instruments — Results of the Uruguay Round, vol. 31, 33 I.L.M. 1197 (1994).

[7]   Adopted in Paris on 20 March 1883, last revised by the Paris Union on 28 September 1979, 828 U.N.T.S. 305, 21 U.S.T. 1583, art. 2.

In other words, the Convention has no penalties when its members violate its provisions, as illustrated by *Havana Club Holding, S.A. v. Galleon, S.A.*[8]

The trade mark HAVANA CLUB originally belonged to the Arechabalas, a Cuban family that fled Cuba after the Castro regime confiscated their distillery. Bacardi bought the trade mark in 1995 and began selling rum under the name HAVANA CLUB. Havana Club International, a joint venture between the Cuban government and France's Pernod Ricard, has also been selling rum under the trade mark HAVANA CLUB since 1994. Since Havana Club International could not sell its rum in the United States, as U.S. law prohibits the sale of Cuban products in the United States, it sued in a U.S. court to enjoin Bacardi from selling rum in the United States under the trade mark HAVANA CLUB. Havana Club International was able to bring this lawsuit in the U.S. court because the U.S., Cuba and France are all signatories to the Convention.

The U.S. court ruled that Havana Club International could not assert its trade mark rights to the name HAVANA CLUB in the United States because the U.S. 1998 *Omnibus Appropriations Act*[9] provided that trade mark and trade name rights are essentially unenforceable with respect to marks and names that were confiscated by the Cuban government. In particular, subsection 211(a) prohibited U.S. courts from recognizing, enforcing or otherwise validating any assertion of rights based on common law rights or registration by certain persons in respect of confiscated marks and names, and subsection 211(b) prohibited recognition, enforcement or other validation of treaty rights in respect of such property. However, this was a clear violation of the national treatment principle of the Convention. Unfortunately, the Convention lacked the enforcement provisions required to substantively protect trade marks on an international scale.

(b) Agreement on Trade-Related Aspects of Intellectual Property Rights

As another international agreement for trade mark protection, TRIPs gives more extensive protection to trade marks in foreign countries than the Convention because it has enforcement provisions to back up its protection of trade marks. TRIPs provides that trade mark owners may

---

[8] 62 F. Supp. 2d 1085 (S.D.N.Y. 1999), aff'd 203 F.3d 116 (2nd Cir. 2000) [hereinafter "*Havana Club*"].

[9] Pub. L. No. 105-277, 105th Cong.

obtain injunctions and provisional measures against infringers in foreign countries,[10] as illustrated in the MCDONALD'S case.[11]

As a participant in the embargo to protest apartheid in South Africa, McDonald's had no restaurants in that country. Capitalizing on the absence of McDonald's within the country, a South African company attempted to register several McDonald's trade marks, including the "golden arches" and the "Big Mac". McDonald's sued successfully in a South African court to enjoin the South African company from using its trade marks based on the provisions of TRIPs. This case demonstrates how compliance with TRIPs' enforcement provisions is essential to international protection of well-known trade marks. In addition, member countries violating TRIPs face penalties determined and enforced by the World Trade Organization. As a result, the enforcement provisions under TRIPs are the strongest international protections currently available for well-known trade marks.

The limitation to TRIPs is that only countries, not individuals, can be members to the agreement; therefore, only countries may file complaints under the agreement. Since a business is not a member of and does not have the right to file a complaint under TRIPs, it must have a member country do so on its behalf instead. However, a member country is unlikely to file a complaint unless the trade mark infringements are significant enough to impact the country's economy. The result is that a majority of trade mark infringements are never addressed by TRIPs, and even if a complaint were filed under TRIPs, any relief resulting from a successful complaint would be awarded to the country bringing the complaint, not to the specific business that suffered the loss. Thus, a business seeking relief for infringement of its well-known trade mark will not find any under TRIPs.[12]

(c) Suing in foreign courts

Another means of foreign trade mark protection is for the trade mark owner to bring a lawsuit in the foreign country where the trade mark infringement

---

[10] 15 April 1994, Marrakesh Agreement establishing the World Trade Agreement, Annex, 1C, Legal Instruments — Results of the Uruguay Round, vol. 31, 33 I.L.M. 1197 (1994), art. 44 and 50.

[11] Stuart Gardinar, "McDonald's Triumphs in South Africa" IP Worldwide (Nov.-Dec. 1996) at 15 (citing to the appellate case of *McDonald's Corporation v. Joburgers Drive-Inn Restaurant,* 1997 (1) SA 1 (A)).

[12] E. Brooke Brinkerhoff, "International Protection of U.S. Trademarks: A Survey of Major International Treaties" (2001) 2 Rich. J. Global L. & Bus. 109 at 123.

is taking place. A trade mark owner can only hope that the foreign country whose citizens are infringing its well-known trade mark has updated its trade mark laws to bring it in line with international standards, such as those set out in TRIPs. Then the trade mark owner may sue in the foreign country for relief just as McDonald's sued in South Africa. This means of foreign trade mark protection may prove the best chance for obtaining relief when a trade mark owner cannot establish Canadian jurisdiction over an infringer and bring the lawsuit in a Canadian court.

When bringing a lawsuit in the foreign country where the trade mark infringement is taking place, it is important to be aware of local laws. After all, action that is legal in one country may be considered illegal in another country, as illustrated in *Prince plc v. Prince Sports Group, Inc.*[13] Prince Sports Group, a U.S. company, registered the trade mark PRINCE in the United Kingdom and was trying to use it also in a domain name when it discovered that Prince plc, a British company, was already using the domain name. The U.S. company then sent a cease and desist letter to the British company warning it to stop using the domain name. The British company responded by suing the U.S. company for an unjustified threat alleging trade mark infringement. It argued that British trade mark law allowed it to use the domain name, since the two companies traded in different types of products; that is, the U.S. company was a tennis manufacturer while the British company was an information technology provider. The Court agreed and enjoined Prince Sport Group from issuing further threats of trade mark infringement.

(d) Suing in domestic courts

In addition to the means of foreign trade mark protection discussed above, another means of trade mark protection is for a trade mark owner to bring a lawsuit in its domestic courts for whatever actions are available in home country. For example, Amazon.com brought a lawsuit in a U.S. court against Amazon.gr, an online book-selling site in Greece.[14] In the lawsuit, Amazon.com alleged trade mark and service mark infringement, unfair competition, false designation of origin and trade mark dilution.

The limitation of domestic means of trade mark protection is that it may be difficult to establish Canadian jurisdiction over a trade mark infringer in another country. One way to establish jurisdiction is to locate property in

---

[13] [1997] E.W.J. No. 1619, 21 FSR (H.C.J.(Ch. D.)).

[14] Tom Schoenberg, "Amazon.com v. Greg Lloyd Smith, et al." *Legal Times* (20 September 1999) at 13.

Canada owned by the foreign company. In the above example, Amazon.com was able to assert U.S. jurisdiction over the Greek company because it had a registered agent in the U.S.

Despite the availability of alternative means of foreign trade mark protection, it is still important for charitable or not-for-profit organizations to give serious consideration to obtaining a trade mark registration in each country in which they operate, since such registration will provide the most comprehensive protection in each country.

SUMMARY

Although this chapter has focused on the process for registering a trade mark in the United States and Europe, the principle remains the same for other jurisdictions: it is essential to ensure that the charitable or not-for-profit organization obtains trade mark protection in all countries in which the organization intends to operate.

Understandably, the importance of obtaining such protection will necessarily have to be weighed against the time and expense required to make the requisite applications in possibly multiple jurisdictions. However, as this chapter has discussed, a charitable or not-for-profit organization operating in Canada can take advantage of the savings provided in the U.S. and European systems, as well as under the Convention, in order to limit the costs involved with making such applications. These savings include being able to file a trade mark application in a Convention country within six months of filing the application in Canada, and filing a single application for the European Community rather making individual applications for each country. As such, despite the expense, serious consideration should be given to registering a trade mark in each jurisdiction the charitable or not-for-profit organization intends to operate. Organizations will find that there are many similarities between the various trade mark systems, but it is important to seek professional assistance in order to guide the organization through the intricacies of each system. This is especially crucial when the organization is faced with strict timelines that could force the dismissal of an application.

CHAPTER 7

PROTECTING THE BRAND THROUGH TRADE MARK SELECTION AND SEARCHING

1. Trade Mark Selection
   (a) Inherently strong marks
   (b) Inherently weak marks
   (c) Suggestive marks
   (d) Compound word marks
   (e) Marks that have acquired a secondary meaning
2. Trade Mark Registrability
   (a) Name or surname
   (b) Descriptive or misdescriptive
   (c) Name in any language
   (d) Confusingly similar
   (e) Sections 9 and 10
   (f) Public misconception
3. Trade Mark Searching
   (a) When to do a trade mark search
   (b) Why do a trade mark search?
   (c) Types of trade mark searches
   (d) The trade mark search opinion
   (e) Expunging competing trade marks

Summary

Chapter 1 discussed the importance of branding to a charitable or not-for-profit organization. Effective branding of an organization not only attracts the right clients to the service, but it attracts donors and supporters who can identify with the cause and the overall strength and integrity of the organization. While branding encompasses more than an organization's trade mark, the trade mark becomes one of the most visible and enduring connections between the organization, its services and its users, donors and supporters. An effective trade mark allows the public to instantly identify the organization. For example, few people will not think of the Swiss charity WORLD WIDE FUND FOR NATURE (formerly the WORLD WILDLIFE FUND) when they see its panda design trade mark. As such, the selection of the trade mark is an important consideration for the charitable or not-for-profit organization. In addition to selecting a mark that conveys the appropriate message to the public, the organization must also concern itself with selecting a mark that conforms with the statutory requirements of the *Trade-marks Act*,[1] ensuring the mark or a similar mark is not already registered by another organization.

1.   TRADE MARK SELECTION

Often a lawyer will have the opportunity to work with a charitable or not-for-profit organization when it is initially created. This will normally involve obtaining and reviewing a NUANS (Newly Upgraded Automated Name Search) computerized corporate name search to be used in the application for incorporation. In such situations, the lawyer can and should explain to the charitable and not-for-profit organization the strengths and weaknesses of the proposed name to be used by the organization. Such an explanation should be prefaced by the lawyer first explaining that the name selected for the organization will become one of its most important assets, and therefore the selection of the name needs to be done with care. This is particularly so for the charitable or not-for-profit organization that may want to apply either now or in the future for trade mark registration for all or a portion of the corporate name it has chosen.

Generally speaking, the selection of trade marks can be broken down into five broad categories: inherently strong marks, inherently weak marks, suggestive marks, compound word marks and marks that have acquired a second meaning, each of which are discussed below.

---

[1]   R.S.C. 1985, c. T-13.

(a) Inherently strong marks

The strongest trade marks for a charitable or not-for-profit organization are those that have no inherent dictionary meaning; they are creative and do not describe the quality or features of the goods or services they represent. As some commentators have suggested, marks that are inherently distinctive clearly represent intellectual property and merit the highest level of protection.[2] Popular examples of such inherently strong marks are coined or fanciful words like ZELLERS, XEROX, KODAK or EXXON. These marks convey no other information other than a specific brand. Other marks that are considered inherently strong are those using dictionary words that have no reference to the goods in association with which they are used, such as CITIZEN when used in relation to watches. Other such arbitrary marks include TIME for a magazine and BLUE DIAMOND for nuts.

(b) Inherently weak marks

Inherently weak marks those that use dictionary words that merely describe a characteristic or quality of the underlying goods or services. For example, SUPER GLUE used in conjunction with glue products, ARTISTIC DANCING for a ballet program or LEMONADE for lemonade would all be inherently weak marks. Inherently weak marks are generally not entitled to trade mark protection unless it can be demonstrated that it has acquired a secondary meaning over time. Many charitable and not-for-profit organizations have initially very descriptive names, which may serve a useful purpose for attracting clients and donors, but the descriptive name may eventually acquire distinctiveness through long term use, such as the CANADIAN CANCER SOCIETY.

(c) Suggestive marks

Suggestive marks are not "clearly descriptive" and require some exercise of the imagination to associate the word or words with the underlying product or service. But because the mark is "suggestive" of products they are also not considered to be inherently strong marks, yet they are still considered deserving of protection. Examples of a suggestive mark are SHAKE AND BAKE for chicken coating products or COPPERTONE for suntan oils and creams. However, like inherently weak marks, suggestive

2   Jacob Jacoby, "The Psychological Foundations of Trademark Law: Secondary Meaning, Genericism, Fame, Confusion and Dilution" (2001) 91 Trademark Rep. 1013.

marks can acquire a secondary meaning where they gain sufficient market recognition.

(d) Compound word marks

Compound word marks are commonly marks that are comprised of two or more distinct words or words and syllables that are presented as one word. A compound word mark may also be represented by a combination of a distinctive word with a descriptive word. For instance, COCA-COLA would be considered to be a compound word mark since COLA would be a distinctive mark, whereas the word COCA would be descriptive of the drink product. Other examples of compound word marks are POWERBOOK and THINKPAD, both of which are used in association with portable computers.

(e) Marks that have acquired a secondary meaning

As indicated above, an inherently weak trade mark can become distinctive through length of usage by virtue of acquiring a secondary meaning. In other words, once the consuming public comes to associate the trade mark with the producer rather than with the underlying product, the trade mark has risen above its status as an inherently weak mark and becomes a mark that has acquired a secondary meaning. Examples include FRIGIDAIRE for fridges or HOLIDAY INN for hotels, which are both *prima facie* inherently weak marks because they are descriptive of the underlying product or service. However, with usage and the passage of time, the public has come to recognize FRIGIDAIRE as a distinctive trade mark for fridges and HOLIDAY INN as a distinctive trade mark for hotels.

2.   TRADE MARK REGISTRABILITY

When the charitable or not-for-profit organization selects a trade mark, it is also important to understand what barriers may be encountered in obtaining trade mark registration. The sections of the *Trade-marks Act* dealing with registration of a trade mark are very complex and are well beyond the scope of this book. However, for the purposes of a general overview, the following is a brief synopsis of the statutory provisions of the *Trade-marks Act* that describe what trade marks cannot be registered.[3]

(a) Name or surname

A trade mark will not be registrable if it is a word that is "primarily merely the name or the surname of an individual who is living or has died within the preceding thirty years".[4] For example, a trade mark for SMITH would not be registrable because it is "primarily merely a surname". In contrast, the trade mark ELDER may be registrable because there may be another meaning for ELDER beyond that of a surname that could be registrable. In determining whether a proposed trade mark is primarily merely the name or surname of an individual, searches of telephone directories and dictionaries in various languages may need to be conducted. However, as with other unregistrable marks noted above, a mark that is primarily merely a name or surname may become registrable over time if it can acquire a secondary meaning. As such, we see such examples as E.D. SMITH, MCDONALD'S, TOMMY HILFIGER and RALPH LAUREN as marks that are afforded trade mark protection even though they are primarily merely a name or surname of an individual.

(b) Descriptive or misdescriptive

A trade mark will not be registrable if it is a word that is "clearly descriptive or deceptively misdescriptive in the English or French language of the character or the quality of the wares or services, the condition of or the persons employed in their production or of their place of origin".[5] For instance, SWEET for ice cream is "clearly descriptive" and therefore is not registrable; ALL SILK for non-silk fabrics is "deceptively misdescriptive" and therefore is not registrable; and PARIS FASHION indicates a place of origin and is not registrable. The exception is where a secondary meaning has developed to overcome the descriptive nature of the mark. There is no similar exception for a deceptively misdescriptive mark; it cannot be overcome through acquisition of distinctiveness because it is considered to be misleading to the public.

---

[3] *Trade-marks Act*, R.S.C. 1985, c. T-13, s. 12.

[4] *Ibid.*, s. 12(1)(a).

[5] *Ibid.*, s. 12(1)(b).

(c) Name in any language

A trade mark will not be registrable if it is "the name in any language of any of the wares or services in connection with which it is used or proposed to be used".[6] For instance, SHREDDED WHEAT for cereal products cannot be registered because it is the name of the item that is the subject matter of the trade mark. In addition, HOLY BIBLE for Bibles cannot be registered as a trade mark because it is the name of the item in question.

(d) Confusingly similar

A trade mark may not be registrable if it is confusing with a previously registered, applied for or used trade mark or trade name. The test in this regard is whether the trade marks look or sound alike or suggest a similar idea, and whether they are used to market similar wares or services. It is only necessary that there be a likelihood of confusion for the Canadian Intellectual Property Office ("CIPO") to refuse the application. CIPO will consider various factors, including:

(a) the inherent distinctiveness of the trade marks or trade names and the extent to which they have become known;

(b) the length of time the trade mark or trade names have been in use;

(c) the nature of the wares, services or businesses;

(d) the nature of the trade; and

(e) the degree of resemblance between the trade marks or trade names in appearance, sound, or in the ideas suggested by them.[7]

(e) Sections 9 and 10

A trade mark will not be registrable if it is a mark under section 9 or 10 of the *Trade-marks Act* as explained in Chapter 2. Section 9 sets out various prohibited marks, including official marks of a university or a public authority for which public notice has been given; the coats of arms for the Royal Family;[8] the RCMP;[9] emblems of the Red Cross and the Red Crescent; the words or seals of the United Nations, as well as other similar types of government marks.

---

[6]   *Ibid.*, s. 12(1)(c).
[7]   *Ibid.*, s. 6(5)(a)–(e).
[8]   For example, Canadian Intellectual Property Office, Application Number 0972026: State Emblem of the United Kingdom.
[9]   Canadian Intellectual Property Office, Application Number 0907128.

**Figure 1 — State emblem of the United Kingdom is a prohibited
mark registered by the Prince of Wales**

Figure 2 — Coat of arms of the Royal Canadian Mounted Police

Section 10 prohibits the adoption of a mark which by ordinary and
bona fide commercial use has become recognized in Canada designating
the kind, quality, quantity or origin of a trade mark, (*e.g.*, HARRIS
TWEED)[10].

HARRIS TWEED

Figure 3 — The Harris Tweed certification mark

---

[10] Canadian Intellectual Property Office, Registration Number TMA270898. The certification
mark, originally granted in the United Kingdom in 1909, refers to a tweed made from
pure virgin wool produced in Scotland. It was spun, dyed and finished in the Outer
Hebrides and handwoven by the islanders at their own homes in the islands of Lewis,
Harris, Uist, Barra and their several appurtenances.

(f) Public misconception

Lastly, there is another barrier to trade mark registrability that has particular application to charitable and not-for-profit organizations as a result of a frequently held misconception. The *Trade-marks Act* defines a trade mark as "a mark that is used by a person for the purpose of distinguishing or so as to distinguish *wares or services manufactured, sold, leased, hired or performed by him from those manufactured, sold, leased, hired or performed by others*".[11] Many charitable and not-for-profit organizations have mistakenly read a commercial requirement into the section, interpreting the section as applying only to wares and services used in the normal course of business. However, it is important for charitable and not-for-profit organizations to recognize that there is nothing in the definition requiring the services provided to be commercial in nature. In addition, the courts have held that the term "services" should be interpreted liberally.[12] As such, an organization that provides counselling, babysitting, transportation, food or other similar services on a not-for-profit basis would be able to register their trade marks even though they are not carried out on a commercial basis.

3. TRADE MARK SEARCHING

Once a charitable or not-for-profit organization has settled on a trade mark, and after reviewing the strength and weaknesses of the trade mark, a search should be conducted so as to ensure that no one else is already using the trade mark and to determine the registrability of the trade mark.

(a) When to do a trade mark search

There is a general misconception that a trade mark search only needs be done when a charitable or not-for-profit organization wishes to obtain a trade mark registration. There are a number of other instances where a trade mark search should also be performed, particularly if the information that is produced by a NUANS computerized name search does not provide a comprehensive or up-to-date report on trade mark

---

[11] *Trade-marks Act*, R.S.C. 1985, c. T-13, s. 2 [emphasis added].
[12] *Kraft Ltd. v. Canada (Registrar of Trade Marks)*, [1984] F.C.J. No. 910, 1 C.P.R. (3d) 457 (F.C.T.D.); *Société nationale des chemins de fer français v. Venice Simplon-Orient-Express Inc.*, [2000] F.C.J. No. 1897 (T.D.); *Renaud Cointreau & Co. v. Cordon Bleu International Ltd.*, [2000] F.C.J. No. 882 (T.D.), aff'd (2002) 11 C.P.R. (4th) 95 (F.C.A.).

registrations. The following are examples of when an organization should consider conducting a trade mark search:

- If an organization has an unregistered trade mark, they may wish to obtain the enhanced benefits of obtaining a registered trade mark. This not only provides access to better enforcement mechanisms through the *Trade-marks Act*, but it also enhances the scope of protection by providing exclusive use of the mark in association with the ware or service throughout Canada;

- Whether non-profit or commercial, significant resources are expended in developing a brand and its marketing ventures. A charitable or not-for-profit organization can avoid the expense of having to revamp branding or marketing initiatives by conducting trade mark searches prior to selecting a future trade mark or logo for its operations;

- Similar to the situation of an organization going through a rebranding or marketing initiative, a charitable or not-for-profit organization would be wise to conduct a trade mark search when the organization is choosing a new or amended corporate name so as to ensure there are no conflicts with other organizations or businesses;

- The organization will also want to avoid conflicts when choosing a new name for an operating division of the organization;

- When choosing a domain name to use on the Internet, the organization is opening up to competition on a global scale which may expose the organization to other commercial or non-commercial organizations that are antithetical to the charitable or not-for-profit organization's goals or beliefs; and

- When the organization is licencing its name to another organization, it may involve the use of the trade mark in geographical locations for which the organization has no right to the use of the trade mark due to the limited geographical scope of an unregistered trade mark.

(b) Why do a trade mark search?

There are a variety of reasons why it is advisable to conduct a trade mark search. A trade mark search determines the strengths of an existing unregistered trade mark before proceeding with the expense of actually applying for trade mark registration. A search also determines if there are any pre-existing trade marks in CIPO's records that are potentially confusing with the trade mark to be used by the client. This should either be avoided or possibly challenged based upon the earlier entitlement of the charitable or not-for-profit organization to the trade mark based on prior usage, provided the challenge is brought within a five-year period from the date of the competing trade mark registration.[13] Even if there is already an existing trade mark with the same name, a trade mark search will help to determine the extent of wares and services that have been claimed in relation to existing trade marks and, therefore, enable counsel to advise as to which wares and services are left open for exclusive identification with the trade mark of the organization. Finally, a trade mark search will enable an organization to avoid possible trade mark infringement actions as a result of intentionally or unintentionally misappropriating existing registered trade marks for similar wares and services from the holder of the trade mark rights.

(c) Types of trade mark searches

A general misunderstanding about trade mark searches is that there is only one type of search. There are in fact two types of trade mark searches.

The first search is a preliminary search which only reviews CIPO's records. This type of search is done to see if there is an identical mark already registered or pending with CIPO. In addition, there are now several companies that offer services in determining whether or not one's trade mark can be registered. Some companies have even created their own database based upon CIPO's records, with added value such as translation of French trade marks into English, classification of trade marks into specific classes of goods or services and cross-referencing of variations on the spelling of the trade marks.

The other type of search is a more comprehensive search which reviews CIPO's records for identical or confusingly similar trade marks, as well as common law sources, such as corporate registries, trade directories, dictionaries, phone books and domain registries for identical or confusingly similar unregistered trade marks across Canada. Since owners of unregistered trade marks have protection at common law, failure to conduct a comprehensive search may result in the owner of an existing unregistered trade mark being able to oppose the application to

---

[13] *Trade-marks Act*, R.S.C. 1985, c. T-13, s. 17.

register a trade mark or, alternatively, to have the trade mark expunged after it has been issued.

A U.S. case, *International Star Class Yacht Racing Ass'n v. Tommy Hilfiger, U.S.A. Inc.*,[14] emphasizes the importance of common law trade mark searches. In that decision, a not-for-profit corporation alleged infringement of their STAR CLASS trade mark by the defendant clothing designer. The Court found the defendant had intentionally infringed the plaintiff's trade mark by its failure to conduct a full trade mark search, including a common law search, despite a recommendation from the defendant's attorney that a full search be conducted. This case has placed an onus on U.S. trade mark attorneys to recommend that a full trade mark search, which includes a common law search, be undertaken. Whether or not this case will be followed in Canada is not known; however, failure to complete a comprehensive search, including a common law search, could result in a successful challenge to the trade mark.

Although Canada does not have an effective single source for common law searches of a trade mark as there is in the United States, there are various ways in which a common law search could be conducted, either by the organization or its lawyer. Some possible searches that should be considered include:

1. a NUANS name search of all corporations, partnerships and business names in Canada;

2. a business name search in each province;

3. a review of trade journals and magazines;

4. a review of the Yellow Pages directory in telephone books in major cities; and

5. a search of domain names on the Internet.

(d) The trade mark search opinion

The written opinion of a trade mark agent resulting from a search of registered trade marks will normally be qualified by a statement that it does not include a common law trade mark search. However, if requested, the search can include the results of a NUANS name search and/or an Internet domain name search. The written opinion of the trade mark agent should state whether the trade mark in question is capable of registration as a Canadian trade mark and whether or not the client is free to adopt the

---

[14] 38 U.S.P.Q. 2d at 1369 (1996), aff'g in part 33 U.S.P.Q. 2d at 1610.

name and use it as a trade mark in Canada. Although there are obviously no guarantees that the trade mark application will ultimately be successful, the search will at least advise the charitable or not-for-profit organization of the probabilities of success if a trade mark application is made or whether the trade mark can continue to be used as an unregistered trade mark in Canada without fear of an action being brought against the organization for passing off.

(e) Expunging competing trade marks

Often the trade mark registrability opinion will indicate that there is an existing registered trade mark that is potentially confusing with the charitable or not-for-profit organization's trade mark because the name and application to wares and services is similar to that of the organization. However, that does not necessarily mean the organization has to forego applying for a registered trade mark. There are strategies that can be followed to challenge an existing competing trade mark that should be reviewed with legal counsel.

A popular method of expunging a competing trade mark is to rely upon section 45 of the *Trade-marks Act* to require the owner of a competing trade mark to produce an affidavit showing that the trade mark has been in use or explaining non-use during the previous three-year period. CIPO can make the request at any time and at the request of a third party three years after the trade mark is registered. If the trade mark owner does not file a response within three months, then the registered trade mark will automatically be expunged.

SUMMARY

As considerable resources of the charitable or not-for-profit organization will go into registering and promoting its trade marks, it is fitting to expend sufficient time and resources into selecting an appropriate trade mark; one that not only meets the technical requirements of the *Trade-marks Act*, but will enable potential clients and donors to instantly recognize the organization. A charitable or not-for-profit organization would be mistaken to take its cue from many of the trade marks that exist today, as they only qualify as trade marks since they have acquired distinctiveness through the length of time they have been in use. Organizations would be wise to carefully examine the restrictions that are placed on the registration of trade marks through the *Trade-marks Act*, and then ensure their trade mark agent performs a search of the trade marks database as well as a common law search to ensure the registrability of organization's trade mark.

CHAPTER 8

PROTECTING THE BRAND THROUGH TRADE MARK USE AND MONITORING

1. Trade Mark Use
    (a) Ensure continued use
    (b) Ensure proper marking
    (c) Ensure identification of licenses
    (d) Use distinctively
    (e) Use as an adjective
    (f) Use with a generic name
    (g) Use consistently
    (h) Amend applicant name
    (i) Amend wares and/or services
    (j) Educate staff and board members
2. Trade Mark Monitoring
    (a) Ensure parallel registrations
    (b) Monitor infringement
    (c) Stop infringement
    (d) Protect unregistered trade marks
    (e) Protect registered trade marks
    (f) Ensure use of trade marks
Summary

As the previous chapters have indicated, a trade mark becomes the focal point for the organization's communication with the outside world; if it is carefully selected, it will come to embody the organization's business, ethos and wares collectively in one focal point. The directors of a charitable or not-for-profit organization also owe a fiduciary duty to the organization to protect its assets, the breach of which may result in significant consequences for the directors. Although a charitable or not-for-profit organization may obtain a registered trade mark, it will be of little use if the organization does not understand how to properly use and protect the trade mark in order to obtain its maximum benefit. The organization must take steps to protect the valuable asset that it has acquired.

1. TRADE MARK USE

Trade mark use involves a more concerted effort than occasionally including the mark on documents or wares that will reach the public. The following discussion reviews some of the considerations that should be communicated to a charitable or not-for-profit client in this regard.

(a) Ensure continued use

It is important that the trade mark continue to be used. A trade mark is used in regard to wares if it is displayed on the wares themselves or their packaging and are sold or distributed to customers. A trade mark is used in connection with services if it is displayed during the performance of the services or in advertising or promotional materials for the services. After its third anniversary, a trade mark may be vulnerable to cancellation or amendment if the trade mark is not in use in Canada with all of the wares and/or services covered by the registration. A registration may also be expunged if it can be found that the owner intended to abandon the trade mark.

(b) Ensure proper marking

Canada has no specific legal requirement for a trade mark notice; however, use of the symbols ® and ™ beside the trade mark is encouraged (*e.g.*, on labels or packaging or in advertising or promotional materials). A charitable or not-for-profit organization should designate an unregistered trade mark with the symbol ™, which stands for "trade mark". In Quebec, the English ™ symbol would be replaced with the symbol ^{MC}, which stands for "marque de commerce". After registration, the appropriate symbol to use is ®, which stands for "registered trade mark". In Quebec, the English ® symbol would be replaced with the symbol ᴹᴰ, which stands for "marque déposé". However, any wares or services that are being offered in the United States should not be marked with the symbol ® if the trade mark has not been registered in the United States. If a charitable or not-for-profit organization that operates on an international level cannot be certain that the wares or services will not be offered into the United States, it should consider using the symbol ™ instead of the symbol ®.

It is important that the organization clearly identify the trade mark by consistently using the appropriate symbol on all advertising, letterhead, publications, tapes, videos, receipts and solicitations, with a brief note that the mark in question is a trade mark of the named charitable or not-for-profit organization.

(c) Ensure identification of licenses

A license arrangement should be shown whenever the licensed trade mark is used (further discussion on trade mark licensing can be found in Chapter 10). The licensor should make sure that the licensee is giving the requisite public notice by clearly identifying the owner of the trade mark and advising that the trade mark is being used under license. This can be done by a footnote or legend which indicates that the mark is a registered trade mark, identifies the registered owner by name and indicates, where applicable, that use of the trade mark is under license. For example:

ABC RELIEF AGENCY ®

"ABC Relief Agency" is a registered trade mark of ABC Relief Agency International used under license by ABC Relief Agency of Canada.

The use of the trade mark by an authorized licensee is an acceptable means in order to maintain the registration, but only to the extent that the registered owner has direct or indirect control of the character or quality of the wares or services. Furthermore, section 50 of the *Trade-marks Act*[1] provides that to the extent that public notice is given of the licensed use and the identity of the owner, there is a presumption that the character or quality of the wares or services is under the control of the owner unless proven otherwise. The license arrangement should be in writing.

---

[1] R.S.C. 1985, c. T-13.

(d) Use distinctively

In addition to correct marking, it is important that the trade mark be used in a manner to distinguish it from descriptive or generic words. This can be done by either showing the trade mark in distinctive type, bold type or capitalized lettering or putting the trade mark in a prominent position on the letterhead.

Failure to maintain the distinctiveness of the trade mark may lead to expungement of the registration. Loss of distinctiveness may occur through improper use, improper licensing or failure to restrain infringement of the trade mark by others.

(e) Use as an adjective

Generic use of a trade mark may render it indistinctive and vulnerable to expungement; therefore, it is important to ensure that a trade mark is used as an adjective and never as a noun. When a mark is used as a noun, it will eventually become generic and unenforceable, as happened with several well-known trade marks, such as LINOLEUM, ZIPPER, ESCALATOR and CELLOPHANE.

A trade mark should always be followed by a word or words which identify the wares or services for which it has been registered, such as BAND-AID bandages instead of simply BAND-AID, or the reference to JELL-O gelatin instead of simply JELL-O.

(f) Use with a generic name

When a trade mark is new or substantially different from an existing one, it may be necessary to create or choose a suitable generic name to follow the trade mark. In this regard, generic names should be highly descriptive, relatively short and easily pronounceable. An example would be the use of the generic name of "copiers" when used in conjunction with the trade mark XEROX (*e.g.*, XEROX copiers).

(g) Use consistently

It is important that the trade mark always appear in the form in which it was registered and with the wares or services for which it was registered, without significant variation. Otherwise, its enforceability may be seriously affected as a result of possible dilution of the trade mark, or it may become vulnerable to cancellation for non-use. For example, it is important to avoid varying the trade mark and using it in the plural or possessive form, such as "COCA-COLA's great taste".

(h) Amend applicant name

In the event a charitable or not-for-profit organization changes its name, it is essential that a change of name of the owner of the registered trade mark be filed with the Canadian Intellectual Property Office ("CIPO") as soon as possible. In addition, the organization's change of name must be shown on all markings. Failure to do so may result in the loss of trade mark rights.

(i) Amend wares and/or services

If the trade mark will be used with wares and/or services other than those covered by the current registration, the registration should be amended to extend coverage to such other wares and/or services to maintain full protection for the trade mark.

As explained in Chapter 1, failure to use the trade mark in association with the wares and/or services covered in the registration could result in CIPO expunging the trade mark because the trade mark was abandoned. Using a trade mark in association with wares and/or services that are not covered in the registration will not protect the trade mark registration from expungement, because the *Trade-marks Act* only provides protection for trade marks in relation to the wares and/or services listed in the registration. Consequently, should a charitable or not-for-profit organization desire to use the trade mark in relation to a different set of wares and/or services, the registration would have to be amended in order to extend protection to the other wares and/or services.

(j) Educate staff and board members

Since staff and board members of a charitable or not-for-profit organization tend to change on a regular basis, it is necessary that there be a consistent program of education and a written style/use guide provided for new board members, executive staff and other staff involved in the media and publications. This training should cover the importance of trade mark rights, the steps that need to be taken to protect them and the means by which trade mark protection can be implemented.

This education process should be mandatory for every new board member and relevant staff member; it should be included as part of a written policy and updated as necessary every few years.

2.   TRADE MARK MONITORING

Trade mark protection involves looking at trade mark rights at various levels, including, of course, obtaining a registered trade mark.

(a) Ensure parallel registrations

Unfortunately, many charitable and not-for-profit organizations think that because they have a corporate name or they have registered the name under the Ontario *Business Names Act*[2] these steps are sufficient. This, however, does not provide the protection of a registered trade mark and consideration should be given to obtaining a registered trade mark and/or a section 9 official mark.

In addition, if a charitable or not-for-profit organization is operating in another country, consideration should also be given to registration of trade marks in foreign jurisdictions, as discussed in Chapter 6. Finally, it is also important to remember to secure domain names as soon as possible for the trade marks.

(b) Monitor infringement

Even if a charitable or not-for-profit organization obtains a registered trade mark, the organization will still have to be proactive in monitoring potential infringement of its trade mark by others. This would include regular review of:

- Competing trade marks in the *Trade marks Journal*, although this is not a practical option for most small organizations unless they are prepared to pay a trade mark agent to do so on their behalf;
- Trade journals, magazines and newspapers;
- Corporate and business name registration, conducted through regular NUANS name searches;
- Names in telephone books in major cities;

---

[2]   R.S.O. 1990, c. B.17.

- Internet domain names to see if there are domain names of other organizations that are identical or potentially confusing to that of the charitable or not-for-profit organization; and
- Names of registered charities with Canada Revenue Agency, or with a company that provides trade mark watching services, as discussed in Chapter 6.

(c) Stop infringement

Where a charitable or not-for-profit organization becomes aware of a confusing trade mark, it is essential that the organization take steps to stop the infringement, otherwise the organization may eventually lose its entitlement to the registered trade mark. Some steps that can be taken to avoid this from happening include sending a polite but firm letter to the offending party advising that an infringement is occurring and requesting that it change its name. If that is not successful, then have legal counsel send a formal letter of complaint to the other party.

If the other party is not prepared to stop using the trade mark, then suggest granting a license of the trade mark in question, or enter into a binding agreement that limits the use of the offending trade mark. The charity WORLD WILDLIFE FUND successfully employed this method albeit short-term, in its dispute with the former WORLD WRESTLING FEDERATION over its use of the initials "WWF". The two bodies entered into an agreement that limited the wrestling organization's use of the initials in its marketing and promotional activity. Although the wrestling body did not adhere to the agreement after several years, the agreement was at the bases of legal proceedings initiated by the charity, which sought to protect its global brand and reputation from any unsavoury connection with professional wrestling. The English Court of Appeal eventually upheld an injunction that forced the wrestling organization to keep to the strict terms of the agreement.[3]

Should negotiations fail, entering into an alternative dispute resolution process should be proposed. Finally, if all else fails, the charitable or not-for-profit organization may need to proceed with litigation to protect its trade mark rights or accept the fact that, if it fails to enforce its rights in court, it may lose any rights it has to the trade mark in question.

---

[3] *WWF — World Wide Fund for Nature v. World Wrestling Federation Entertainment Inc.*, [2002] E.W.J. No. 830, [2002] EWCA Civ. 196.

This is the very situation in which THE NATIONAL BALLET SCHOOL/L'ÉCOLE NATIONALE DE BALLET found itself. The National Ballet School/L'École nationale de ballet ("NBS") was the first user of and owned the official marks to both "The National Ballet School" and "L'École nationale de ballet". When NBS became aware that another ballet school was planning to change its name to ÉCOLE NATIONALE DE BALLET CONTEMPORAIN, NBS wrote to the ballet school to protest the similarity between the names and request that the ballet school immediately cease and desist from using the similar name. When the ballet school proceeded with its name change anyway, NBS applied for a permanent injunction enjoining the ballet school from using the name "École nationale de ballet contemporain", on the grounds that the name was identical to "L'École nationale de ballet" and was likely to confuse (and had in fact confused) the public with respect to the two organizations. The Court found that there was confusion and, accordingly, granted a permanent injunction enjoining the ballet school from using the name "École nationale de ballet contemporain" and awarded damages in the amount of $1,000 to NBS.[4]

As mentioned in Chapter 1, a U.S. organization, MAKE-A-WISH FOUNDATION,[5] had to do damage control after it learned a car salesman solicited funds on behalf of the organization without permission, used the foundation's logo in advertisements and kept all of the proceeds. Make-A-Wish Foundation originally turned down the man's request to start a charity program with the foundation, but the man went ahead and did it anyway. Following an investigation by the Ohio Attorney General's office, in which it was confirmed that consumers who had donated cars thought the profits were going to the charity, the car salesman was charged with fraud. The case demonstrates how easy it is for an organization to not only lose goodwill through the fraudulent acts of others, but how important it is to continually monitor the use of an organizations's trade marks.

On a commercial level, the Coca-Cola Company was forced to bring an action in 1972 to enjoin another company from printing, distributing and selling a poster which consisted of a reproduction of the company's ENJOY COCA-COLA trade mark with the script changed to ENJOY COCAINE.[6]

---

[4]   *National Ballet School/École nationale de ballet c. École nationale de ballet contemporain*, [2006] J.Q. no 747, 2006 QCCS 459.

[5]   "Did You Ever Wonder?" (2005) 13 Canadian Not-For-Profit News 5.

[6]   *Coca-Cola Co. v. Gemini Rising, Inc.*, 346 F. Supp. 1183 (E.D.N.Y. 1972).

Figure 1 — Coca-Cola's rights to its trade mark ENJOY COCA-COLA were found to be infringed in this parody

Although the defendant claimed a parody defence, the Court was convinced that the defendant's use of the mark impinged directly on Coca-Cola's own use of their trade mark in advertising and caused confusion, and as such violated Coca-Cola's rights in their trade mark. In granting the relief requested, the Court approved of remarks made in another trade mark infringement case, saying "[t]o the plaintiff its name is at stake, and continued injury to its reputation and good will would be a far more serious blow to it than the curtailment of the sale by the defendants would be to them".[7]

(d) Protect unregistered trade marks

Notwithstanding the fact that charitable and not-for-profit organizations should obtain registered trade mark protection, the fact is that most do not obtain a registered trade mark and may not do so for some time in the future. In such situations, a charitable or not-for-profit organization will need to know what steps can be taken to protect an unregistered trade mark. Some factors in this regard are as follows:

- **Protection under corporate law** — Both federal and provincial incorporating legislation, and provincial business name legislation, generally have a mechanism that may provide some protection. In the event another organization has a confusing corporate name to that of a charitable or not-for-profit organization, the holder of a unregistered trade mark should file a complaint to the Companies Branch of the particular jurisdiction concerning the confusion, requesting that the other corporate entity be required to change its

---

[7] *Estée Lauder, Inc. v. Watsky*, 323 F. Supp. 1064 at 1068 (S.D.N.Y. 1970).

name. However, a business name registration is not enough in itself to protect the unregistered trade mark. Provincial registrars of business names have taken the position that registration of a business name does not provide any protection for the name. This position is founded upon the principle that the purpose of business name registration is to protect the public; *i.e.*, to record the owner's use of the business name and inform the public of the owner's identity upon request.

- **Expunging a competing registered trade mark** — As indicated earlier, in the event there is already a competing registered trade mark, steps can be taken under the *Trade-marks Act* to have the registered trade mark expunged. This can be done through a notice under section 45 of the *Trade-marks Act* requiring the owner of the registered trade mark to establish use of the trade mark within the immediately proceeding three years. Alternatively, the charitable or not-for-profit organization can apply to expunge a trade mark under section 17, based upon evidence the organization has a prior claim to that trade mark, provided the application is brought within a period of five years of the registration of the offending trade mark.

- **"Passing-off" action at common law** — Although a common law "passing-off" action is difficult to prosecute, lengthy and expensive, it may provide an avenue of protection to a charitable or not-for-profit organization with an unregistered trade mark. However, as already indicated, a passing-off action is limited to the local geographical area in which the trade mark is used.

(e) Protect registered trade marks

When a trade mark has been registered, the available protection is considerably enhanced because of the ability to enforce the trade mark by bringing an action in the Federal Court of Canada, instead of in a provincial court. In addition, the protection afforded to a registered trade mark is not limited to a specific geographical area. Finally, and most importantly, the trade mark infringement action does not require the owner of a trade mark to confirm that it owns the trade mark, since this is already presumed by virtue of the trade mark being registered.

(f) Ensure use of trade marks

Since anyone can require CIPO to send a notice under section 45 of the *Trade-marks Act* to require evidence of usage of a trade mark, it is essential that a charitable or not-for-profit organization understand it is not sufficient to simply obtain a registered trade mark. The trade mark must in fact be used, otherwise the organization faces the real possibility that its trade mark will be expunged. The adage of "use it or lose it" is very much applicable in the context of protecting trade marks. In this regard, the charitable or not-for-profit organization needs to keep detailed records of usage of the trade mark after registration in order to be able to respond to a section 45 challenge.

To have a trade mark expunged for abandonment under common law, it is necessary to show not only the discontinuance of use but also an intention to abandon. The discontinuance of use can be shown by virtue of a charitable or not-for-profit organization's failure to use the trade mark in association with the goods and services referred to in the trade mark registration. For example, there is a discontinuance of use if the trade mark is not displayed on the goods or their packaging and the goods are sold or distributed to customers, or if the trade mark is not displayed during the performance of the services or in advertising or promotional materials for the services. The intention to abandon can be implied. Abandonment will result in the loss of both registered and unregistered trade mark rights. As such, it is important for charitable and not-for-profit organizations to use the trade marks in order to stem off allegations of abandonment.

SUMMARY

Once a charitable or not-for-profit organization obtains a registered trade mark, the work must begin to ensure the valuable asset is used appropriately and protected from becoming a wasting asset for the organization. A trade mark owner cannot become complacent in the use or monitoring of its trade marks. As discussed, a mark can lose its distinctive character as a trade mark when it is only used in a generic sense or when licensees are not properly constrained. Similarly, organizations need to monitor the use of the trade mark and any similar marks that may cause confusion for donors or clients. Improper usage of the charitable or not-for-profit organization's trade mark, or the use of a confusingly similar trade mark, must be avoided as it may result in the loss of entitlement to the trade mark.

CHAPTER 9

PROTECTING THE BRAND THROUGH DOMAIN NAMES

1. What is a Domain Name?
2. Importance of Domain Names
   (a) Communicating
   (b) Fundraising
   (c) Events
   (d) Recruitment
   (e) Advocacy
3. Domain Name Conflicts
   (a) Conflicts between domain names
   (b) Conflicts between domain names and trade marks
   (c) ICANN's dispute resolution
   (d) CIRA's dispute resolution
4. Securing Domain Names
   (a) Obtain domain names as soon as possible
   (b) Obtain as many domain names as possible
   (c) Register with multiple domain names
   (d) Register multiple domain names
   (e) Conduct trade mark search
   (f) Register trade mark
   (g) Monitor and renew domain names
5. Contesting Domain Names
   (a) Identical or confusingly similar
   (b) Legitimate interest
   (c) Bad faith

6.   Licensing Domain Names
Summary

The Internet is seen by many as a vastly underutilized tool for a charitable or not-for-profit organization's communication, brand development and donor support.[1] With the prevalence and growth of Internet consumerism, it is a natural stage on which to develop philanthropy; the Internet holds great potential for providing the cost-effect branding initiatives that are generally lacking in charitable and not-for-profit organizations. But the lower cost for communications and marketing should not be seen as a license to ignore the fundamental branding and trade mark issues related to an organization's Internet presence.

As entire volumes have been dedicated to the issue of branding initiatives on the Internet, space does not allow a thorough discussion of the relevant issues. However, the following is an important introduction to the issue of electronic branding and trade marks in the context of charitable and not-for-profit organizations.

1.   WHAT IS A DOMAIN NAME?

A domain name is the numeric electronic address used to locate a computer on the Internet. It is the equivalent of a telephone number for a computer. A domain name registration has been described as "an inchoate proprietary right because it affords exclusive use of the name in electronic commerce on the information highway".[2]

There are two portions to a domain name: the top level domain and the second level identifying name. The original seven generic top level domains were:

1.   .com (commercial)

2.   .org (organization)

3.   .net (network)

4.   .edu (education)

---

[1]   Ted Hart, James M. Greenfield & Michael Johnston, *Nonprofit Internet Strategies: Best Practices for Marketing, Communications, and Fundraising* (New Jersey: John Wiley & Sons, Inc., 2005) at 102.
[2]   Andrea F. Rush, "Internet Domain Name Protection: A Canadian Perspective" (1996) 11 I.P.J. 1 at 2.

5. .gov (government)

6. .int (international)

7. .mil (military)

The domain name system is regulated by the Internet Corporation for Assigned Names and Numbers (ICANN). ICANN, in turn, has assigned the registration of generic top level domain names to InterNIC Networks Solutions, Inc., the only domain name registrar accredited by ICANN. However, due to the explosive increase in domain name registrations, ICANN accredited more registrars to assist in regulating the domains. At present, there are at least 191 accredited registrars.

However, as will be explained in more detail later in this chapter (in the section regarding conflicts between domain names and trade marks), there can only be one "www.charity.com" for all the charities that operate throughout the world. In addition, there are only so many ways that "www.charity.com" can be varied into "www.charities.com" or "www.charitable.com". The consequence is that there will be more demand than supply, resulting in fierce competition for the few effective domain names available. Some of the resulting competition for effective domain names has been relieved by the creation of new generic top level domains, such as:

• .biz (business)

• .info (information)

• .pro (professional)

• .name (name)

• .museum (museum)

• .coop (co-operative)

• .aero (members of the aviation community)

However, it will only be a matter of time before these additional domains also become as crowded as the current list. What is not clear, though, is whether any of the additional domains will be as popular as the original seven domains of .com or .org.

There are also regional top level domains used for each country, such as .ca for Canada, .us for the United States, .uk for the United Kingdom, as well as .eu for the European Union. The .ca top level domain used to be managed by the University of British Columbia, but management was transferred to the Canadian Internet Registration Authority (CIRA) on November 8, 2000. In addition, there are regional top level domains for provinces such as .on for Ontario and .qc for Quebec. If possible, it is preferable to obtain a generic top level domain as opposed to a regional top level domain.

The other portion of a domain name (*i.e.*, the second level identifying name), can consist of up to 26 letters that identify the organization or business. Some businesses and organizations will choose to use the initials of their full name to describe themselves in the second level identifying name, such as the Law Society of Upper Canada's website "www.lsuc.on.com", even though it does not have any meaning on its own. Other organizations are careful to ensure they have their corporate identity clearly shown in the second level identifying name, such as "www.microsoft.com", "www.mcdonalds.com", "www.xerox.com", "www.ibm.com", *etc.*

2. IMPORTANCE OF DOMAIN NAMES

Participation on the Internet is no longer seen as an option for a charitable or not-for-profit organization if it intends to be noticed in the increasingly competitive marketplace. This is due to the exponential growth of the Internet and the increase in websites and domain names that have accompanied it.

- **Internet** — In 1996, there were 50 million people using the Internet worldwide. Since then, the number of Internet users worldwide has increased exponentially to 391 million people in 2000 and 941 million people in 2004. For 2005, it is projected that 1.1 billion people will use the Internet.[3]

- **Websites** — The exponential growth of the Internet has been matched by a parallel increase of global commerce taking place on the Internet. The future is now seen in terms of electronic commerce with the Internet moving from an informational source to a transactional forum. This is evidenced by the number of unique websites on the Internet: there were 1.7 million unique websites on the Internet in 1993; 43 million unique websites on the Internet in 1999; and over 317 million unique websites on the Internet in 2005.[4]

- **Domain names** — Organizations beginning to realize the exponential growth of the Internet and the parallel increase of global commerce taking place on the Internet are starting to

---

[3]   Global Reach, online <http://www.glreach.com/globstats>.
[4]   Internet Systems Consortium, online <http://www.isc.org>.

register domain names for their organizations. As a result, 15.7 million domain names were registered in March 2000, with 9.7 million of those being .com domain names; and 64.5 million domain names were registered in 2004, with half of those being .com domain names.[5]

Integral to a charitable or not-for-profit organization having an effective presence on the Internet is its ability to secure an effective domain name as its permanent computer address. It is essential for a donor using the Internet to be able to connect with the website of the organization with as little confusion as possible. This can be accomplished by using a domain name that is easy to remember by including the name of the organization, *e.g.*, "www.redcross.org" or "www.salvationarmy.org". It can also be accomplished if the organization has a generic description for a domain name (*e.g.*, "www.arthritis.ca" or "www.charity.ca") that will enable a donor to quickly find the website when using a search engine. The importance of securing an effective domain name cannot be emphasized enough, as an effective domain name will assist a charitable or not-for-profit organization in the following areas.[6]

(a) Communicating

The Internet can reach the greatest number of people in the world, given the high number of Internet users. Potentially, a charitable or not-for-profit organization that has an effective domain name could attract and communicate to a worldwide audience through the Internet. This would require the organization to invest in the creation and maintenance of a website that effectively gets the organization's brand out in the open. Such organizations must be careful to update the website regularly in order to ensure it provides relevant, current information. This would encourage anyone visiting the website or receiving the organization's email to pass along the website or email information, thereby increasing circulation. Although it is not a charitable or not-for-profit organization, THE GLOBE AND MAIL realizes this and has an "email this article" option at the end of every article posted on its website. The chances are simply greater that someone receiving an email from a trusted family

---

[5] VeriSign, Quarterly Domain Name Report, online <http://www.verisign.com/verisign-inc/news-and-events/news-archive/us-news-2004/page_015910.html>.

[6] Ted Hart, James M. Greenfield & Michael Johnston, *Nonprofit Internet Strategies: Best Practices for Marketing, Communications, and Fundraising* (New Jersey: John Wiley & Sons, Inc., 2005) at 8.

member or friend would read the email, whereas that same person might be inclined to delete the same email if sent by an organization. The Globe and Mail also provides an option to leave a comment and to join a discussion group at the end of every article. This is a creative way of engaging the public in the communication.

In addition, the Internet is the fastest means of communication. Websites, blogs, chat rooms, bulletin boards and email provide organizations with instantaneous modes of communication. The Internet enabled WORLD VISION to act quickly in alerting Canadians to the tsunami that devastated Indonesia on December 26, 2004, and informing Canadians on what could be done in response. This gave the WORLD VISION brand a lot of publicity in relation to international relief efforts, which is one of World Vision's mission objectives. The one drawback to an Internet presence is that supporters who join the charitable or not-for-profit organization via the Internet may expect an instantaneous response to their communications.

Finally, the Internet is the least expensive means of communication. Websites and email enable organizations to communicate with a much wider audience at minimal cost. The value of this cannot be underestimated for charitable or not-for-profit organizations that have little start-up financial resources. Although email is cost-effective and efficient, such organizations should be careful to observe applicable privacy legislation that may govern their activities when compiling their email lists. For starters, an organization should not assume that an individual consents to being placed on its email lists. Even where the individual has provided consent or has voluntarily opted to join the email list, organizations should still provide an easy method of opting out of the email list.

As a word of caution, charitable and not-for-profit organizations should not abandon all other means of communication. The Internet should not be seen as the only means of communication, but as a complementary means which supplements conventional methods such as direct mail, telephone, radio, television and personal visits. Not only has the Internet not replaced conventional means of communication, it has not revolutionized conventional means of successful communication. Just as charitable and not-for-profit organizations must work at attracting brand interest, maintaining brand interest and developing brand loyalty among its potential supporters with the off-line "bricks and mortar" world, they must also do the same with the online "cyberspace" world.

(b) Fundraising

Many charitable and not-for-profit organizations have a section on their website for fundraising. Whether donors sign up for a one-time gift or a monthly plan, the Internet makes it quick and convenient for them to support the organization of their choice. Not only does this self-serve style of donation save the organization time and effort in collecting donations, it can also benefit participants by saving them from the hassle of asking for and collecting pledges.

In order to benefit from online fundraising, organizations must ensure their websites are both secure and private. Many protect their donors' financial and personal information through encryption codes, or have a certification mark such as VERISIGN SECURED to signal the charitable or not-for-profit organization has chosen one or more VeriSign SSL Certificate or online payment solutions to improve the security of e-commerce and other confidential information on its website. Charitable and not-for-profit organizations must also protect their donors' privacy by implementing a privacy policy in accordance with applicable privacy legislation, promising to use the financial and personal information only for the purposes for which it was provided, and allowing donors to control, amend or remove the financial and personal information collected.

In addition, the Internet itself can be a source of fundraising. Some organizations have sponsorship advertisements on their website, and the funding they receive from their sponsor will depend upon the popularity of the website; that is, the more web traffic the organization has, the more funding the organization will receive.

(c) Events

The Internet can make it easier to promote an organization's brand through upcoming events, campaigns, programs, seminars, shows, *etc.* Since the individuals visiting the website and receiving the organization's email are already interested in the organization's mission objectives, it is likely the individuals would also be more responsive to the website advertisement or email invitation regarding upcoming activities.

In addition to the promotional benefits, it is also easier to organize responses to and registrations for the activities being promoted. If a charitable or not-for-profit organization does not have the technical capabilities for such organizational management, it can take advantage of the many Internet services now available. One simple example is "www.evite.com", which offers free online invitations and event planning tips, all to help you "create and manage your invitations and RSVP's — all in one place".

Finally, the Internet can assist a charitable or not-for-profit organization in improving its brand by surveying its event attendees after the event is over. These surveys can be useful in getting feedback on what was done well, areas that could be improved and complaints that need to be addressed, as well as provide suggestions for future planning. If the organization sets up the survey online with the right survey tools, it can save itself a lot of time from having to tabulate the results.

(d) Recruitment

In addition to communicating with the public, recruiting donations or reinforcing their brand, charitable and not-for-profit organizations can also recruit the public for volunteers. For example, GREENPEACE has a section on its website for recruiting volunteers, with information on the necessary requirements and the application process.

If an organization does not have the technical capabilities to create and manage its own online volunteer database, there are online resources that will match volunteers with charitable or not-for-profit organizations. For example, VOLUNTEERMATCH offers a variety of online services to support charitable organizations, claiming to welcome millions of visitors a year and having become the preferred Internet recruiting tool for more than 30,000 charitable and non-profit organizations.[7]

(e) Advocacy

Depending on the type of organization, advocacy at the grassroots levels may be the primary or a major objective. The Internet could be used to send information to the organization's supporters, amass electronic petitions from the public and send email calling for change to the targeted audience. The Internet, or email in particular, are more effective than conventional means of mass communication because it is easier and less expensive for an individual to forward an Internet link or an email message to a friend or family member than it is for the same individual to photocopy and mail a letter to the same person.

The convenience of the Internet can increase opportunities for advocacy. For example, Greenpeace has an action forum where its supporters can sign

---

[7]   VolunteerMatch, online: <http://www.volunteermatch.org>.

up to receive its newsletter and learn how to become a "cyber activist", as well as a regular activist "to help win campaigns for the environment".[8] For organizations such as Greenpeace, the Internet is an excellent forum to advocate for change and rally support at the grassroots level.

3.   DOMAIN NAME CONFLICTS

As was discussed earlier, an effective domain name is essential to a charitable or not-for-profit organization's Internet presence. Since a more recognizable domain name will be easier to find on the Internet, the choice of a domain name which contains the name of the organization will significantly enhance the goodwill and the international recognition of that organization. The difficulty, however, is that there can be only one domain name for the multiple organizations that own similar names. For example, both CHRISTIAN BLIND MISSION and CANADIAN BAPTIST MINISTRIES refer to themselves in the short form as "CBM", however, there; can only be; one "www.cbm.org". In addition, there are only so many ways a domain name can be varied within the same domain and divided among the multiple organizations that own similar names; that is, "www.cbm.com" can only be varied into the less desirable "www.c-b-m.org" or "www.c.b.m.org". The result will be fierce competition for the few effective domain names available. As such, charitable and not-for-profit organizations need to be proactive and diligent in registering its domain names as quickly as possible or risk losing the domain name.

(a) Conflicts between domain names

MCDONALD'S learned the lesson about conflicts between domain names the hard way a number of years ago when it was repeatedly contacted by a computer expert to see if it was intending to obtain a domain name for "www.mcdonald's.com". When the company did not show any interest in this regard, the individual reserved the name himself, requiring McDonald's to negotiate with him to obtain a return of the domain name. Following an unsuccessful court battle, McDonald's was only able to obtain the domain name by agreeing to make a donation to a charity designated by the computer expert.[9]

---

[8]   Greenpeace, online: <http://www.greenpeace.org/international/about/volunteers>.
[9]   Stanford University, online: <http://cse.stanford.edu/classes/cs201/projects/domain-names/problems/grabbing.html>.

The computer expert toying with McDonald's was seeking to make a point about the necessity of being proactive and diligent in registering domain names, but others have not been motivated by such benign considerations. A classic example of competitive grabbing of a domain name would be the KAPLAN case. When THE PRINCETON REVIEW, a competitor of Kaplan, first decided to establish an Internet presence, it registered the names "www.review.com" and "www.princeton.com" to set up as websites. Realizing that "www.kaplan.com" was also available, The Princeton Review also decided to register Kaplan's domain name for the purpose of hosting a complaint website about Kaplan's products and services. Kaplan took the case to court and an arbitrator decided to give the domain name to Kaplan.[10]

In other cases, companies have been forced to spend significant sums of money on legal fees in order to obtain the domain name matching their corporate name or trade mark. While the United States has enacted laws to extend some measure of protection for trade marks into the realm of domain names, there is still plenty of room for conflict and grey areas. Just as large businesses have had to learn the hard way about the importance of securing an effective domain name, charitable and not-for-profit organizations will also need to be diligent to avoid a similar result.

Domain name conflicts, though, do not all result from multiple organizations competing for the same domain name or from one organization grabbing its competitor's domain name, as described above. Domain name conflicts also arise from competition between:

- Trade mark owners who have similar trade marks with similar domain names. An example of this would be CANADIAN BLIND MISSION's "www.cbm.org" and CANADIAN BAPTIST MINISTRIES' "www.cbmin.org".

- Trade mark owners and "cybersquatters" who only register the domain name for the sole purpose of selling them to the trade mark owners for a profit. An example would be an individual registering "www.benandjerrys.com" for no reason, with no intent to ever use the domain name, and then selling it to BEN & JERRY'S for profit.

- Trade mark owners and "typosquatters" who register misspelled domain names to reroute searches for popular websites. An example would be someone operating a search engine and registering the website as "www.yahho.com" to redirect traffic

---

[10] *Ibid.*

from "www.yahoo.com". By looking at the website, it is clear that "www.yahho.com" offers similar products to or is in competition with "www.yahoo.com".

(b) Conflicts between domain names and trade marks

In addition to conflicts between domain names, there can also be conflicts between domain names and trade marks. Although the registrars will require the domain names to be unique before they can be registered, the registrars will not take into account or make decisions concerning the legality of the domain names; that is, whether the domain name conflicts with a trade mark. Not surprisingly, in recent years there has been increasing conflicts between registered trade marks and domain names. The tension arises out of a number of factors:

- Trade marks are creatures of statute and therefore national in scope, whereas domain names are international in nature and transcend national borders and trade mark laws. The result is that a restaurant calling itself CHINESE BUFFET in Canada would find itself competing for the same "www.chinesebuffet.com" as a restaurant in the U.S. or a restaurant in Europe operating under the same generic name. The international nature of domain names was exhibited in the dispute over "www.ottawa.biz" wherein a Texas company with a trade mark in the word OTTAWA was awarded the domain name regardless of the fact that the national capital of Canada is the same name.[11]

- Trade marks are restricted to a specific list of wares and services, whereas domain names have no restrictions concerning their application. The result is that there can be more multiple NIKE trade mark owners, since one owner could use NIKE for sportswear while another owner could use NIKE for telephone equipment and a third owner could use NIKE for plant food products. However, all three NIKE trade mark owners would want the one "www.nike.com" domain name.

- Trade mark law permits multiple people to use the same mark simultaneously, whereas there is only one owner of a particular domain name on a worldwide basis. The result is that there can be multiple NIKE trade mark owners, all using NIKE to operate a

---

[11] Michael Geist, "Domain name policy absurd when it comes to trademarks" *The Globe and Mail* (25 July 2002).

sportswear store through a franchise agreement. If the franchisor or head office does not take the initiative or is not providing strong control and leaves it to the franchisees to establish their own websites, all three NIKE trade mark owners will be competing for the same "www.nike.com" domain name.

- Trade marks in some countries such as Canada and the U.S. are acquired by establishing entitlement based upon a claim of "first to use" basis, whereas domain names are acquired on a "first come, first serve" basis.

- Trade marks are difficult to obtain; trade mark applicants must go through a rigorous application and examination process before receiving statutory protection for their trade marks. However, whereas domain names can be obtained relatively easily; domain name applicants need only provide a name, street address, email address and credit card.

(c) ICANN's dispute resolution

As a result of the obvious real and potential conflicts between domain names and trade marks, ICANN developed the Uniform Domain Name Dispute Resolution Policy ("UDRP").[12] The UDRP is intended to provide a procedure to resolve conflicts between owners of domain names and owners of trade marks. This was done by necessity, since it is not uncommon for domain name registrars to be named as defendants in domain name disputes.[13]

The UDRP sets out the following procedure for resolving disputes between trade mark owners and domain name owners:

- The complainant must have grounds to assert the following three elements: (1) the domain name is identical or confusingly similar to a trade mark in which the complainant has rights; (2) the domain name owner has no rights or legitimate interests in respect of the domain name; and (3) the domain name has been registered and is being used in bad faith. As can be seen from these three elements, the UDRP does not specifically require the complainant to have a registered trade mark in order to contest a domain name.

---

[12] <http://www.icann.org/dndr/undrp/policy.htm>.
[13] John-Paul Hoffman, "Domain Names Test Boundaries of Trade Mark Law" *Law Times* (6 October 1996) at 15.

The complainant could just as well contest a domain name on the basis of its common law rights in an unregistered trade mark.

- The complainant then forwards a copy of the complaint to a dispute-resolution service provider approved by ICANN, at which time the dispute-resolution service provider will then notify the domain name owner of the complaint received.

- The domain name owner must then submit a response to the dispute-resolution service provider within 20 days of the commencement of the administrative proceeding.

- The administrative proceeding will result in three possible decisions: (1) cancellation of the domain name; (2) rejection of the complaint; or (3) an order directing the transfer of the domain name from the domain name owner to the trade mark owner. The UDRP does not award damages, interest or costs.

- After a decision is made, the dispute-resolution service provider will communicate the full text of the decision to each party, the concerned domain name registrar(s) and ICANN. The concerned domain name registrar(s) will then set a date for implementing the decision; however, the party wishing to dispute the decision can do so by commencing an action in a court of competent jurisdiction within 10 days of the decision. This is the only recourse available as the UDRP does not have an appeal board.

(d) CIRA's dispute resolution

In 2003, CIRA also set up its own Domain Name Dispute Resolution Policy ("CIRA's Policy"),[14] to deal with disputes concerning names registered with the .ca regional top level domain. CIRA's Policy is very similar to the UDRP, including the three elements that a complainant must meet when contesting a domain name. CIRA's Policy, like the UDRP, does not specifically require the complainant to have a registered trade mark in order to contest a domain name, which is in keeping with Canadian trade mark law and allows for both infringement actions with respect to registered trade marks and passing-off actions with respect to unregistered trade marks.

There are, however, three main differences between CIRA's Policy and the UDRP that should be noted. First, although CIRA's Policy does

---

[14] <http://www.cira.ca/en/documents/q4/CDRP_Policy_2003-12-04_en_final.pdf>.

not award damages, interest or costs, it does award a penalty of up to $5,000 to the domain name owner if the complainant is found to have brought the complaint in bad faith. The complainant will also be ineligible to file another complaint with CIRA until it pays the amount owing. Second, CIRA's Policy recognizes official marks in the same way it recognizes regular trade marks. As such, a complaint can use an official mark as a basis for contesting a domain name, and, conversely, a domain name owner can use an official mark as proof of having a legitimate interest in the domain name. Third, CIRA's Policy restricts the complaint process only to those complainants who meet the Canadian Presence Requirements, namely, complainants who are:[15]

(a)   Canadian citizens;

(b)   Permanent residents;

(c)   Legal representatives of (a) or (b) above;

(d)   Canadian corporations, either federally or provincially incorporated;

(e)   Trusts established under the laws of a province or territory in Canada, whose trustees meet 66 per cent of the requirements set out in (a) to (d) above;

(f)   Partnerships registered under the laws of Canada, whose partners meet more than 66 per cent of conditions (a) to (d) above;

(g)   Unincorporated associations where at least 80 per cent of members meet conditions (a) to (f) above and at least 80 per cent of directors or other representatives are ordinarily resident in Canada;

(h)   Trade unions recognized under the laws of Canada with a head office in Canada;

(i)   Political parties registered under relevant electoral laws of Canada;

(j)   Educational institutions, located in Canada and recognized or licensed under an Act of the legislature of a province or territory in Canada;

(k)   Libraries, archives and museums located in Canada, which are not established for profit;

(l)   Hospitals located in Canada and approved or licensed to operate as such under the laws of Canada;

---

[15]   <http://www.cira.ca/en/documents/q3/CanadianPresenceRequirementsForRegistrants-EffectiveDateJune52003.pdf>.

(m) Her Majesty the Queen and successors, as well as governments in Canada;

(n) Aboriginal peoples and Indian bands, as defined; and

(o) Owners of registered trade marks or official marks in Canada.

Notwithstanding the intent to resolve disputes, the UDRP and CIRA's Policy will obviously not satisfy every trade mark owner who believes, rightly or wrongly, that its trade mark rights are being infringed upon. At present, there have been several Canadian court cases that have dealt with disputes between domain name owners and trade mark owners.[16] The emerging case law highlights the fact that domain names are not immune from trade mark law. As a result, if a court is satisfied that there has been an actual infringement of a trade mark, notwithstanding compliance with the UDRP or CIRA's Policy, it will intervene. Thus far, Canada has protected trade marks from infringement, including infringement by a domain name, on the basis of: (1) imitation; (2) confusion; (3) depreciation of goodwill; and (4) passing-off.

4. SECURING DOMAIN NAMES

It is important to carefully select a domain name, since the resulting domain name will become one of the most important assets in developing the charitable or not-for-profit organization's brand and carrying out its operations. The domain name will also become more valuable the longer the domain name is used and the association between the domain name and the organization or cause is strengthened. The right choice of domain name will also enhance fundraising on the Internet; therefore, it is important to take proactive steps to secure and protect domain names and consider the following strategies in making that selection.

---

[16] See, for example, *Peinet Inc. v. O'Brien (c.o.b. Island Services Network (ISN))*, [1995] P.E.I.J. No. 68 (S.C. (T.D.)); *Fitzwilliam v. Rolls-Royce plc*, [1999] F.C.J. No. 527 (T.D.); *Bell Actimedia Inc. v. Puzo (Communications Globe Tête)*, [1999] F.C.J. No. 683 (T.D.); *Canada Post Corp. v. Epost Innovations Inc.*, [1999] F.C.J. No. 1297 (T.D.); *Epost Innovations Inc. v. Canada Post Corp.*, [1999] B.C.J. No. 2060 (S.C.); *Toronto.com v. Sinclair (c.o.b. Friendship Enterprises)*, [2000] F.C.J. No. 795 (T.D.); *Innersense International Inc. v. Manegre*, [2000] A.J. No. 613 (Q.B.); *Pro-C Ltd. v. Computer City, Inc.*, [2001] O.J. No. 3600 (C.A.), rev'g [2000] O.J. No. 2823 (Sup. Ct.); *Black v. Molson Canada*, [2002] O.J. No. 2820 (Sup. Ct.); *ITV Technologies, Inc. v. WIC Television Ltd.*, [2003] F.C.J. No. 1335 (T.D.).

(a) Obtain domain names as soon as possible

It is imperative that a charitable or not-for-profit organization obtain a domain name as soon as possible. As was already mentioned, there are only a limited number of effective domain names available for the preferred top level domains of .com, .net, .org, .info, .biz and .us. Therefore, although there may be multiple organizations operating under similar names, there cannot be any duplication of identical domain names in each category. This will result in competition between trade mark owners who have similar trade marks.

(b) Obtain as many domain names as possible

Multiple domain names will insulate key domain names used by a charitable or not-for-profit organization by creating a "safe zone" around the key domain names. Multiple domain names will also assist donors in finding the organization on the Internet through both regular searches and search engines. Finally, multiple domain names will preclude others from misappropriating a similar domain name of the organization.

(c) Register with multiple domain names

When obtaining as many domain names as possible, the charitable or not-for-profit organization should register with multiple top level domains. If possible, an organization should obtain the most popular generic top level domains, such as the "trilogy" of .com, .net and .org. After the desired generic top level domain names are obtained, consideration should also be given to registering with regional top level domains for each country and geographic region in which the organization operates. Even if not all the domain names can be used at present, their availability may prove useful in the future. By securing multiple domain names now, an organization may avoid potential confusion that might otherwise result if the domain names in issue were used by another organization.

Such a scenario is presently playing out in a legal action launched by the WATCH TOWER BIBLE AND TRACT SOCIETY OF CANADA and its U.S. parent organization against a former member of the organization. Although the religious organization obtained the website "www.watchtower.org", in 1997, it did not obtain the same domain name under the different top level domains. In 2000, a former member of the organization registered the domain name "www.watchtower.ca", a website that redirects users to another website that reproduces and discusses Watch

Tower publications, which Watch Tower claims trades on the significant reputation and goodwill associated with Watch Tower's trade marks and attempts to embarrass the organization.[17] Whether anything comes of the action remains to be seen, but it serves as a valuable lesson for charitable and not-for-profit organizations to consider the impact of failing to register multiple domains.

(d) Register multiple domain names

When obtaining as many domain names as possible, the charitable or not-for-profit organization should also register multiple second level identifying names with the same top level domain. First, the organization should use its full trade mark as the second level identifying name. It is also important to remember to register French domain names for the organization's French trade marks where a charitable or not-for-profit organization has operations in Quebec. As noted in Chapter 5, the organization is advised to translate its English name(s) into French in order to comply with Quebec's language legislation. Any corporate or business names or slogans not registered as trade marks should also be used as second level identifying names. As an example, THE RED CROSS could also register the slogan "www.thegiftoflife.org". This will preclude others from misappropriating the goodwill attached to those names or slogans. Second, the organization should also consider registering as many slight variations on the second level identifying name as possible. Registering "www.red-cross.org" and "www.redcrosses.org" will reduce the potential for confusion with "www.redcross.org". Third, the organization should also consider registering popular misspellings of their second level identifying names, especially in light of emerging typosquatters who register misspelled domain names to reroute searches for popular websites. Finally, the charitable or not-for-profit organization should also consider using generic descriptions as the second level identifying name. This will direct donors conducting general searches on the Internet to the appropriate website. An example of this would be "www.giveblood.org" for the Red Cross.

---

[17] *Watch Tower Bible and Tract Society of Canada et al. v. Peter Anthony Mosier* (September 2005), 05-CV-296308PD2 at 9-10 (Ont. Sup. Ct.).

(e) Conduct trade mark search

If the charitable or not-for-profit organization has not already conducted a trade mark search for its second level identifying name, then it should be advised to do so, since the use of a domain name that is the same or similar to a registered trade mark may constitute a trade mark infringement. In this regard, trade mark searches should be done in all countries in which the organization will be carrying on operations in order to determine whether or not there is the potential for trade mark infringement in that jurisdiction.

(f) Register trade mark

Once a decision has been made to obtain a particular domain name, the organization should apply for trade mark registration in Canada, and possibly in foreign jurisdictions (as discussed in Chapter 6), for its exact second level identifying name in order to protect the domain name from future challenges under the UDRP or CIRA's Policy.

(g) Monitor and renew domain names

Domain name registrations are only valid for a specific period of time and will expire unless renewed. It is important to set up a reminder system to renew domain names well in advance of the expiry date. One way is to establish a staff member as a domain name portfolio manager for the charitable or not-for-profit organization to keep track of its multiple domain name renewal dates. Another way is to register with companies such as NAMEPROTECT at "www.nameprotect.com" to provide notification of forthcoming expiration dates. Failure to renew domain names in a timely fashion could result in major embarrassment for the charitable or not-for-profit organization.

In a process that has been given the moniker "porn-napping", owners of pornography websites have been known to purchase expired domain names and then have them redirect traffic to their own sites. Sometimes they will sell the domain name back to the forgetful original owner, but likely at an exorbitant price. Such reputable organizations as ERNST & YOUNG, the UNITED NATIONS and the U.S. DEPARTMENT OF EDUCATION have all fallen victim to porn-napping. In the case of Ernst & Young, their website dedicated to children's money management, which had been listed as one of the top picks in the book *300 Incredible Things for Kids on the Internet*, lapsed and was quickly purchased by an

Armenian pornographer who redirected traffic to a porn site.[18] The clerical error resulted in a "brand-management disaster" for the firm as well as an undisclosed payment to the pornographer in order to secure the domain name's return.

Similarly, a small U.S. not-for-profit organization dedicated to educating elderly citizens about health benefits lost their original domain name to an Eastern European pornographer who wanted $3,000 to $5,000 for its return.[19] Such a price was too much for the organization, which was forced to obtain a new domain name.

5.   CONTESTING DOMAIN NAMES

Since the availability of effective domain names will become more and more restricted, consideration may need to be given to what steps can be taken to challenge an existing domain name that a charitable or not-for-profit organization has failed to secure. In this regard, there are two strategies that can be followed:

1.   One option is to commence a trade mark infringement action against the domain name owner in the U.S. (where ICANN is located) or against the domain name owner in Canada (where CIRA is located) for a .ca domain name. However, this is obviously an expensive and time-consuming process, one that is not going to be easily adopted. This in turn emphasizes the importance of securing an effective domain name now, while the desired domain name may still be available, instead of waiting until the name has been secured by another organization and having to consider expensive litigation in order to obtain entitlement to the desired domain name.

2.   Another option is to use the procedure under the UDRP or CIRA's Policy. This would require the organization to prove that: (1) the domain name is identical or confusingly similar to a trade mark to which the organization has rights; (2) the domain name owner has no rights or legitimate interests in respect of the

---

[18]   Jerry Ropelato, "Tricks Pornographers Play" (2003), online: Family Safe Media <http://www.familysafemedia.com/tricks_pornographers_play.html>; Jane Black, "Invasion of the 'Porn Nappers'" (7 March 2002), online: Business Week Online <http://www.businessweek.com/bwdaily/dnflash/mar2002/nf2002037_2837.htm>.

[19]   Jane Black, "Invasion of the 'Porn Nappers'" (7 March 2002), online: Business Week Online <http://www.businessweek.com/bwdaily/dnflash/mar2002/nf2002037_2837.htm>.

domain name; and (3) the domain name has been registered and is being used in bad faith.

(a) Identical or confusingly similar

There does not appear to be a consistent test for "confusingly similar". Domain names have been found to be confusingly similar for a variety of reasons:

- The domain name was a misspelled variation of a well-known trade mark; *e.g.*, "www.tdwatergouse.com" and "dwaterhouse.com" were confusingly similar with TD WATERHOUSE;[20]

- The domain name had a punctuation added to the trade mark; *e.g.*, "www.twilight-zone.net" was confusingly similar with TWILIGHT ZONE;[21] and

- The domain name had a space omitted from the trade mark; *e.g.*, "www.victoriasecret.org" was confusingly similar with VICTORIA'S SECRET.[22]

The closest thing to a consistent test for "confusingly similar" might be the test found in *AMF, Inc. v. Sleekcraft Boats*,[23] which the UDRP has followed on several subsequent occasions. That test sets out eight factors to be considered:

1. strength of the mark;
2. proximity of the goods;
3. similarity of the marks;
4. evidence of actual confusion;

---

[20] *Toronto-Dominion Bank v. Kapachev* (15 January 2001), WIPO Case No. D2000-1571, online: World Intellectual Property Organization <http://arbiter.wipo.int/domains/decisions/html/2000/d2000-1571.html>.

[21] *CBS Broadcasting, Inc. v. LA-Twilight-Zone* (19 June 2000), WIPO Case No. D2000-0397, online: World Intellectual Property Organization <http://arbiter.wipo.int/domains/decisions/html/2000/d2000-0397.html>.

[22] *V Secret Catalogue, Inc. v. Artco, Inc.* (9 May 2000), Forum File No. FA94342, online: National Arbritration Forum <http://www.arbforum.com/domains/decisions/94342.html>.

[23] 599 F.2d 341 (9th Cir. 1979) [hereinafter "*AMF*"]. This test has been applied in *Arthur Guinness Son & Co. (Dublin) Ltd. v. O'Donnell* (9 February 2001), WIPO Case No. D2000-1710, online: World Intellectual Property Organization <http://arbiter.wipo.int/domains/decisions/html/2000/d2000-1710.html> and *Wal-Mart Stores, Inc. v. Walsucks and Walmarket Puerto Rico* (20 July 2000), WIPO Case No. D2000-0477, online: World Intellectual Property Organization <http://arbiter.wipo.int/domains/decisions/html/2000/d2000-0477.html>.

5.   marketing channels used;

6.   type of goods and the degree of care likely to be exercised by the purchaser;

7.   defendant's intent in selecting the mark; and

8.   likelihood of expansion of the product lines.[24]

There is no clear rule on whether "sucks" websites are confusingly similar. The minority of cases have held that a "sucks" domain name cannot be confusingly similar with a trade mark, since it is clear that the purpose of the website hosted at the domain name was to criticize or disparage the goods and services associated with the trade mark; e.g., "www.walmartcanadasucks.com"[25] or "www.crappytire.com".[26] The majority of cases, however, have found that "sucks" domain names can be confusingly similar with a trade mark as search engines will retrieve both the "sucks" website and the trade mark owner's website; e.g., "adtsucks.com"[27] and "wachoviasucks.com".[28]

(b) Legitimate interest

In order to prove legitimate interest, the domain name owner must prove any one of the following three elements:

1.   It used or was prepared to use the name in connection with a good faith offering of goods or services;

2.   It is commonly known by that name; or

3.   It is making legitimate non-commercial or fair use of the name, with no intent for commercial gain.

It is not clear whether websites that criticize or disparage the goods and services associated with a trade mark is a legitimate interest,

---

[24]   *AMF, ibid.*

[25]   *Wal-Mart Stores, Inc. v. Walmarket Canada* (2 May 2000), WIPO Case No. D2000-0150, online: World Intellectual Property Organization <http://arbiter.wipo.int/domains/decision/html/2000/d2000-0150.html>.

[26]   *Canadian Tire Corp. Ltd. v. McFadden*, (24 May 2001), WIPO Case No. D2001-0383, online: World Intellectual Property Organization <http://abiter.wipo.int/domains/decisions/html/2001/d2001-0383.html>.

[27]   *ADT Services AG v. ADT Sucks.com*, (23 April 2001), WIPO Case No. D2001-0213, online: World Intellectual Property Organization<http://arbiter.wipo.int/domains/decisions/html/2001/d2001-0213.html>.

[28]   *Wachovia Co. v. Alton Flanders*, (19 September 2003), WIPO Case No. D2003-0596, online: World Intellectual Property Organization <http://arbiter.wipo.int/domains/decisions/html/2003/d2003-0596.html>.

especially if there is no commercial gain or diversion of customers involved. There is case law saying that such websites are legitimate interests; *e.g.*, "www.tmpworldwide.net" and "tmpworldwide.org".[29] The majority of cases, however, find that such websites do divert customers, since the search engines will retrieve both the critical and disparaging website along with the trade mark owner's website; *e.g.*, "adtsucks.com"[30] and "wachoviasucks.com".[31]

(c) Bad faith

Although the following list sets out guidelines for finding bad faith, it is not an exhaustive list:

- Circumstances indicating the domain name owner registered or acquired the domain name primarily for the purpose of selling, renting or otherwise transferring the domain name registration to the owner of the trade mark or to a competitor of the owner, for valuable consideration in excess of the domain name owner's documented out-of-pocket costs directly related to the domain name;

- The domain name owner registered the domain name in order to prevent the owner of the trade mark from using the mark in a corresponding domain name, if the domain name owner has engaged in a pattern of such conduct;

- The domain name owner registered the domain name primarily for the purpose of disrupting the business of a competitor; or

- By using the domain name, the domain name owner intentionally attempted to attract, for commercial gain, Internet users to the website or other online location by creating a likelihood of confusion with the trade mark owner's mark as to the source,

---

[29] *TMP Worldwide Inc. v. Potter* (5 August 2000), WIPO Case No. D2000-0536, online: World Intellectual Property Organization <http://arbiter.wipo.int/domains/decisions/html/2000/d2000-0536.html>.

[30] *ADT Services AG v. ADT Sucks.com* (23 April 2001), WIPO Case No. D2001-0213, online: World Intellectual Property Organization <http://arbiter.wipo.int/domains/decisions/html/2001/d2001-0213.html>.

[31] *Wachovia Corp. v. Flanders* (19 September 2003), WIPO Case No. D2003-0596, online: World Intellectual Property Organization <http://arbiter.wipo.int/domains/decisions/html/2003/d2003-0596.html>.

sponsorship, affiliation or endorsement of the website or of a product or service on the website. [32]

6. LICENSING DOMAIN NAMES

After obtaining a domain name, it is important for the charitable or not-for-profit organization to protect the use of the domain name through a license agreement when:

- An organization permits an Internet link from its website to the website of another similar organization;

- A Canadian charitable or not-for-profit organization is set up on a national basis with chapters, and these chapters are able to use geographic divisions of the main domain name; *e.g.*, the national charity has "www.arthritis.ca" and the provincial charities have "www.arthritis.on.ca";

- A religious denomination across Canada wants to retain control over the use of the denominational domain names by local churches;

- A charitable or not-for-profit organization expands to other countries and wishes to use similar domain names in those countries, such as "www.redcross.us" from the U.S.; or

- A charitable or not-for-profit organization permits its domain name to be used by business for web links or for advertising the domain name of the business in conjunction with the domain name of the organization.

The licensing of the domain name can be done either through a trade mark license agreement or through a separate license agreement, depending upon the circumstances.

SUMMARY

In the increasingly competitive charitable market, the Internet is one platform that charitable and not-for-profit organizations cannot ignore. Although it is a cost-efficient means of communicating with donors, developing and supporting the organization's brand and providing a means for donors and members to show their support, the Internet is a

---

[32] Uniform Domain Name Dispute Resolution Policy (24 October 1999), online: <http://www.icann.org/dndr/udrp/policy.htm>.

tool that must be carefully developed and managed. Trade marks will play an essential role in developing the charitable or not-for-profit organization's online brand. As such, organizations must carefully and thoughtfully select and manage domain names, license its use in appropriate situations and fight to protect its integrity where warranted.

CHAPTER 10

PROTECTING THE BRAND THROUGH TRADE MARK LICENSING

1.   What is Licensing?
2.   When is Licensing Relevant?
     (a)   Co-branding
     (b)   Sponsorship
     (c)   Recommendations
     (d)   Risks
3.   Licensing Requirements
     (a)   Registered user system
     (b)   Controlled licensing system
     (c)   Current licensing requirements
4.   Licensing Considerations
     (a)   Type of license
     (b)   Scope of license
     (c)   Licensee's undertaking
     (d)   Licensee's standing
     (e)   Licensor's warranties
     (f)   Licensor's control
     (g)   Royalties
     (h)   Assignment and sub-license
     (i)   Indemnifications
     (j)   Confidentiality

(k)   Termination

Summary

Licensing of a charitable or not-for-profit organization's trade marks is becoming an increasing reality in the modern world as organizations band together to improve the success of promotions for both organizations. In many cases, charitable and not-for-profit organizations get to expand the scope of their audience, and for-profit corporations get a chance to improve their image by being associated with a worthy cause. The common law of trade marks and Canada's own *Trade-marks Act*[1] has had to mature alongside this development, as such practices were not always possible. In fact, prior to the introduction of the *Trade-marks Act* in Canada in 1953, a trade mark owner could not license the trade mark's use by any third party, as such use ran contrary to Canada's theory of trade marks. In other words, if a trade mark was intended to distinguish the wares or services of trade mark owner from that of another individual or corporation, or act as an indication of source or origin, then how could its use by a third party result in anything but confusion in the marketplace?

With the introduction of the *Trade-marks Act* in Canada in 1953, trade mark owners were given a limited right to license a trade mark, which has expanded over time. Today, licensing of a charitable or not-for-profit organization's trade marks can account for a significant percentage of the income derived from trade marks.

There are many benefits to a charitable or not-for-profit organization licensing its trade marks, even if no fees are derived from the arrangement. For example, licensing has the ability to extend the geographic and product scope of the trade mark. However, charitable and not-for-profit organizations must consider the feasibility and advisability of entering into agreements with other similar organizations or for-profit corporations, as the risks may sometimes outweigh the benefits. In some circumstances, there is little choice but to license the trade mark, as in instances when a national organization starts local or associate organizations which will use the trade mark. As this chapter will discuss, entering into a licensing agreement is not a simple or casual matter for the charitable or not-for-profit organization to consider, and thus should be done judiciously.

---

[1]   R.S.C. 1985, c. T-13.

1.   WHAT IS LICENSING?

Licensing occurs when an owner of certain rights permits or authorizes another person to exercise those rights by contract where such exercise would not ordinarily be permitted. Licensing does not create a proprietary right for the licensee, as the owner retains the right in what was licensed and retains the right to revoke the permit or authorization. Examples of different types of licensing are:

- **Franchise** — A right to conduct business or sell a product or service under a name or mark in accordance with the methods and procedures set by the franchisor. This does not grant the licensee any right to the name.[2]

- **Government** — Authority or permission by an appropriate governmental body to do or carry on some trade or business which would otherwise be unlawful. This does not confer upon the licensee contractual, vested or property rights.[3]

- **Patents** — Authority granted by the owner of a patent empowering another person to make or use the patented article for a limited period or in a limited territory. This does not affect the licensor's monopoly with respect to the rest of the world.[4]

- **Real Property** — A mere personal or revocable privilege to perform an act or series of acts on the land of another. This does not operate to confer on or vest in the licensee any title, interest or estate in such property.[5]

- **Trade Marks** — Permission to use a trade mark in association with a product or service. This does not affect the licensor's ownership of the trade mark or the validity of the trade mark.[6]

The licensor is the party granting the right through the license, and the licensee is the party receiving the right through the license.

---

[2] *H & R Block, Inc. v. Lovelace*, 208 Kan. 538, 493 P.2d 205, 211.

[3] *Rosenblatt v. California State Board of Pharmacy*, 69 Cal. App. 2d 69, 158 P.2d 199, 203; *American States Water Service Co. of California v. Johnson*, 31 Cal. App. 2d 606, 88 P.2d 770, 774.

[4] *De Forest Radio Telephone & Telegraph Co. v. Radio Corporation of America*, 9 F.2d 150, 151 (D.C.Del.); *L.L. Brown Paper Co. v. Hydroiloid, Inc.*, 32 F. Supp. 857, 867, 868 (D.C.N.Y.).

[5] *Hennebont Co. v. Kroger Co.*, 221 Pa. Super. 65, 289 A.2d 229, 231; *Timmons v. Cropper*, 40 Del. Ch. 29, 172 A.2d 757, 759.

[6] *E.F. Prichard Co. v. Consumers Brewing Co.*, 136 F.2d 512, 521 (C.C.A.K.).

2. WHEN IS LICENSING RELEVANT?

To understand when licensing is relevant, one must first understand why licensing is necessary. It must be remembered that a trade mark registration gives the owner the right to use the trade mark to the exclusion of everyone else; that is, the trade mark owner can stop others from using the same or a confusingly similar trade mark in association with the same or confusingly similar wares and services. As such, a license is necessary for the trade mark owner to grant another party permission to use the trade mark and to limit the trade mark owner's exclusive right *vis-à-vis* that party.

In the commercial context, licensing is usually relevant for the purpose of generating income. Specifically, a trade mark owner may consider licensing because the market demand has surpassed what the trade mark owner can supply. Since the trade mark owner is unable to satisfy market demand, licensing may be one way of increasing the number of suppliers. Conversely, a trade mark owner may consider licensing in order to increase market demand by expanding into other territories.

Some of the same principles of meeting market demand or expanding into new territories are relevant to charitable and not-for-profit organizations as well. There are a number of other situations in which such an organization should consider the licensing of a trade mark in order to maintain ownership and control of the mark. These would include, for example, the following situations:

- Setting up local chapters of the charitable or not-for-profit organization;
- A Canadian organization expanding its operations into other countries, or vice versa;
- An organization wishing to permit other such organizations to use its trade mark as evidence of membership or maintenance of standards; *e.g.*, CANADIAN COUNCIL OF CHRISTIAN CHARITIES;
- Using a trade mark in conjunction with a fundraising event conducted by other organizations;
- Entering into a sponsorship agreement; or
- A religious denomination wanting to retain control over the use of the denominational name by local churches.

In all situations, the trade mark owner would grant limited rights to the use of the trade mark through some form of licensing agreement, all the while maintaining the ownership and control of its trade mark on an international basis.

(a) Co-branding

Licensing may also be relevant in situations where two or more trade mark owners decide to use their trade marks together; that is, when two or more brands are used at the same time. Organizations are entering into increasing numbers of co-branding arrangements as they realize that two brands may be better than one when it comes to increasing exposure and credibility, which will lead to increased market demand and business profits. In addition, co-branding may reduce costs because organizations can now instantly transfer the image, message, appeal and value of one brand from one organization to another, instead of spending money on research and development or marketing to re-create the same image, message, appeal or value.

One reason for co-branding may be to complement the products, where an organization seeks to improve its sales by co-branding with another organization whose wares or services complement those of the organization. Examples of this type of co-branding include:

- YAHOO! and SBC COMMUNICATIONS, because people using Internet search engines also want high-speed Internet portal services;[7]

- MCDONALD'S and COCA-COLA, because food complements beverages;

- HOLIDAY INN motels and PIZZA HUT restaurants, because travellers also need to eat, especially since they cannot cook while travelling;[8]

- ST. LAWRENCE HOMES and JOHN DEERE, because people who buy homes are also likely to buy lawn maintenance products. The arrangement involved St. Lawrence Homes' sale signs featuring John Deere, while John Deere provide landscaping work to St. Lawrence Homes. While St. Lawrence Homes expects to sell their properties faster as a result of John Deere's endorsement of and implicit stamp of approval for its landscaped

---

[7] Paul F. Nunes, Stephen F. Dull & Patrick D. Lynch, "When Two Brands are Better than One" (January 2003), online: Accenture <http://www.accenture.com>.

[8] Emery P. Dalesio, "John Deere Homes Add New Wrinkle" (24 June 2005), online: ABC News <http://abcnews.go.com/Business/wireStory?id-877417>.

properties, John Deere expects to sell more riding lawnmowers, leaf-blowers and other yard equipment as a result of St. Lawrence Homes' publicity;[9]

- STARBUCKS and CHAPTERS, because having a coffee is an activity which often accompanies reading a book; and

- STARBUCKS, T-MOBILE and HEWLETT-PACKARD, because the availability of a wireless Internet connection brings in customers.[10]

A second reason for co-branding may be to gain entry into markets that were previously unavailable for the charitable or not-for-profit organization, especially if an organization seeks to associate itself with new wares and services. Examples of this type of co-branding include:

- RANDOM HOUSE and OPRAH WINFREY, as her televised recommendations could boost sales in ways that no other form of marketing or advertisement could;[11]

- CREST and THE AMERICAN DENTAL ASSOCIATION, because the trusted institution's endorsement of the toothpaste as "an effective decay-preventative dentifrice that can be of significant value" enhanced the brand;

- TARGET and MICHAEL GRAVES, to enhance Target's reputation as a retailer of attractive, good-quality products;[12]

- JOHN DEERE and ST. LAWRENCE HOMES, because John Deere wanted to expand its product line. Traditionally known for selling large equipment such as tractors and lawnmowers, John Deere wanted consumers to broaden the association to include smaller products such as plants and grass seeds. Co-branding with St. Lawrence Homes was one way of featuring its lesser-known products so that consumers would come to associate John Deere with all yard maintenance products instead of only large machinery;[13] and

- MOTOROLA's co-branding with the NATIONAL FOOTBALL LEAGUE broadened its image from merely a cellphone provider

---

[9] *Ibid.*
[10] Paul F. Nunes, Stephen F. Dull & Patrick D. Lynch, "When Two Brands are Better than One" (January 2003), online: Accenture <http://www.accenture.com>.
[11] *Ibid.*
[12] *Ibid.*
[13] Online Emery P. Dalesio, "John Deere Homes Add New Wrinkle" (24 June 2005), online: ABC News <http://abcnews.go.com/Business/wireStory?id-877417>.

to that of a communications provider. The arrangement involved Motorola designing more effective and comfortable headphones for football coaches, and the National Football League permitting Motorola to place its logo prominently on the headphones, which are generally seen on game broadcasts all across North America.[14]

This type of co-branding can also be used by competitors, as demonstrated by the arrangement between BORDERS and AMAZON.COM.[15] Borders, a traditional bricks-and-mortar bookseller, has established itself as a giant in the industry with more than 1,200 stores around the world and annual sales over $3.9 billion.[16] Yet, despite its success off-line, the company failed to effectively launch itself into the Internet bookselling world. In fact, prior to its alliance with its online competitor, Amazon.com, the Borders Online website had lost more than $18 million.[17] In 2001, Borders teamed with Amazon.com to launch a co-branded site, called "Borders Teamed with Amazon.com", which quickly became profitable. As the website's promotional material states, "[w]e think it's a great match: the premier international retailer of books, music, and movies partnered with the leader in online commerce".[18] As some commentators have suggested, the two companies continue to be fierce competitors while benefiting from the union as it advances both companies' strategic goals:

> Borders gained an online presence that serves its customers well and drops profits, not losses, to its bottom line. Amazon, for its part, gained an additional revenue source, and also took a valuable step toward establishing itself as a viable supplier of outsourced online retailing capability. And both companies have ended up better positioned against common entrenched rivals.[19]

Another reason for co-branding may be to identify partners, especially if a product's character or quality depends upon the sub-products of which it is composed. Examples of this type of co-branding include:

---

[14] Paul F. Nunes, Stephen F. Dull & Patrick D. Lynch, "When Two Brands are Better than One" (January 2003), online: Accenture <http://www.accenture.com>.

[15] *Ibid.*

[16] Borders Group, online: <http://www.bordersgroupinc.com/about/index.html>.

[17] Paul F. Nunes, Stephen F. Dull & Patrick D. Lynch, "When Two Brands are Better than One" (January 2003), online: Accenture <http://www.accenture.com>.

[18] Amazon, online: <http://www.amazon.com/exec.obidos/tg/stores/static/-/borders/amazon-borders-partnership/103-8186077-1566202> (date accessed: March 3, 2006).

[19] Paul F. Nunes, Stephen F. Dull & Patrick D. Lynch, "When Two Brands are Better than One" (January 2003), online: Accenture <http://www.accenture.com>.

- ADIDAS producing sneakers with rubber soles made by GOODYEAR;[20]
- OCEAN SPRAY producing drinks with sweeteners made by SPLENDA;
- WRIGLEY producing sugar-free gum and COCA-COLA producing diet pop with sweeteners made by NUTRASWEET;[21] and
- DELL and COMPAQ producing computers with computer chips made by INTEL.

The Dell, Compaq and Intel co-branding initiative remains the classic example of this type of co-branding.[22] Today's computer consumers are well aware of Intel products, but few had heard of the brand prior to the early 1990s. This was largely due to the company's original marketing strategy that was directed solely at computer manufacturers and design engineers.

Marketing executives for the company eventually recognized the pivotal role the computer's processing chip played in consumer's choices for personal computers. After two years of failed attempts to develop a better way of communicating with end users, and after failing to secure trade mark protection for its two main processors — the 386 and the 486 — Intel's marketing executive came up with the now well-known co-branding initiative "Intel Inside".[23] Computer makers such as Dell and Compaq benefited from this initiative, as it generated a new form of consumer awareness and demand for the processing-chip maker's components. Intel also offered co-marketing dollars for those companies that included the INTEL INSIDE logo in their advertising. Today, although the co-branding initiative has seen Intel spend more than $7 billion on its advertising program, it now has more than 2,600 computer makers licensed to use the company's logo, and many homes and businesses contain computers with the familiar logo pasted on its front as a constant reminder.[24]

Although the examples above relate to for-profit businesses, charitable and not-for-profit organizations should not consider the door closed to them when it comes to co-branding initiatives. In fact, many consumers

---

[20] Emery P. Dalesio, "John Deere Homes Add New Wrinkle" (24 June 2005), online: ABC News <http://abcnews.go.com/Business/wireStory?id-877417>.
[21] Paul F. Nunes, Stephen F. Dull & Patrick D. Lynch, "When Two Brands are Better than One" (January 2003), online: Accenture <http://www.accenture.com>.
[22] *Ibid.*
[23] *Ibid.*
[24] *Ibid.*

are beginning to show a preference for charitable and not-for-profit organizations to benefit from co-branding relationships when it comes to choosing such things as credit card preferences. Instead of consumers obtaining benefits by using a co-branded card for grocery stores or oil companies, there is a developing trend to have favourite charitable or not-for-profit oganizations benefit from consumers' spending habits. For example, MBNA claims to now have over 5,000 co-branding relationships with various colleges and universities and charitable and not-for-profit organizations.[25] In Canada, credit card holders can automatically have donations made to their chosen organization with every purchase they make with the card, with no additional cost to the consumer. Organizations that have benefited from such arrangements include DUCKS UNLIMITED, the HUMANE SOCIETY OF CANADA, and THE ROYAL CANADIAN GEOGRAPHICAL SOCIETY. In Europe, MBNA offers the same type of program, benefiting such organizations as the BRITISH HEART FOUNDATION, CHILDLINE, NATIONAL AIDS TRUST and UNICEF. The co-branding initiative between WORLD WIDE FUND FOR NATURE (WWF) and MBNA has already generated more than £5,000,000 in essential support for the organization's conservation work around the world.[26]

(b) Sponsorship

Licensing can also be relevant where a business decides to endorse a charitable or not-for-profit organization, usually through financial support, in exchange for advertising or publicity; or vice versa, where a charitable or not-for-profit organization endorses a business' products. As more corporations discover that sponsoring charitable and not-for-profit organizations may improve their public image, the public will see more examples of the different forms sponsorship make take.

In the wake of several natural disasters, including the tsunami in Southeast Asia in December 2004, or the hurricanes in the Southern United States in the summer of 2005, the public has seen many examples of corporations donating their wares and services to aid in relief efforts. Following the devastating tsunami, pharmaceutical companies provided antibiotics, soft drink makers provided bottled water and courier companies provided transportation services for the medicine and supplies

---

[25]   MBNA Canada, online: <http://www.mbna.com/canada/about_index.html>.
[26]   MBNA Europe, online: <http://www.mbna.com/europe/creditcards/partner_charitygroups .html>.

donated.[27] Similarly, following the hurricanes, corporations lined up to ensure the needed wares and services reached those affected.

Natural disaster relief, however, is not the only project which corporations sponsor. Corporations may support charitable and not-for-profit organizations by sponsoring their event, activity or campaign, as in the case of PROCTOR & GAMBLE and the LEAGUE AGAINST CANCER/LIGA CONTRA EL CANCER.[28] Wanting to penetrate the Hispanic market in Florida, Procter & Gamble approached the community-based provider of free medical care for cancer patients without financial resources or health insurance. The League Against Cancer/Liga Contra el Cancer asked the corporation to sponsor the printing of the 250,000 raffle tickets required for its annual raffle and included a Proctor & Gamble coupon with each ticket; as a result, both organizations benefited.

Another creative example involved THE PRESS GALLERY and THE EDMONTON OPERA,[29] which went beyond the basic arrangement of sponsorship in return for free opera tickets. The Press Gallery, an Edmonton dry cleaning company, took on the practice of creating contests promoted through the *Edmonton Sun* newspaper to give away opera tickets.

> Instead of simply handing out free opera tickets to their customers the year they sponsored *Madame Butterfly*, The Press Gallery created a contest in which people submitted the name of their favourite opera to a local columnist at the *Edmonton Sun*. Winners of a random drawing met at The Press Gallery for a champagne reception and then took limos to the opera house, where they enjoyed a dinner catered by a local Thai restaurant before seeing the performance. They also met cast members at the postproduction party and received dry cleaning and opera gift certificates.
>
> For *La Traviata*, which happened to be produced during the month of Verdi's birthday, The Press Gallery sponsored a "Happy Birthday Verdi" contest through the newspaper. Readers sent birthday cards to Verdi via the columnist, who collected them and drew six winners. The lucky opera-lovers enjoyed limo service to the opera and after the production were surprised with an invitation to gather onstage for champagne and a birthday cake that sported Verdi's portrait.[30]

Alternatively, corporations may support sports organizations by sponsoring an event, such as CONESCO sponsoring the NASCAR races, or by sponsoring a building, such as AIR CANADA sponsoring The Air Canada Centre, the official home of the NBA's Toronto Raptors,

---

[27] Marcie Good, "The Giving Game" *BCBusiness* (July 2005) 137.
[28] Mary Ellen Collins, "Good Deal!" *Advancing Philanthropy* (September/October 2005) 20.
[29] *Ibid.*
[30] *Ibid.*

the NHL's Toronto Maple Leafs and the NLL's Toronto Rock, and SCOTIABANK sponsoring Scotiabank Place (formerly the Corel Centre, sponsored by Corel), the official home of the NHL's Ottawa Senators.

Corporations may also choose to sponsor trusted institutions, as in the case of OCEAN SPRAY's statement on its website[31] that it is the proud sponsor of the AMERICAN DIABETES ASSOCIATION, or BECEL's support of the HEART AND STROKE FOUNDATION.

An interesting development in terms of sponsorship is that which is related to loyalty rewards programs. For many years, credit card companies and businesses have operated loyalty reward programs as part of their own marketing initiatives. In the ever-expanding marketplace, businesses are discovering that it is far cheaper to keep a customer than to acquire a new one. By offering rewards that consumers desire, a business can not only retain customers, but attract new customers. While consumer preference focused on travel and merchandise rewards in the 1990s, charitable and not-for-profit organizations are now beginning to reap the rewards of consumer loyalty programs.[32] In Canada, both the ROYAL BANK OF CANADA and AMERICAN EXPRESS CANADA have added charitable organizations as an option for consumers cashing in their reward points. While American Express customers can support HOPE AIR and CHILDREN'S WISH FOUNDATION by donating their loyalty reward points, Royal Bank customers can support as Olympic athletes as well as Hope Air. Also, charitable and not-for-profit organizations seem to be the significant winners when it comes to "orphan points": points collected by consumers who do not collect frequently enough to obtain any of the major rewards.[33]

(c) Recommendations

When approaching a corporation to sponsor a charitable event, activity or campaign, it is essential to keep in mind that not all corporations understand the concept of sponsorship. Charitable and not-for-profit organizations might find themselves having to educate corporations on the business benefits, as most corporations may wrongly assume that the only benefit is having their logo displayed. In preparation for the solicitation for sponsorship, a charitable or not-for-profit organization

---

[31] <http://www.oceanspray.com>.
[32] "Charities reap rewards: More card holders are steering points toward favourite causes" *The Globe and Mail* (22 November 2005) E2.
[33] *Ibid.*

should "do its homework" in order to target the appropriate sponsor and convey the appropriate message that will ensure the deal goes through.

One of the first projects a charitable or not-for-profit organization should undertake is to identify its assets and the benefits of sponsorship. Although donations are made with no expectation of return, sponsorships carry with them an expectation of benefits in exchange for the financial contribution. The WHITAKER CENTER FOR SCIENCE AND THE ARTS provides an excellent example of how to successfully attract sponsors.[34] The Center started from a position of strength by conducting market research in the surrounding area. The results of the survey were an important component of the sponsorship pitch to potential sponsors, as they indicated that the Center had high name recognition, drew visitors from all the surrounding areas and had a positive reputation amongst those surveyed. The Center followed up on these positive survey results by purchasing two plasma screen monitors on which to display the sponsors' ads and creating an asset inventory to which they put a dollar value on each item. By doing this, they were able to show sponsors the true business value of the sponsorship apart from the "feel-good" sensation of supporting a cultural asset.

After identifying the organization's assets and the benefits of sponsorship, charitable or not-for-profit organizations should determine what the sponsor will receive in return for their sponsorship. Just as donations of varying amounts receive different recognition, so sponsorships at varying levels should receive different benefits. Not only does this avoid dissatisfaction among sponsors should they talk to each other, it also avoids the risk that a charitable or not-for-profit organization will give away too much for too little, which is a practical problem under the federal *Income Tax Act*,[35] especially for registered charities. Registered charities are prohibited from giving away their charitable resources to other entities that are not "qualified donees".[36] This may be an opportunity

---

[34] Mary Ellen Collins, "Good Deal!" *Advancing Philanthropy* (September/October 2005) 20.

[35] R.S.C. 1985 (5th Supp.), c.1.

[36] Subsection 149.1(1) of the *Income Tax Act* provides that "qualified donees" are organizations that can issue official donation receipts for gifts that individuals and corporations make to them. Qualified donees consist of: registered charities in Canada; registered Canadian amateur athletic associations; housing corporations that provide low-cost housing for the aged; federal and provincial governments; municipalities; the United Nations and its agencies; prescribed universities outside Canada; charitable organizations outside Canada to which the federal government has made a gift during the fiscal period or in the 12 months immediately preceding the period; and registered national arts service organizations. In July 2005, municipal or public bodies performing a function of government in Canada are also proposed to be added to the list.

for the organization to demonstrate creativity, as sponsors may be willing to sponsor an organization in return for a wide variety of forms of recognition, from naming rights for buildings or research chairs to recognition in advertising or programs.

However, it should be noted that any such benefits should not include the issuance of charitable donation receipts to the sponsors. Whether a payment is a gift or a sponsorship fee depends on the facts and the understating of the parties in each case. It must be understood that gifts and sponsorship fees are mutually exclusive concepts. Charitable donation receipts may only be provided by registered charities in return for gifts received. Sponsorship fees, however, are not gifts but are amounts paid to a registered charity in exchange for advertising or some other consideration and, therefore, must not involve any donation receipts in return.[37]

It is important to recognize that in order to obtain sponsorships that will be beneficial to both the sponsor as well as the charitable or nor-for-profit organization, it is crucial to research potential sponsors for suitability. As will be discussed in more detail in the following section, there are risks involved whenever one organization allows itself to be linked with another organization. In a worst-case scenario, the charitable or not-for-profit organization may inadvertently align itself with a corporate sponsor that is antithetical to the organization's core beliefs or objects. An example of this would be an environmental group unwittingly aligning itself with a corporate sponsor that fails to abide by environmental regulations. A poor match such as this could be disastrous for the charitable or not-for-profit organization's reputation and future donor prospects. As such, charitable or not-for-profit organizations must research the corporation's personal interests by reviewing their websites, mission statements, philanthropic goals and community service activities. If possible, the organization should also research the corporation's marketing goals by reviewing their marketing materials, promotional materials and advertising campaigns.

When the organization is ready to approach a sponsor, it is crucial to contact the right decision-maker. Although donations are usually handled by a corporation's foundation or community department, sponsorships are usually handled by the marketing or advertising department. It is also important to understand whether a corporation is more locally oriented or nationally controlled, in order to market the solicitation for sponsorship

---

[37]   See Canada Revenue Agency, Summary Policy CSP-S13 (3 September 2003), online: <http://www.cra-arc.gc.ca/tax/charities/policy/csp/csp-s13-e.html>.

to the right decision-maker. By approaching the wrong individual, the organization will only waste valuable resources and time.

Finally, when approaching a sponsor, it is important to schedule the meeting at the right time; that is, at an appropriate time in the corporation's budget cycle, so as to ensure the charitable or not-for-profit organization will be considered during the budget-planning stage. Otherwise, the budget may already be finalized and the organization will have to wait until the following year's budget-planning season to approach a corporate sponsor. In addition, it is also important to be aware of when the corporation will be reviewing its budget or whether the corporation is already sponsoring other charitable or not-for-profit organizations. This may help a charitable or not-for-profit organization to understand how to make future requests for sponsorship more successful.

(d) Risks

Although there are many benefits to co-branding and sponsorships, there are also great risks involved. From a marketing perspective, just as one brand's positive attributes can be increasing exposure and credibility, leading to increased market demand and business profits, so can a brand's negative attributes create infamy and scepticism, leading to decreased public appeal and business profits. The main concerns for any charitable or not-for-profit organization are dilution and devaluation.

A brand is diluted when it loses consumer appeal.[38] The loss of consumer appeal is not due to any negative publicity, but to lack of publicity. Likewise, consumers do not have any negative association with the brand, but merely have no association with or a lack of interest in the brand. In such a case, the co-brand or sponsored brand is not negatively affected, but the co-branding or sponsorship arrangement has lost its purpose or value.

On the other hand, a brand is devalued when it loses consumer appeal and incurs consumer distaste.[39] The loss of consumer appeal is the result of negative publicity and, as such, consumers have a negative association with the brand. In such a case, not only has the co-branding or sponsorship arrangement lost its value as an asset, it has also become a liability.

From a trade mark perspective, it is important to ensure co-branding or sponsorship does not result in public confusion. The moment the public becomes confused as to who owns the trade marks, the marks lose their

---

[38] Paul F. Nunes, Stephen F. Dull & Patrick D. Lynch, "When Two Brands are Better than One" (January 2003), online: Accenture <http://www.accenture.com>.
[39] *Ibid.*

distinctiveness and, as a result, lose their protection under the *Trade-marks Act* because a trade mark should indicate the source of the wares and/or services with which it is associated or the character and quality that can be expected of those wares and/or services. In order to reduce the likelihood of public confusion, the co-branding or sponsorship arrangement should ensure all trade marks are strictly identified. For example, lawnmowers manufactured by YARD-MAN and distributed by SEARS can be identified by both the manufacturer's and the distributor's trade marks in the following manner so as to avoid public confusion regarding the owner or source of the respective trade marks:[40]

> Product of YARD-MAN, INC. ... for SEARS, ROEBUCK & CO.

Or

> Produced by YARD-MAN, INC. ... for distribution by SEARS, ROEBUCK & CO.

The co-branding or sponsorship agreement should also ensure the trade marks and the wares and/or services with which they are associated are complementary but not identical or very closely related. For example, there is no confusion as to which wares and/or services are associated with Starbucks and which are associated with Chapters. However, the public would likely and understandably experience confusion if Starbucks were to co-brand with COFFEE TIME or TIM HORTONS.

Finally, the agreement should ensure the business operations are in separate and well-defined areas. For example, although Starbucks and Chapters are under the same roof, there is a clear separation between the two business operations: different interior designs, different employees and electronic detectors accompanying the sign reading, "Unpurchased products from Chapters are not permitted in Starbucks".

3.　　LICENSING REQUIREMENTS

As noted above, trade marks historically could not be licensed and any licensing of a trade mark would destroy its validity. This was in keeping with the source theory of trade marks; that is, the purpose of a trade mark was to inform the public that the wares or services bearing the trade mark come from a particular "source". Therefore, licensing the trade mark and allowing another party to produce wares and services in association with the trade mark would render the trade mark incapable of identifying the

---

[40] *Yardman, Inc. v. Getz Exterminators Inc.*, 157 U.S.P.Q. 100 (T.T.A.B. 1968).

source of the wares and services and would mislead the public. This point was clearly settled and enunciated in 1913 by the House of Lords:

> The object of the law is to preserve for a trader a reputation he has made for himself, not to help in disposing that reputation as of itself a marketable commodity, independent of his goodwill, to some other trader. If that were allowed, the public would be misled, because they might buy something in the belief that it was the make of a man whose reputation they knew, whereas it was the make of someone else.[41]

As a result, the only way a trade mark could be passed on to another party was to sell or assign the trade mark, along with the business which produced the wares or performed the services used in association with the trade mark.

(a) Registered user system

Wanting to enable the licensing of trade marks, Canada amended its trade mark legislation in 1953 to introduce the system of registered user agreements. As a result, the owner of a registered trade mark could license the trade mark by completing and filing a registered user agreement to record the licensee as a registered user with the trade marks office. One drawback with the registered user system was that only registered trade marks could be licensed, as common law trade marks were not registered and therefore no user agreement could be registered for those trade marks. Another drawback was that, generally, the formalities of completing and filing a registered user agreement were the primary focus in determining whether or not a proper license of a trade mark had occurred, as opposed to looking at the substance of the relationship between the licensor and the licensee; that is, whether the licensor was controlling the licensee's use of the trade mark.

(b) Controlled licensing system

In order to jettison the cumbersome and unpopular registered user agreements, and in order to restore the concept that the public ought to be able to rely upon a trade mark as an indication of the quality of the wares and services, Canada amended its trade mark legislation in 1993. In particular, section 50 of the *Trade-marks Act* dealing with licensing was

---

[41] *Boweden Wire Ltd. v. Bowden Brake Co. (No. 1)* (1914), 31 R.P.C. 385.

significantly amended and, as a result, registered user agreements were no longer necessary. Instead, subsection 50(1) states:

> For the purposes of this Act, if an entity is licensed by or with the authority of the owner of a trade-mark to use the trade-mark in a country and the owner has, under the licence, direct or indirect control of the character or quality of the wares or services, then the use, advertisement or display of the trade-mark in that country as or in a trade-mark, trade-name or otherwise by that entity has, and is deemed always to have had, the same effect as such a use, advertisement or display of the trade-mark in that country by the owner.

The controlled licensing system applies equally to both licensing and sub-licensing. The fact that the licensee must be licensed "by or with the authority of the owner of a trade-mark" indicates that section 50 contemplates both direct licensing and sub-licensing, as well as the appointment by the trade mark owner of some entity to enter into licensing agreements on the trade mark owner's behalf.[42]

The controlled licensing system applies equally to both use in Canada and use outside Canada. The phrase "to use the trade-mark in a country" applies to the use of a licensed trade mark in any country. As a result, a trade mark application based on the ground of actual use in Canada can now rely upon use in Canada by a controlled licensee. Similarly, a trade mark application based on the ground of foreign country application or registration and use abroad can now rely upon use abroad by a controlled licensee. Finally, a trade mark application based on the ground of proposed use in Canada can now rely upon a statement in the trade mark application that either the trade mark applicant or its licensee, or both, intend to use the trade mark in Canada. Before the amendments to section 50, use for any trade mark applications would have to be used by the trade mark owner and/or by the trade mark owner's predecessor in title.[43]

The controlled licensing system applies equally to both past and future use of the trade mark by a controlled licensee. The Federal Court of Appeal has held that section 50 applies retroactively, thus curing defects from past licensing of trade marks that did not meet the strict statutory requirements of the registered user system.[44]

One of the greatest benefits of the controlled licensing system is the extension of subsection 50(1) to unregistered trade marks. The controlled licensing system, as opposed to the registered user system, applies equally

---

[42] Donna G. White, *Selecting and Protecting Trade marks* (Toronto: Carswell, 1994) at 107–108.

[43] *Ibid.* at 108.

[44] *Eli Lilly & Co. v. Novapharm Ltd.* (2000), 10 C.P.R. (4th) 10 (F.C.A.), leave to appeal refused (2001), 275 N.R. 200 (note) (S.C.C.).

to both registered trade marks and common law trade marks. As such, a trade mark need not be registered to benefit from the provision of section 50, and common law trade marks enjoy the same rights and protection as registered trade marks.

Another benefit of the controlled licensing system is the presumption provided in subsection 50(2), which states that:

> to the extent that public notice is given of the fact the use of the trade mark is a licensed use and of the identity of the owner, it shall be presumed, unless the contrary is proven, the use is licensed by the owner of the trade mark and the character and quality of the wares or services is under the control of the owner.

Yet another benefit of the controlled licensing system is the protection provided in subsection 50(3), which states that:

> Subject to any agreement subsisting between an owner of a trade mark and a licensee of the trade mark, the licensee may call on the owner to take proceedings for infringement thereof, and, if the owner refuses or neglects to do so within two months after being so called on, the licensee may institute proceedings for infringement in the licensee's own name as if the licensee were the owner, making the owner a defendant.

(c) Current licensing requirements

This section provides a brief outline of some of the more important considerations that need to be established in a trade mark license agreement. Although not exhaustive, current trade mark licensing requirements under section 50 can be summarized as follows:

1. There must be a licensing arrangement between the licensor and the licensee. Although the *Trade-marks Act* does not require the license arrangement to be written, a written license agreement is always advisable as it clearly sets out the terms and conditions of the licensing agreement.

2. The license must be granted by the owner of the trade mark. As such, the license agreement should identify every license use and the licensee should ensure the licensor is the actual trade mark owner as listed on the trade mark register. Furthermore, sub-licensees should ensure the sub-license is permitted not only by the licensee but also by the licensor.

3. The owner must maintain direct or indirect control over the character, quality and use of the trade mark in association with the wares or services in question. The trade mark owner must actually exercise the contractual right of control as provided in

the license agreement. This means setting meaningful quality standards by which the licensee must comply, reviewing the licensee's activities to ensure compliance and terminating the license agreement if the licensee fails to comply by the quality standards.

4.   The use of the trade mark by a licensee must clearly identify the owner of the trade mark and that the trade mark is being used under license. This is because the law views licensing agreements as weakening a trade mark's distinctiveness, which may result in the invalidation of the registered trade mark. Section 50 balances this view with a rebuttable presumption that the owner has retained control over the trade mark to the extent public notice is given of the fact the use of the trade mark is a licensed use and of the identity of the owner. A suggested way of identifying this relationship is as follows:

> HELP THE CHILDREN ®
>
> "Help the Children" is a registered trade mark of Help the Children International used under license by Help the Children Canada.

4.   LICENSING CONSIDERATIONS

When a trade mark license agreement is entered into, there are certain key considerations that need to be in place in order to protect the integrity of the trade mark even if they are not specifically required by the *Trade-marks Act*. These considerations can be summarized by the following factors.

(a) Type of license

The trade mark license agreement should stipulate what type of license the licensor is granting to the licensee. There are three basic types of licenses:

1.   An **Exclusive License**, which gives the licensee permission to use the trade mark to the exclusion of all others, including the licensor/trade mark owner;

2.   A **Non-Exclusive License**, which gives the licensee permission to use the trade mark, but not to the exclusion of anyone else;

that is, the licensor/trade mark owner can still use the trade mark and also license the trade mark to other licensees; and

3. A **Sole License**, which is the middle ground between the two prior extremes. It gives the licensee permission to use the trade mark to the exclusion of all others, except the licensor/trade mark owner; that is, the licensor/trade mark owner can still use the trade mark but cannot license the trade mark to other licensees.

(b) Scope of license

The trade mark license agreement should be clear concerning the scope of the license. Specifically, the following issues should be addressed in the agreement:

*   **Trade Marks** — If multiple trade marks are owned, define which of the trade marks are being licensed, and if appropriate, which trade marks are not being licensed;
*   **Rights** — Define which use, advertisement, display and other trade mark rights are being licensed;
*   **Wares/Services** — Define the wares and/or services with which the trade mark can be used, as well as limit, restrict or prohibit the wares and/or services with which the trade mark cannot be used;
*   **Territory** — Define which geographic region or which market area the license is effective for; and
*   **Time** — Define the duration or term of the license.

When it comes to defining the wares and/or services with which the trade mark can be used, the wares and/or services covered in the trade mark license agreement should correspond to those covered in the trade mark application or registration. Although the trade mark license agreement can have a more limited list, it cannot have a more extensive list of wares and/or services than that which is provided in the trade mark application or registration.

The trade mark license agreement should also contain clauses dealing with any limitations, such as restrictions to a particular field, prohibitions on uses, limits on quantity or volume, prohibitions on export or restrictions on transferability.[45]

(c) Licensee's undertaking

The licensee's undertaking is a formal promise on the part of the licensee with respect to various issues concerning the trade marks which are being licensed. The undertaking, which should be included in the written agreement, should include the following agreements:

- To co-operate in maintaining the validity of the trade mark;
- To abide by the quality standards set out by the licensor;
- Not to alter, modify, dilute or otherwise misuse the trade mark; and
- To co-operate if the licensor requires assistance in registering, renewing or defending the trade mark.

The undertaking should also include the following warranties:

- Not to commit any act or omission adverse or injurious to the licensor's trade mark rights;
- Not to attack the validity of the trade mark;
- Not to dispute the trade mark owner's rights pursuant to the trade mark;
- Not to oppose the renewal of the trade mark; and
- Not to challenge any extension of the wares or services pursuant to the trade mark.

Furthermore, the licensee should acknowledge and agree that any rights or goodwill which attach to the trade mark as a result of the licensee's use will enure to the licensor and for the licensor's benefit. In the event the licensee uses the trade mark in respect of wares and/or services beyond the scope of the trade mark license agreement, the agreement should specify that any resulting rights also enure to the licensor based upon the actions of the licensee as agent of the licensor. In furtherance of this, the licensee must acknowledge and agree to give public notice of the fact the use of the trade mark is a licensed use and to identify the licensor as the trade mark owner.

---

[45] Gordon Sustrik & Emery Jamieson, *Trade mark Transactions: Assignments, Licences and Security Interests* (Sponsored by the Patent and Trademark Institute of Canada, 1999) at 12.

(d) Licensee's standing

Section 50 of the *Trade-marks Act* gives a licensee standing to sue for infringement in the licensee's own name as if the licensee were the owner, and naming the trade mark owner as a defendant, if the trade mark owner fails to enforce the trade mark rights. As such, the trade mark license agreement should set out the scope and limits on what right or standing, if any, the licensee will have to commence legal proceedings for enforcing trade mark rights.

In addition, the trade mark license agreement should also specify whether the licensee has any right or standing to deal with the protection and enforcement of the licensed trade marks, even where there is no infringement. For example, what role should the licensee play in filing, prosecuting and paying for trade mark applications; renewing and paying the filing fee for registered trade marks; monitoring for infringement of trade marks; litigating infringement and passing-off actions; or ensuring appropriate use of the ™ and ® symbols.

(e) Licensor's warranties

The benefit a licensee receives from licensing a trade mark depends on the value of the trade mark licensed. As such, it is imperative that a licensee ensures a number of warranties and representations are covered in the trade mark license agreement.[46] This will include representations and warranties that the licensor has full right and title to the trade marks; the trade marks have been in continuous use; the trade marks have been used properly, both in form and with respect to the associated wares and/or services; proper notice of ownership of the trade mark was given when the trade mark was used; all trade mark applications and registrations are valid and in good standing; there are no prior undisclosed assignments or licenses; there are no existing infringement or passing-off claims; and there are no anticipated infringement or passing-off claims to the best of the licensor's knowledge.

(f) Licensor's control

It is essential that the owner of the trade mark establish and monitor the standards for the trade mark in question or appoint someone to act on its behalf in this regard. In addition to exercising control, either directly or indirectly, over the character and quality of the wares and/or services, it

---

[46] *Ibid.* at 13.

is essential for the trade mark owner to exercise control over the use of the trade mark itself. Consequently, it is important to remember that the owner is presumed to be exercising some control as long as public notice is given of the fact the use of the trade mark is a licensed use and of the identity of the owner.

At a minimum, the licensor should establish a standard of quality and ensure the licensee is complying with the standard of quality.[47] These standards can be set directly by the licensor or by reference to regulatory standards, industry standards, *etc*. In ensuring the licensee's compliance, the license should include the right to examine and inspect production facilities, the right to obtain and inspect samples of wares and the right to obtain and inspect samples of trade mark use.

(g) Royalties

The trade mark license agreement should stipulate what kind of compensation the licensor will receive from the licensee for the licensing of the trade mark. The agreement should be clear on the following with respect to payment:

- What kind of payment will be required — A flat fee or a percentage of profits? If it is a flat fee, will there be an initial upfront lump sum, periodical fixed instalments or minimum royalties? If it is a percentage of profits, what happens if there are no profits?

- How the payment will be calculated — If it is a percentage of profits, should royalties be calculated based on production volumes, units sold, gross sales, net sales or some other criteria?

- When payment will be calculated or required — How often and at what times; *e.g.*, monthly, quarterly or annually?

- Does compensation include equity in the licensee?

If the trade mark license agreement is for use in foreign jurisdictions, there should be a clause dealing with currency exchanges and applicable tax withholdings.

If the payment is calculated in terms of a percentage of profits, the agreement should address the issue of what happens if there are no profits, establishing minimum requirements. For example, a minimum royalty, or a minimum sales quota or minimum marketing efforts should be required. With respect to marketing efforts, there should be clearly

---

[47] *Ibid*. at 14.

delineated obligations respecting marketing, such as the requirement to maintain a sales office, have a sales force or spend a certain budgetary amount on advertising.

Finally, charitable and not-for-profit organizations should be aware that there may be Goods and Services Tax/Harmonized Sales Tax ("GST/HST") liability under the federal *Excise Tax Act*[48] with respect to the royalties or payments they make to a licensor as a result of the license agreement. In general, where there is a licensing of trade marks from a business entity or non-profit organization, it is subject to GST/HST based upon the consideration given in exchange for the trade marks licensed, but where the licensing of trade marks is from a registered charity, the licensing is usually GST/HST exempt. However, where the licensing is subject to GST/HST and the licensor is not at an arm's length with the licensee, the Canada Revenue Agency may challenge the value of the license for GST/HST purposes and may assess GST/HST based on a deemed fair market value of the trade marks licensed as determined by the Canada Revenue Agency.

However, where a charity is licensing its trade marks within the context of a sponsorship arrangement, such transactions may be exempt from GST/HST. The following are examples of sponsorships that are not taxable because they are not considered to be payment the charities receive from a sponsor as payment for a good or service:[49]

- When a business financially supports the activities of a registered charity in return for which the charity promotes the business. For example, a charity organizes a softball team and agrees to feature a sponsor's trade name on the team's uniforms or to publish an acknowledgment of the sponsor in the event's program.

- When a charity receives funding from a business in return for allowing the sponsor the right to use the charity's logo. For example, a corporation uses a national charity's logo in its advertising campaign.

The sponsorship and licensing arrangement in each case should be reviewed carefully to determine whether the particular transaction in question is subject to GST/HST.

---

[48] R.S.C. 1985, c. E-15.
[49] See Canada Revenue Agency, *GST/HST Information for Charities* (9 September 2005), online: <http://www.cra-arc.gc.ca/E/pub/gp/rc4082/rc4082-05e.pdf>.

(h) Assignment and sub-license

Since section 50 states that control may be direct or indirect, a licensee may assign, transfer or sub-license the trade mark with the consent of the licensor, because the licensee may be considered a person licensed by or with the authority of the owner to control the character or quality of the wares and/or services. Therefore, the license agreement should state whether or not the licensor agrees to the assignment, transfer or sub-licensing of the trade mark and on what terms. In particular, the license agreement should state that any assignment or sub-license by the licensee would require the written consent of the licensor.

The licensor will normally retain the right to assign its rights in the trade mark to another party. In this regard, the licensee may want to impose some terms to protect its interest in the event of an assignment of the trade mark by the licensor.

(i) Indemnifications

The agreement should indicate the licensor remains liable for the registrability of the licensed trade mark; however, the licensee should be made liable for misuse of the trade mark. Notwithstanding this provision, it is important that the licensor maintain appropriate liability insurance in the event a claim is made against the licensor for actions of the licensee arising out of misuse of the trade mark.

When it comes to trade marks which are being licensed in relation to wares, the licensee may be required to maintain a comprehensive public and product liability insurance policy. Furthermore, the requirement of section 50 that the licensor have direct or indirect control over the character or quality of the wares may increase the licensor's liability for the wares produced by the licensee. The product liability policy should cover any claims, actions or damages which may arise as a direct result or the indirect result of the use of the products produced by the licensee in association with the licensor's trade mark.

(j) Confidentiality

The trade mark license agreement should include a non-disclosure clause, whereby the licensee agrees to keep confidential any information obtained as a result of the license agreement. Such a confidentiality agreement is particularly important in terms of licensing agreements that will divulge proprietary information that the organization would not want passed on to competitors. This duty of confidentiality should survive the life of the agreement.

(k) Termination

The trade mark license agreement needs to provide for a specific termination date, together with provisions allowing the license agreement to be renewed at the option of either party. In addition, a trade mark license agreement should set out a right in favour of the licensor to terminate the agreement in the event of a breach of the agreement. Regardless of the reasons for termination, it is important to specify:

- The rights and obligations of the parties in the event of a breach of the agreement; for example, can the licensor immediately terminate the agreement or must the licensee be granted a period of time to cure the default?
- Any rights of termination on notice; for example, can the parties immediately terminate the agreement or must the parties provide a specific amount of notice to the other party? Furthermore, what are the acceptable means of communicating the notice and to where should the notice be directed?
- The rights and obligations respecting inventory upon termination. Depending on whether the licensee was paying a flat fee or a percentage of the profits to the licensor, the licensee may be permitted to keep or may be required to return the inventory.
- The effect of termination on any sub-licensees.

Usually, the trade mark license agreement would state that upon the termination of the license agreement, the licensee ceases to have the right to use the trade mark; the licensee agrees to return all items with the trade mark on it; and the licensee and the licensor will issue a joint public statement if deemed necessary by the licensor.

SUMMARY

Licensing a charitable or not-for-profit organization's trade marks through co-branding or sponsorship initiatives can prove to be an effective method of expanding the scope of the organization's recognition, which can lead to new donors, new clients and new products and/or services. Both non-profit and for-profit organizations have proven that co-branding and sponsorship arrangements can be very beneficial, as each organization can play upon the strengths of the other. However, entering into licensing agreements is something that should be done with great thought and care, as the trade mark owner inevitably gives up a measure of control over the public perception of the organization by virtue of the licensee's actions.

Accordingly, any charitable or not-for-profit organization that chooses to enter into licensing agreements must take the initial step of doing their homework in order to determine what the organization has to offer the licensee and whether the licensee will make an appropriate match for the organization's values and goals. Once an appropriate match is made, the care should continue in the drafting of the license agreement so as to ensure the organization retains the control necessary to protect its valuable assets.

CONCLUSION

Effective branding enables the public to immediately identify a charitable or not-for-profit organization, protecting both the organization and donors by distinguishing the organization from other organizations and leading to an increased market share. An effectively controlled brand can create value for the charitable or not-for-profit organization by attracting corporate sponsors who want to be associated with the positive values the organization portrays. With increasing reliance placed upon the goodwill associated with an organization's name for potential fundraising and even related business activities, where permissible for registered charities, the protection of the organization's brand name and trade marks is becoming a significant aspect in advising the charitable or not-for-profit client.

If they are not already aware, directors of charitable and not-for-profit organizations should be instructed concerning the importance of protecting and developing the organization's trade marks. In the non-profit world, trade marks will be one of the most significant assets the organization will ever possess. The strength of the mark will dictate the organization's ability to attract appropriate donors and will draw the clients whom the organization wants to serve. Any dilution or devaluation of the trade mark will not only affect the organization but those whom it serves.

Directors of charities have the additional concern of ensuring they do not breach their fiduciary duty to the charity to protect the assets of the organization. Canadian courts have held that directors of charities act as quasi-trustees of the charitable property, owing a fiduciary duty to the charities, the donors, as well as the creditors. Thus, directors of charities are held to the highest possible standard of care. As part of their fiduciary duty, directors of a charity have a primary obligation to exercise due diligence in overseeing and managing the charity and its charitable property. Exercising due diligence includes attending board meetings, supervising operations, monitoring compliance with corporate objects and ensuring board resolutions are adopted by informed decisions of the directors.

Although it is not necessary for a lawyer who advises a charitable or not-for-profit organization to be a registered trade mark agent, it is important that the lawyer be able to identify some of the key issues involved in trade mark protection. In this regard, some of the more important considerations discussed in this book that should be communicated by the lawyer to a charitable or not-for-profit client can be summarized as follows:

1. Trade marks, as well as other forms of intellectual property, are an essential asset of any organization. An effectively controlled branding initiative, with trade marks as an essential component, brings value to the organization as it enables donors, clientele and constituents to immediately identify and distinguish the organization from competitors or fraudulent organizations.

2. Trade marks can be lost if they are not properly protected. If a mark is no longer able to perform its function of identifying and distinguishing the wares and services of an organization, it is no longer considered a trade mark. Charitable and not-for-profit organizations can lose their trade marks in a number of ways, including: if they fail to use them; if they fail to use them consistently; if they fail to restrain others from using them; or if they fail to limit the number of organizations who are licensed to use the trade marks.

3. A charitable or not-for-profit organization needs to be proactive in protecting its trade marks or risk losing its trade mark rights by default. Being proactive in protecting a trade mark includes instituting a system of reviewing the use of the trade mark by the organization and its licensees, as well as reviewing the use of confusingly similar trade marks. Should any infringement be discovered, the charitable or not-for-profit organization needs to take action.

4. Registration of a corporate name or business name does not by itself give trade mark protection. Such registration is intended for consumer protection, not protection of the organization.

5. Trade mark rights exist at common law, but those rights may be better protected by trade mark registration under the *Trade-marks Act*. Registered trade mark protection enables the trade mark holder to occupy the field, and the test for infringement is less complicated than a passing-off action for common law trade marks. Common law trade marks are also limited in their geographic scope.

6. Separate trade mark registration must be done in each country in which the charitable or not-for-profit organization is operating. Failure to do so may result in the loss of trade mark rights in foreign jurisdictions.

7. It is essential to properly use and license trade marks. A mark can lose its distinctive character as a trade mark when it is only used in a generic sense or if licensees are not properly constrained.

8. An infringement of a trade mark by others, even if done unintentionally, must be immediately challenged.

9. The board members and executive staff of a charitable or not-for-profit organization need to be informed of the importance of trade mark rights, and policies must be in place to effectively monitor, renew and protect the organization's trade marks.

10. In addition to obtaining a trade mark registration, a charitable or not-for-profit organization should secure a domain name as soon as possible using its trade mark as part of the domain name.

The diligence that a charitable or not-for-profit organization's legal counsel exhibits in informing the client on trade mark issues may provide an immeasurable benefit to the organization in the long run. In so doing, the lawyer will have transformed trade mark rights from a wasting asset into one of the most valuable assets the organization will ever own.

APPENDIX

TRADE-MARKS ACT

(R.S.C. 1985, c. T-13)

Note: For your convenience, where the Act refers to another piece of legislation not otherwise reproduced in this publication, the cite and/or text of that other piece of legislation is reproduced after the referencing section.

Amendments: S.C. 1990, c. 14, s. 8, in force June 12, 1990; S.C. 1990, c. 20, ss. 79-81, in force August 1, 1990; S.C. 1992, c. 1, ss. 133-135, in force February 28, 1992; S.C. 1993, c. 15, ss. 57-64, 67-71 in force June 9, 1993, ss. 65-66 in force January 15, 1994; S.C. 1993, c. 44, ss. 225-238, in force January 1, 1994; S.C. 1994, c. 47, ss. 190-201, in force January 1, 1996; S.C. 1995, c. 1, s. 62, in force March 29, 1995; S.C. 1996, c. 8, s. 32, in force July 12, 1996; 2001, c. 27, s. 271, in force June 28, 2002; S.C. 2002, c. 8, s. 177, in force July 2, 2003; SOR/2004-85 filed April 22, 2004, gazetted May 5, 2004, ss. 1(3) and (4), which repeal ss. 11.18(3)(*l*) to (*v*) and 11.18(4)(*a*) and (*c*), in force April 22, 2004, s. 1(2), which repeals ss. 11.18(3)(*f*) to (*k*), in force December 31, 2008, and s. 1(1), which repeals ss. 11.18(3)(*a*) to (*e*), in force December 31, 2013; S.C. 2005, c. 38, ss. 142(*j*) and 145(2)(*j*), in force December 12, 2005.

SHORT TITLE

1. Short Title—This Act may be cited as the *Trade-marks Act.*

INTERPRETATION

2. Definitions—In this Act,

"certification mark" means a mark that is used for the purpose of distinguishing or so as to distinguish wares or services that are of a defined standard with respect to

    (*a*) the character or quality of the wares or services,

    (*b*) the working conditions under which the wares have been produced or the services performed, (*c*) the class of persons by whom the wares have been produced or the services performed, or

(*d*) the area within which the wares have been produced or the services performed,

from wares or services that are not of that defined standard;

"confusing", when applied as an adjective to a trade-mark or trade-name, means a trade-mark or trade-name the use of which would cause confusion in the manner and circumstances described in section 6;

"Convention" means the Convention of the Union of Paris made on March 20, 1883 and any amendments and revisions thereof made before or after July 1, 1954 to which Canada is party;

"country of origin" means

(*a*) the country of the Union in which the applicant for registration of a trade-mark had at the date of the application a real and effective industrial or commercial establishment, or

(*b*) if the applicant for registration of a trade-mark did not at the date of the application have in a country of the Union an establishment as described in paragraph (*a*), the country of the Union where he on that date had his domicile, or

(*c*) if the applicant for registration of a trade-mark did not at the date of the application have in a country of the Union an establishment as described in paragraph (*a*) or a domicile as described in paragraph (*b*), the country of the Union of which he was on that date a citizen or national;

"country of the Union" means

(*a*) any country that is a member of the Union for the Protection of Industrial Property constituted under the Convention, or

(*b*) any WTO Member; [1994, c. 47, s. 190(1).]

"distinctive", in relation to a trade-mark, means a trade-mark that actually distinguishes the wares or services in association with which it is used by its owner from the wares or services of others or is adapted so to distinguish them;

"distinguishing guise" means

(*a*) a shaping of wares or their containers, or

(*b*) a mode of wrapping or packaging wares

the appearance of which is used by a person for the purpose of distinguishing or so as to distinguish wares or services manufactured, sold, leased, hired or performed by him from those manufactured, sold, leased, hired or performed by others;

"geographical indication" means, in respect of a wine or spirit, an indication that

(*a*) identifies the wine or spirit as originating in the territory of a WTO Member, or a region or locality of that territory, where a quality, reputation or other characteristic of the wine or spirit is essentially attributable to its geographical origin, and

(*b*) except in the case of an indication identifying a wine or spirit originating in Canada, is protected by the laws applicable to that WTO Member; [1994, c. 47, s. 190(2).]

"owner", in relation to a certification mark, means the person by whom the defined standard has been established;

"package" includes any container or holder ordinarily associated with wares at the time of the transfer of the property in or possession of the wares in the course of trade;

"person" includes any lawful trade union and any lawful association engaged in trade or business or the promotion thereof, and the administrative authority of any country, state, province, municipality or other organized administrative area;

"person interested" includes any person who is affected or reasonably apprehends that he may be affected by any entry in the register, or by any act or omission or contemplated act or omission under or contrary to this Act, and includes the Attorney General of Canada;

"prescribed" means prescribed by or under the regulations;

"proposed trade-mark" means a mark that is proposed to be used by a person for the purpose of distinguishing or so as to distinguish wares or services manufactured, sold, leased, hired or performed by him from those manufactured, sold, leased, hired or performed by others;

"protected geographical indication" means a geographical indication that is on the list kept pursuant to subsection 11.12(1); [1994, c. 47, s. 190(2).]

"register" means the register kept under section 26;

"registered user" [Repealed by S.C. 1993, c. 15, s. 57.]

"registered trade-mark" means a trade-mark that is on the register;

"Registrar" means the Registrar of Trade-marks appointed under section 63;

"related companies" means companies that are members of a group of two or more companies one of which, directly or indirectly, owns or controls a majority of the issued voting stock of the others;

"representative for service" means the person or firm named under paragraph 30(*g*), subsection 38(3), paragraph 41(1)(*a*) or subsection 42(1);

"trade-mark" means

(*a*) a mark that is used by a person for the purpose of distinguishing or so as to distinguish wares or services manufactured, sold, leased, hired or performed by him from those manufactured, sold, leased, hired or performed by others,

(*b*) a certification mark,

(*c*) a distinguishing guise, or

(*d*) a proposed trade-mark;

"trade-name" means the name under which any business is carried on, whether or not it is the name of a corporation, a partnership or an individual;

"use", in relation to a trade-mark, means any use that by section 4 is deemed to be a use in association with wares or services;

"wares" includes printed publications;

"WTO Agreement" has the meaning given to the word "Agreement" by subsection 2(1) of the *World Trade Organization Agreement Implementation Act*;*

"WTO Member" means a Member of the World Trade Organization established by Article I of the WTO Agreement. [1993, c. 15, s. 57; 1994, c. 47, s. 190(2).]

***World Trade Organization Agreement Implementation Act*, S.C. 1994, c. 47**

2. *Definitions*—(1) In this Act,

"Agreement" means the Agreement Establishing the World Trade Organization, including

(*a*) **the agreements set out in Annexes 1A, 1B, 1C, 2 and 3 to that Agreement, and**

(*b*) **the agreements set out in Annex 4 to that Agreement that have been accepted by Canada,**

all forming an integral part of the Final Act Embodying The Results Of The Uruguay Round Of Multilateral Trade Negotiations, signed at Marrakesh on April 15, 1994;

---

3. When deemed to be adopted—A trade-mark is deemed to have been adopted by a person when that person or his predecessor in title commenced to use it in Canada or to make it known in Canada or, if that person or his predecessor had not previously so used it or made it known, when that person or his predecessor filed an application for its registration in Canada.

4. When deemed to be used—(1) A trade-mark is deemed to be used in association with wares if, at the time of the transfer of the property in or possession of the wares, in the normal course of trade, it is marked on the wares themselves or on the packages in which they are distributed or it is in any other manner so associated with the wares that notice of the association is then given to the person to whom the property or possession is transferred.

(2) *Idem*—A trade-mark is deemed to be used in association with services if it is used or displayed in the performance or advertising of those services.

(3) *Use by export*—A trade-mark that is marked in Canada on wares or on the packages in which they are contained is, when the wares are exported from Canada, deemed to be used in Canada in association with those wares.

5. When deemed to be made known—A trade-mark is deemed to be made known in Canada by a person only if it is used by that person in a country of the Union, other than Canada, in association with wares or services, and

(*a*) the wares are distributed in association with it in Canada, or

(*b*) the wares or services are advertised in association with it in

(i) any printed publication circulated in Canada in the ordinary course of commerce among potential dealers in or users of the wares or services, or

> (ii) radio broadcasts ordinarily received in Canada by potential dealers in or users of the wares or services,

and it has become well known in Canada by reason of the distribution or advertising.

6. When mark or name confusing—(1) For the purposes of this Act, a trade-mark or trade-name is confusing with another trade-mark or trade-name if the use of the first mentioned trade-mark or trade-name would cause confusion with the last mentioned trade-mark or trade-name in the manner and circumstances described in this section.

(2) *Idem*—The use of a trade-mark causes confusion with another trade-mark if the use of both trade-marks in the same area would be likely to lead to the inference that the wares or services associated with those trade-marks are manufactured, sold, leased, hired or performed by the same person, whether or not the wares or services are of the same general class.

(3) *Idem*—The use of a trade-mark causes confusion with a trade-name if the use of both the trade-mark and trade-name in the same area would be likely to lead to the inference that the wares or services associated with the trade-mark and those associated with the business carried on under the trade-name are manufactured, sold, leased, hired or performed by the same person, whether or not the wares or services are of the same general class.

(4) *Idem*—The use of a trade-name causes confusion with a trade-mark if the use of both the trade-name and the trade-mark in the same area would be likely to lead to the inference that the wares or services associated with the business carried on under the trade-name and those associated with the trade-mark are manufactured, sold, leased, hired or performed by the same person, whether or not the wares or services are of the same general class.

(5) *What to be considered*—In determining whether trade-marks or trade-names are confusing, the court or the Registrar, as the case may be, shall have regard to all the surrounding circumstances including

> (*a*) the inherent distinctiveness of the trade-marks or trade-names and the extent to which they have become known;
>
> (*b*) the length of time the trade-marks or trade-names have been in use;
>
> (*c*) the nature of the wares, services or business;
>
> (*d*) the nature of the trade; and

(*e*) the degree of resemblance between the trade-marks or trade-names in appearance or sound or in the ideas suggested by them.

UNFAIR COMPETITION AND PROHIBITED MARKS

7. Prohibitions—No person shall

(*a*) make a false or misleading statement tending to discredit the business, wares or services of a competitor;

(*b*) direct public attention to his wares, services or business in such a way as to cause or be likely to cause confusion in Canada, at the time he commenced so to direct attention to them, between his wares, services or business and the wares, services or business of another;

(*c*) pass off other wares or services as and for those ordered or requested;

(*d*) make use, in association with wares or services, of any description that is false in a material respect and likely to mislead the public as to

(i) the character, quality, quantity or composition,

(ii) the geographical origin, or

(iii) the mode of the manufacture, production or performance of the wares or services; or

(*e*) do any other act or adopt any other business practice contrary to honest industrial or commercial usage in Canada.

8. Warranty of lawful use—Every person who in the course of trade transfers the property in or the possession of any wares bearing, or in packages bearing, any trade-mark or trade-name shall, unless before the transfer he otherwise expressly states in writing, be deemed to warrant, to the person to whom the property or possession is transferred, that the trade-mark or trade-name has been and may be lawfully used in connection with the wares.

9. Prohibited marks—(1) No person shall adopt in connection with a business, as a trade-mark or otherwise, any mark consisting of, or so nearly resembling as to be likely to be mistaken for,

(*a*) the Royal Arms, Crest or Standard;

(*b*)   the arms or crest of any member of the Royal Family;

(*c*)   the standard, arms or crest of His Excellency the Governor General;

(*d*)   any word or symbol likely to lead to the belief that the wares or services in association with which it is used have received, or are produced, sold or performed under, royal, vice-regal or governmental patronage, approval or authority;

(*e*)   the arms, crest or flag adopted and used at any time by Canada or by any province or municipal corporation in Canada in respect of which the Registrar has, at the request of the Government of Canada or of the province or municipal corporation concerned, given public notice of its adoption and use;

(*f*)   the emblem of the Red Cross on a white ground, formed by reversing the federal colours of Switzerland and retained by the Geneva Convention for the Protection of War Victims of 1949 as the emblem and distinctive sign of the Medical Service of armed forces and used by the Canadian Red Cross Society, or the expression "Red Cross" or "Geneva Cross"; [1993, c. 15, s. 58(1).]

(*g*)   the emblem of the Red Crescent on a white ground adopted for the same purpose as specified in paragraph (*f*) by a number of Moslem countries; [1993, c. 15, s. 58(1).]

(*h*)   the equivalent sign of the Red Lion and Sun used by Iran for the same purpose as specified in paragraph (*f*);

(*h*.1) the international distinctive sign of civil defence (equilateral blue triangle on an orange ground) referred to in Article 66, paragraph 4 of Schedule V to the *Geneva Conventions Act*;* [1990, c. 14, s. 8.]

---

* *Geneva Conventions Act*, **R.S.C. 1985, c. G-3**

Article 66 — Identification

. . .

4. The international distinctive sign of civil defence is an equilateral blue triangle on an orange ground when used for the protection of

civil defence organizations, their personnel, buildings and *matériel* **and for civilian shelters.** [1990, c. 14, s. 6.]

(*i*)　any territorial or civic flag or any national, territorial or civic arms, crest or emblem, of a country of the Union, if the flag, arms, crest or emblem is on a list communicated under article 6ter of the Convention or pursuant to the obligations under the Agreement on Trade-related Aspects of Intellectual Property Rights set out in Annex 1C to the WTO Agreement stemming from that article, and the Registrar gives public notice of the communication; [1993, c. 15, s. 58(2); 1993, c. 44, ss. 226(1), 236(1)(c); 1994, c. 47, s. 191(1).]

(*i.*1)　any official sign or hallmark indicating control or warranty adopted by a country of the Union, if the sign or hallmark is on a list communicated under article 6ter of the Convention or pursuant to the obligations under the Agreement on Trade-related Aspects of Intellectual Property Rights set out in Annex IC to the WTO Agreement stemming from that article, and the Registrar gives public notice of the communication; [1993, c. 44, ss. 226(1), 236(1)(c); 1994, c. 47, s. 191(1).]

(*i.*2)　any national flag of a country of the Union; [1993, c. 15, s. 58(2); 1993, c. 44, ss. 226(1), 236(1)(c).]

(*i.*3)　any armorial bearing, flag or other emblem, or any abbreviation of the name, of an international intergovernmental organization, if the armorial bearing, flag, emblem or abbreviation is on a list communicated under article 6ter of the Convention or pursuant to the obligations under the Agreement on Trade-related Aspects of Intellectual Property Rights set out in Annex 1C to the WTO Agreement stemming from that article, and the Registrar gives public notice of the communication; [1993, c. 15, s. 58(2); 1993, c. 44, ss. 226(1), 236(1)(c); 1994, c. 47, s. 191(2).]

(*j*)　any scandalous, obscene or immoral word or device;

(*k*)　any matter that may falsely suggest a connection with any living individual;

(*l*)　the portrait or signature of any individual who is living or has died within the preceding thirty years;

(*m*)　the words "United Nations" or the official seal or emblem of the United Nations;

(*n*)   any badge, crest, emblem or mark

    (i)   adopted or used by any of Her Majesty's Forces as defined in the *National Defence Act*,*

    (ii)   of any university, or

    (iii)   adopted and used by any public authority, in Canada as an official mark for wares or services,

in respect of which the Registrar has, at the request of Her Majesty or of the university or public authority, as the case may be, given public notice of its adoption and use;

***National Defence Act, R.S.C. 1985, c. N-5**

    2. *Definitions*—

. . .

"Her Majesty's Forces" means the armed forces of Her Majesty wherever raised, and includes the Canadian Forces;

(*n*.1)   any armorial bearings granted, recorded or approved for use by a recipient pursuant to the prerogative powers of Her Majesty as exercised by the Governor General in respect of the granting of armorial bearings, if the Registrar has, at the request of the Governor General, given public notice of the grant, recording or approval; or [1993, c. 15, s. 58(3).]

(*o*)   the name "Royal Canadian Mounted Police" or "R.C.M.P." or any other combination of letters relating to the Royal Canadian Mounted Police, or any pictorial representation of a uniformed member thereof.

(2) *Excepted uses*—Nothing in this section prevents the adoption, use or registration as a trade-mark or otherwise, in connection with a business, of any mark

(*a*)   described in subsection (1) with the consent of Her Majesty or such other person, society, authority or organization as may be considered to have been intended to be protected by this section; or (*b*) consisting of, or so nearly resembling as to be likely to be mistaken for

  (i) an official sign or hallmark mentioned in paragraph (1)(*i*.1), except in respect of wares that are the same or similar to the wares in respect of which the official sign or hallmark has been adopted, or

  (ii) an armorial bearing, flag, emblem or abbreviation mentioned in paragraph (1)(*i*.3), unless the use of the mark is likely to mislead the public as to a connection between the user and the organization. [1993, c. 15, s. 58; 1993, c. 44, ss. 226(2), 236(1)(d).]

10. Further prohibitions—Where any mark has by ordinary and *bona fide* commercial usage become recognized in Canada as designating the kind, quality, quantity, destination, value, place of origin or date of production of any wares or services, no person shall adopt it as a trademark in association with such wares or services or others of the same general class or use it in a way likely to mislead, nor shall any person so adopt or so use any mark so nearly resembling that mark as to be likely to be mistaken therefor.

10.1. Further prohibitions—Where a denomination must, under the *Plant Breeders' Rights Act*,* be used to designate a plant variety, no person shall adopt it as a trade-mark in association with the plant variety or another plant variety of the same species or use it in a way likely to mislead, nor shall any person so adopt or so use any mark so nearly resembling that denomination as to be likely to be mistaken therefor. [1990, c. 20, s. 79.]

---

* S.C. 1990, c. 20

---

11. Further prohibitions—No person shall use in connection with a business, as a trade-mark or otherwise, any mark adopted contrary to section 9 or 10 of this Act or section 13 or 14 of the *Unfair Competition Act*, chapter 274 of the Revised Statutes of Canada, 1952.*

---

* *Unfair Competition Act*, **R.S.C. 1952, c. 274**

13. *Use as trade marks of certain commercial symbols forbidden*— **Where any symbol has by ordinary and *bona fide* commercial usage become recognized in Canada as designating the kind, quality, quantity, destination, value, place of origin or date of production of any wares,**

no person shall adopt it for use as a trade mark for similar wares or use it in such a way as to be likely to mislead.

14. *Use as trade marks of certain emblems, etc., forbidden*—(1) No person is entitled to adopt for use in connection with his business, as a trade mark or otherwise, any symbol consisting of, or so nearly resembling as to be likely to be mistaken for,

(a) the Royal Arms, Crest or Standard;

(b) the arms or crest of any member of the Royal Family;

(c) the national flag in any of its forms;

(d) the standard, arms or crest of His Excellency the Governor General;

(e) the arms or crest adopted and used at any time by Canada or by any province or municipal corporation in Canada;

(f) any national flag, arms, crest or emblem commonly used as such by any foreign state;

(g) the emblem of the Red Cross Society, consisting of a red cross on a white ground or the expression "Red Cross" or "Geneva Cross";

(h) any national, territorial or civic flag, arms, crest, or emblem of the prohibition of which as a commercial device notice has been received and publicly given by the registrar pursuant to the provisions of the Convention more than two months before the adoption of the symbol;

(i) the emblem of any fraternal society, the legal existence of which is recognized under any law in force in Canada;

(j) any symbol adopted and used by any public authority in Canada as an official mark on similar wares; or

(k) the portrait or signature of any person who is living or has died within thirty years.

(2) *Except by permission*—Nothing in this section prevents the use as a trade mark, or otherwise in connection with a business, of any such symbol as aforesaid with the consent and approval of Her Majesty or such other person as may be deemed to have been intended to be protected by the provisions hereof.

11.1. Further prohibitions—No person shall use in connection with a business, as a trade-mark or otherwise, any denomination adopted contrary to section 10.1. [1990, c. 20, s. 80.]

11.11. Definitions—In sections 11.12 to 11.2,

"Minister" means the member of the Queen's Privy Council for Canada designated as the Minister for the purposes of sections 11.12 to 11.2;

"responsible authority" means, in relation to a wine or spirit, the person, firm or other entity that, in the opinion of the Minister, is, by reason of state or commercial interest, sufficiently connected with and knowledgeable of that wine or spirit to be a party to any proceedings in respect of an objection filed under subsection 11.13(1). [1994, c. 47, s. 192.]

11.12. List—(1) There shall be kept under the supervision of the Registrar a list of geographical indications.

(2) *Statement of Minister*—Where a statement by the Minister, setting out in respect of an indication the information mentioned in subsection (3), is published in the *Canada Gazette* and

(*a*) a statement of objection has not been filed and served on the responsible authority in accordance with subsection 11.13(1) and the time for the filing of the statement of objection has expired, or

(*b*) a statement of objection has been so filed and served, but it has been withdrawn or deemed under subsection 11.13(6) to have been withdrawn or it has been rejected pursuant to subsection 11.13(7) or, if an appeal is taken, it is rejected pursuant to the final judgment given in the appeal,

the Registrar shall enter the indication on the list of geographical indications kept pursuant to subsection (1).

(3) *Information*—For the purposes of subsection (2), the statement by the Minister must set out the following information in respect of an
indication:

(*a*) that the Minister proposes that the indication be entered on the list of geographical indications kept pursuant to subsection (1);

(*b*) that the indication identifies a wine or that the indication identifies a spirit;

(*c*) the territory, or the region or locality of a territory, in which the wine or spirit is identified as originating;

(*d*) the name of the responsible authority in relation to the wine or spirit and the address of the responsible authority's principal office or place of business in Canada, if any, and if the responsible authority has no office or place of business in Canada, the name and address in Canada of a person or firm on whom service of any document or proceedings in respect of an objection may be given or served with the same effect as if they had been given to or served on the responsible authority itself; and

(*e*) the quality, reputation or other characteristic of the wine or spirit that, in the opinion of the Minister, qualifies that indication as a geographical indication.

(4) *Removal from list*—The Registrar shall remove an indication from the list of geographical indications kept pursuant to subsection (1) on the publication in the *Canada Gazette* of a statement by the Minister that the indication is to be removed. [1994, c. 47, s. 192.]

11.13. Statement of objection—(1) Within three months after the publication in the *Canada Gazette* of a statement referred to in subsection 11.12(2), any person interested may, on payment of the prescribed fee, file with the Registrar, and serve on the responsible authority in the prescribed manner, a statement of objection.

(2) *Ground*—A statement of objection may be based only on the ground that the indication is not a geographical indication.

(3) *Content*—A statement of objection shall set out

(*a*) the ground of objection in sufficient detail to enable the responsible authority to reply thereto; and

(*b*) the address of the objector's principal office or place of business in Canada, if any, and if the objector has no office or place of business in Canada, the address of the principal office or place of business abroad and the name and address in Canada of a person or firm on whom service of any document in respect of the objection may be made with the same effect as if it had been served on the objector.

(4) *Counter statement*—Within three months after a statement of objection has been served on the responsible authority, the responsible authority may file a counter statement with the Registrar and serve a copy on the objector in the prescribed manner, and if the responsible authority

does not so file and serve a counter statement, the indication shall not be entered on the list of geographical indications.

(5) *Evidence and hearing*—Both the objector and the responsible authority shall be given an opportunity, in the manner prescribed, to submit evidence and to make representations to the Registrar unless

(*a*) the responsible authority does not file and serve a counter statement in accordance with subsection (4) or if, in the prescribed circumstances, the responsible authority does not submit evidence or a statement that the responsible authority does not wish to submit evidence; or

(*b*) the objection is withdrawn or deemed under subsection (6) to have been withdrawn.

(6) *Withdrawal of objection*—The objection shall be deemed to have been withdrawn if, in the prescribed circumstances, the objector does not submit evidence or a statement that the objector does not wish to submit evidence.

(7) *Decision*—After considering the evidence and representations of the objector and the responsible authority, the Registrar shall decide that the indication is not a geographical indication or reject the objection, and notify the parties of the decision and the reasons for the decision. [1994, c. 47, s. 192.]

11.14. Prohibited adoption of indication for wines—(1) No person shall adopt in connection with a business, as a trade-mark or otherwise,

(*a*) a protected geographical indication identifying a wine in respect of a wine not originating in the territory indicated by the protected geographical indication; or

(*b*) a translation in any language of the geographical indication in respect of that wine.

(2) *Prohibited use*—No person shall use in connection with a business, as a trade-mark or otherwise,

(*a*) a protected geographical indication identifying a wine in respect of a wine not originating in the territory indicated by the protected geographical indication or adopted contrary to subsection (1); or

(*b*) a translation in any language of the geographical indication in respect of that wine. [1994, c. 47, s. 192.]

11.15. Prohibited adoption of indication for spirits—(1) No person shall adopt in connection with a business, as a trade-mark or otherwise,

    (*a*)   a protected geographical indication identifying a spirit in respect of a spirit not originating in the territory indicated by the protected geographical indication; or

    (*b*)   a translation in any language of the geographical indication in respect of that spirit.

(2) *Prohibited use*—No person shall use in connection with a business, as a trade-mark or otherwise,

    (*a*)   a protected geographical indication identifying a spirit in respect of a spirit not originating in the territory indicated by the protected geographical indication or adopted contrary to subsection (1); or

    (*b*)   a translation in any language of the geographical indication in respect of that spirit. [1994, c. 47, s. 192.]

11.16. Exception for personal names—(1) Sections 11.14 and 11.15 do not prevent a person from using, in the course of trade, that person's name or the name of the person's predecessor-in-title, except where the name is used in such a manner as to mislead the public.

(2) *Exception for comparative advertising*—Subject to subsection (3), sections 11.14 and 11.15 do not prevent a person from using a protected geographical indication in comparative advertising in respect of a wine or spirit.

(3) *Exception not applicable to packaging*—Subsection (2) does not apply to comparative advertising on labels or packaging associated with a wine or spirit. [1994, c. 47, s. 192.]

11.17. Continued use—(1) Where a Canadian has used a protected geographical indication in a continuous manner in relation to any business or commercial activity in respect of goods or services

    (*a*)   in good faith before April 15, 1994, or

    (*b*)   for at least ten years before that date,

section 11.14 or 11.15, as the case may be, does not apply to any continued or similar use by that Canadian.

(2) *Definition of "Canadian"*—For the purpose of this section, "Canadian" includes

    (*a*)   a Canadian citizen;

(*b*) a permanent resident within the meaning of subsection 2(1) of the *Immigration and Refugee Protection Act* who has been ordinarily resident in Canada for not more than one year after the time at which the permanent resident first became eligible to apply for Canadian citizenship; and

(*c*) an entity that carries on business in Canada. [1994, c. 47, s. 192; 2001, c. 27, s. 271.]

11.18. Exception for disuse—(1) Notwithstanding sections 11.14 and 11.15 and paragraphs 12(1)(*g*) and (*h*), nothing in any of those provisions prevents the adoption, use or registration as a trade-mark or otherwise, in connection with a business, of a protected geographical indication identifying a wine or spirit if the indication has ceased to be protected by the laws applicable to the WTO Member for which the indication is protected, or has fallen into disuse in that Member.

(2) *Exceptions for customary names*—Notwithstanding sections 11.14 and 11.15 and paragraphs 12(1)(*g*) and (*h*), nothing in any of those provisions prevents the adoption, use or registration as a trade-mark or otherwise, in connection with a business, of an indication in respect of a wine or spirit

(*a*) that is identical with a term customary in common language in Canada as the common name for the wine or spirit, as the case may be; or

(*b*) that is identical with a customary name of a grape variety existing in Canada on or before the day on which the Agreement comes into force.

(3) *Exception for generic names for wines*—Notwithstanding sections 11.14 and 11.15 and paragraphs 12(1)(*g*) and (*h*), nothing in any of those provisions prevents the adoption, use or registration as a trade-mark or otherwise, in connection with a business, of the following indications in respect of wines:

(*a*) Champagne;

(*b*) Port;

(*c*) Porto;

(*d*) Sherry;

(*e*) Chablis;

(*f*) Burgundy;

(*g*)   Bourgogne;

(*h*)   Rhine;

(*i*)   Rhin;

(*j*)   Sauterne;

(*k*)   Sauternes;

(*l*)-(*v*) [Repealed by SOR/2004-85, s. 1(3).]

Note: SOR/2004-85, s. 1(2) provides that paragraphs 11.18(3)(*f*) to (*k*) are repealed on December 31, 2008, and s. 1(1) provides that paragraphs 11.18(3)(*a*) to (*e*) are repealed on December 31, 2013.

(4) *Exception for generic names for spirits*—Notwithstanding sections 11.14 and 11.15 and paragraphs 12(1)(*g*) and (*h*), nothing in any of those provisions prevents the adoption, use or registration as a trade-mark or otherwise, in connection with a business, of the following indications in respect of spirits:

(*a*)-(*c*) [Repealed by SOR/2004-85, s. (4).]

(*d*)   Sambuca;

(*e*)   Geneva Gin;

(*f*)   Genièvre;

(*g*)   Hollands Gin;

(*h*)   London Gin;

(*i*)   Schnapps;

(*j*)   Malt Whiskey;

(*k*)   Eau-de-vie;

(*l*)   Bitters;

(*m*)   Anisette;

(*n*)   Curacao; and

(*o*)   Curaçao.

(5) *Governor in Council amendment*—The Governor in Council may, by order, amend subsection (3) or (4) by adding thereto or deleting therefrom an indication in respect of a wine or spirit, as the case may be. [1994, c. 47, s. 192; SOR/2004-85, ss. 1(3), (4).]

11.19. Exception for failure to take proceedings—(1) Sections 11.14 and 11.15 do not apply to the adoption or use of a trade-mark by a person if no proceedings are taken to enforce those sections in respect of that person's use or adoption of the trade-mark within five years after use of the trade-mark by that person or that person's predecessor-in-title has become generally known in Canada or the trade-mark has been registered by that person in Canada, unless it is established that that person or that person's predecessor-in-title first used or adopted the trade-mark with knowledge that such use or adoption was contrary to section 11.14 or 11.15, as the case may be.

(2) *Idem*—In proceedings respecting a registered trade-mark commenced after the expiration of five years from the earlier of the date of registration of the trade-mark in Canada and the date on which use of the trade-mark by the person who filed the application for registration of the trade-mark or that person's predecessor-in-title has become generally known in Canada, the registration shall not be expunged or amended or held invalid on the basis of paragraph 12(1)(*g*) or (*h*) unless it is established that the person who filed the application for registration of the trade-mark did so with knowledge that the trade-mark was in whole or in part a protected geographical indication. [1994, c. 47, s. 192.]

11.2. Transitional—Notwithstanding sections 11.14 and 11.15 and paragraphs 12(1)(*g*) and (*h*), where a person has in good faith

(*a*) filed an application in accordance with section 30 for, or secured the registration of, a trade-mark that is identical with or similar to the geographical indication in respect of a wine or spirit protected by the laws applicable to a WTO Member, or

(*b*) acquired rights to a trade-mark in respect of such a wine or spirit through use,

before the later of the date on which this section comes into force and the date on which protection in respect of the wine or spirit by the laws applicable to that Member commences, nothing in any of those provisions prevents the adoption, use or registration of that trade-mark by that person. [1994, c. 47, s. 192.]

REGISTRABLE TRADE-MARKS

12. When trade-mark registrable—(1) Subject to section 13, a trade-mark is registrable if it is not (*a*) a word that is primarily merely the name or the surname of an individual who is living or has died within the preceding thirty years;

(*b*) whether depicted, written or sounded, either clearly descriptive or deceptively misdescriptive in the English or French language of the character or quality of the wares or services in association with which it is used or proposed to be used or of the conditions of or the persons employed in their production or of their place of origin;

(*c*) the name in any language of any of the wares or services in connection with which it is used or proposed to be used;

(*d*) confusing with a registered trade-mark;

(*e*) a mark of which the adoption is prohibited by section 9 or 10;

(*f*) a denomination the adoption of which is prohibited by section 10.1; [1990, c. 20, s. 81.]

(*g*) in whole or in part a protected geographical indication, where the trade-mark is to be registered in association with a wine not originating in a territory indicated by the geographical indication; and

(*h*) in whole or in part a protected geographical indication, where the trade-mark is to be registered in association with a spirit not originating in a territory indicated by the geographical indication. [1994, c. 47, s. 193.]

(2) *Idem*—A trade-mark that is not registrable by reason of paragraph (1)(*a*) or (*b*) is registrable if it has been so used in Canada by the applicant or his predecessor in title as to have become distinctive at the date of filing an application for its registration.

13. When distinguishing guises registrable—(1) A distinguishing guise is registrable only if

(*a*) it has been so used in Canada by the applicant or his predecessor in title as to have become distinctive at the date of filing an application for its registration; and

(*b*) the exclusive use by the applicant of the distinguishing guise in association with the wares or services with which it has been used is not likely unreasonably to limit the development of any art or industry.

(2) *Effect of registration*—No registration of a distinguishing guise interferes with the use of any utilitarian feature embodied in the distinguishing guise.

(3) *Not to limit art or industry*—The registration of a distinguishing guise may be expunged by the Federal Court on the application of any interested person if the Court decides that the registration has become likely unreasonably to limit the development of any art or industry.

14. Registration of marks registered abroad—(1) Notwithstanding section 12, a trade-mark that the applicant or the applicant's predecessor in title has caused to be duly registered in or for the country of origin of the applicant is registrable if, in Canada, [1994, c. 47, s. 194.]

(*a*) it is not confusing with a registered trade-mark;

(*b*) it is not without distinctive character, having regard to all the circumstances of the case including the length of time during which it has been used in any country;

(*c*) it is not contrary to morality or public order or of such a nature as to deceive the public; or

(*d*) it is not a trade-mark of which the adoption is prohibited by section 9 or 10.

(2) *Trade-marks regarded as registered abroad*—A trade-mark that differs from the trade-mark registered in the country of origin only by elements that do not alter its distinctive character or affect its identity in the form under which it is registered in the country of origin shall be regarded for the purpose of subsection (1) as the trade-mark so registered.

15. Registration of confusing marks—(1) Notwithstanding section 12 or 14, confusing trade-marks are registrable if the applicant is the owner of all such trade-marks, which shall be known as associated trade-marks.

(2) *Record*—Upon the registration of any trade-mark associated with any other registered trade-mark, a note of the registration of each trade-mark shall be made on the record of registration of the other trade-mark.

(3) *Amendment*—No amendment of the register recording any change in the ownership or in the name or address of the owner of any one of a group of associated trade-marks shall be made unless the Registrar is satisfied that the same change has occurred with respect to all the trade-marks in the group, and corresponding entries are made contemporaneously with respect to all those trade-marks.

PERSONS ENTITLED TO REGISTRATION OF TRADE-MARKS

16. Registration of marks used or made known in Canada—(1) Any applicant who has filed an application in accordance with section 30 for registration of a trade-mark that is registrable and that he or his predecessor in title has used in Canada or made known in Canada in association with wares or services is entitled, subject to section 38, to secure its registration in respect of those wares or services, unless at the date on which he or his predecessor in title first so used it or made it known it was confusing with

    (*a*) a trade-mark that had been previously used in Canada or made known in Canada by any other person;

    (*b*) a trade-mark in respect of which an application for registration had been previously filed in Canada by any other person; or

    (*c*) a trade-name that had been previously used in Canada by any other person.

(2) *Marks registered and used abroad*—Any applicant who has filed an application in accordance with section 30 for registration of a trade-mark that is registrable and that the applicant or the applicant's predecessor-in-title has duly registered in or for the country of origin of the applicant and has used in association with wares or services is entitled, subject to section 38, to secure its registration in respect of the wares or services in association with which it is registered in that country and has been used, unless at the date of filing of the application in accordance with section 30 it was confusing with [1994, c. 47, s. 195.]

    (*a*) a trade-mark that had been previously used in Canada or made known in Canada by any other person;

    (*b*) a trade-mark in respect of which an application for registration had been previously filed in Canada by any other person; or

    (*c*) a trade-name that had been previously used in Canada by any other person.

(3) *Proposed marks*—Any applicant who has filed an application in accordance with section 30 for registration of a proposed trade-mark that is registrable is entitled, subject to sections 38 and 40, to secure its registration in respect of the wares or services specified in the application, unless at the date of filing of the application it was confusing with

(a) a trade-mark that had been previously used in Canada or made known in Canada by any other person;

(b) a trade-mark in respect of which an application for registration had been previously filed in Canada by any other person; or

(c) a trade-name that had been previously used in Canada by any other person.

(4) *Where application for confusing mark pending*—The right of an applicant to secure registration of a registrable trade-mark is not affected by the previous filing of an application for registration of a confusing trade-mark by another person, unless the application for registration of the confusing trade-mark was pending at the date of advertisement of the applicant's application in accordance with section 37.

(5) *Previous use or making known*—The right of an applicant to secure registration of a registrable trade-mark is not affected by the previous use or making known of a confusing trade-mark or trade-name by another person, if the confusing trade-mark or trade-name was abandoned at the date of advertisement of the applicant's application in accordance with section 37.

VALIDITY AND EFFECT OF REGISTRATION

17. Effect of Registration in Relation to Previous Use, etc.—(1) No application for registration of a trade-mark that has been advertised in accordance with section 37 shall be refused and no registration of a trade-mark shall be expunged or amended or held invalid on the ground of any previous use or making known of a confusing trade-mark or trade-name by a person other than the applicant for that registration or his predecessor in title, except at the instance of that other person or his successor in title, and the burden lies on that other person or his successor to establish that he had not abandoned the confusing trade-mark or trade-name at the date of advertisement of the applicant's application.

(2) *When registration incontestable*—In proceedings commenced after the expiration of five years from the date of registration of a trade-mark or from July 1, 1954, whichever is the later, no registration shall be expunged or amended or held invalid on the ground of the previous use or making known referred to in subsection (1), unless it is established that the person who adopted the registered trade-mark in Canada did so with knowledge of that previous use or making known.

18. When registration invalid—(1) The registration of a trade-mark is invalid if

(*a*)   the trade-mark was not registrable at the date of registration,

(*b*)   the trade-mark is not distinctive at the time proceedings bringing the validity of the registration into question are commenced, or

(*c*)   the trade-mark has been abandoned,

and subject to section 17, it is invalid if the applicant for registration was not the person entitled to secure the registration.

(2) *Exception*—No registration of a trade-mark that had been so used in Canada by the registrant or his predecessor in title as to have become distinctive at the date of registration shall be held invalid merely on the ground that evidence of the distinctiveness was not submitted to the competent authority or tribunal before the grant of the registration.

19. Rights conferred by registration—Subject to sections 21, 32 and 67, the registration of a trade-mark in respect of any wares or services, unless shown to be invalid, gives to the owner of the trade-mark the exclusive right to the use throughout Canada of the trade-mark in respect of those wares or services.

20. Infringement—(1) The right of the owner of a registered trade-mark to its exclusive use shall be deemed to be infringed by a person not entitled to its use under this Act who sells, distributes or advertises wares or services in association with a confusing trade-mark or trade-name, but no registration of a trade-mark prevents a person from making

(*a*)   any *bona fide* use of his personal name as a trade-name, or

(*b*)   any *bona fide* use, other than as a trade-mark,

(i)   of the geographical name of his place of business, or

(ii)   of any accurate description of the character or quality of his wares or services,

in such a manner as is not likely to have the effect of depreciating the value of the goodwill attaching to the trade-mark.

(2) *Exception*—No registration of a trade-mark prevents a person from making any use of any of the indications mentioned in subsection 11.18(3) in association with a wine or any of the indications mentioned in subsection 11.18(4) in association with a spirit. [1994, c. 47, s. 196.]

21. Concurrent use of confusing marks—(1) Where, in any proceedings respecting a registered trade-mark the registration of which is entitled to the protection of subsection 17(2), it is made to appear to the Federal Court that one of the parties to the proceedings, other than the registered owner of the trade-mark, had in good faith used a confusing trade-mark or trade-name in Canada before the date of filing of the application for that registration, and the Court considers that it is not contrary to the public interest that the continued use of the confusing trade-mark or trade-name should be permitted in a defined territorial area concurrently with the use of the registered trade-mark, the Court may, subject to such terms as it deems just, order that the other party may continue to use the confusing trade-mark or trade-name within that area with an adequate specified distinction from the registered trade-mark.

(2) *Registration of order*—The rights conferred by an order made under subsection (1) take effect only if, within three months from its date, the other party makes application to the Registrar to enter it on the register in connection with the registration of the registered trade-mark.

22. Depreciation of goodwill—(1) No person shall use a trade-mark registered by another person in a manner that is likely to have the effect of depreciating the value of the goodwill attaching thereto.

(2) *Action in respect thereof*—In any action in respect of a use of a trade-mark contrary to subsection (1), the court may decline to order the recovery of damages or profits and may permit the defendant to continue to sell wares marked with the trade-mark that were in his possession or under his control at the time notice was given to him that the owner of the registered trade-mark complained of the use of the trade-mark.

CERTIFICATION MARKS

23. Registration of certification marks—(1) A certification mark may be adopted and registered only by a person who is not engaged in the manufacture, sale, leasing or hiring of wares or the performance of services such as those in association with which the certification mark is used.

(2) *Licence*—The owner of a certification mark may license others to use the mark in association with wares or services that meet the defined standard, and the use of the mark accordingly shall be deemed to be use thereof by the owner.

(3) *Unauthorized use*—The owner of a registered certification mark may prevent its use by unlicensed persons or in association with any wares or services in respect of which the mark is registered but to which the licence does not extend.

(4) *Action by unincorporated body*—Where the owner of a registered certification mark is an unincorporated body, any action or proceeding to prevent unauthorized use of the mark may be brought by any member of that body on behalf of himself and all other members thereof.

24. Registration of trade-mark confusing with certification mark— With the consent of the owner of a certification mark, a trade-mark confusing with the certification mark may, if it exhibits an appropriate difference, be registered by some other person to indicate that the wares or services in association with which it is used have been manufactured, sold, leased, hired or performed by him as one of the persons entitled to use the certification mark, but the registration thereof shall be expunged by the Registrar on the withdrawal at any time of the consent of the owner of the certification mark or on the cancellation of the registration of the certification mark.

25. Descriptive certification mark—A certification mark descriptive of the place of origin of wares or services, and not confusing with any registered trade-mark, is registrable if the applicant is the administrative authority of a country, state, province or municipality including or forming part of the area indicated by the mark, or is a commercial association having an office or representative in that area, but the owner of any mark registered under this section shall permit the use of the mark in association with any wares or services produced or performed in the area of which the mark is descriptive.

REGISTER OF TRADE-MARKS

26. Register—(1) There shall be kept under the supervision of the Registrar

  (*a*) a register of trade-marks and of transfers, disclaimers, amendments, judgments and orders relating to each registered trade-mark; and

  (*b*) the register of registered users that was required to be kept under this subsection as it read immediately before section 61 of the *Intellectual Property Law Improvement Act* came into force.*
      [1993, c. 15, s. 61(1); 1993, c. 44, ss. 227(1), 236(1)(e).]

---

* **S.C. 1993, c. 15**

---

(2) *Information to be shown*—The register referred to in paragraph 1(*a*) shall show, with reference to each registered trade-mark, the following:

(*a*) the date of registration;

(*b*) a summary of the application for registration;

(*c*) a summary of all documents deposited with the application or subsequently thereto and affecting the rights to the trade-mark;

(*d*) particulars of each renewal;

(*e*) particulars of each change of name and address; and

(*f*) such other particulars as this Act or the regulations require to be entered thereon. [1993, c. 15, s. 61(2); 1993, c. 44, ss. 227(2), 236(1)(f).]

27. Register under *Unfair Competition Act*—(1) The register kept under the *Unfair Competition Act*,* chapter 274 of the Revised Statutes of Canada, 1952, forms part of the register kept under this Act and, subject to subsection 44(2), no entry made therein, if properly made according to the law in force at the time it was made, is subject to be expunged or amended only because it might not properly have been made pursuant to this Act.

(2) *Trade-marks registered before Unfair Competition Act*— Trade-marks on the register on September 1, 1932 shall be treated as design marks or word marks as defined in the *Unfair Competition Act*,* chapter 274 of the Revised Statutes of Canada, 1952, according to the following rules:

(*a*) any trade-mark consisting only of words or numerals or both without any indication of a special form or appearance shall be deemed to be a word mark;

(*b*) any other trade-mark consisting only of words or numerals or both shall be deemed to be a word mark if at the date of its registration the words or numerals or both would have been registrable independently of any defined special form or appearance and shall also be deemed to be a design mark for reading matter presenting the special form or appearance defined;

(*c*) any trade-mark including words or numerals or both in combination with other features shall be deemed

(i) to be a design mark having the features described in the application therefor but without any meaning being attributed to the words or numerals, and

(ii) to be a word mark if and so far as it would at the date of registration have been registrable independently of any defined form or appearance and without being combined with any other feature; and

(*d*) any other trade-mark shall be deemed to be a design mark having the features described in the application therefor.

(3) *Trade-marks registered under Unfair Competition Act*—Trade-marks registered under the *Unfair Competition Act*,* chapter 274 of the Revised Statutes of Canada, 1952, shall, in accordance with their registration, continue to be treated as design marks or word marks as defined in that Act.

---

* R.S.C. 1952, c. 274

---

28. Indexes—(1) There shall be kept under the supervision of the Registrar

(*a*) an index of registered trade-marks;

(*b*) an index of trade-marks in respect of which applications for registration are pending;

(*c*) an index of applications that have been abandoned or refused;

(*d*) an index of the names of owners of registered trade-marks;

(*e*) an index of the names of applicants for the registration of trade-marks;

(*f*) a list of trade-mark agents; and [1993, c. 44, ss. 228, 236(2).]

(*g*) the index of the names of registered users that was required to be kept under this subsection as it reads immediately before section 61 of the *Intellectual Property Law Improvement Act** comes into force.

---

* S.C. 1993, c. 15

---

(2) *List of trade-mark agents*—The list of trade-mark agents shall include the names of all persons and firms entitled to represent applicants in the presentation and prosecution of applications for the registration of

a trade-mark or in other business before the Trade-marks Office. [1993, c. 15, s. 62.]

29. Inspection—(1) Subject to subsection (2), the registers, the documents on which the entries therein are based, all applications, including those abandoned, the indexes, the list of trade-mark agents and the list of geographical indications kept pursuant to subsection 11.12(1) shall be open to public inspection during business hours, and the Registrar shall, on request and on payment of the prescribed fee, furnish a copy certified by the registrar of any entry in the registers, indexes or lists, or of any of those documents or applications. [1994, c. 47, s. 197.]

(2) *Register of registered users*—The disclosure of documents on which entries in the register required to be kept under paragraph 26(1)(*b*) are based is subject to the provisions of subsection 50(6), as it reads immediately before section 61 of the *Intellectual Property Law Improvement Act** comes into force. [1993, c. 15, s. 63; 1993, c. 44, ss. 229, 236(1)(g).]

---

* S.C. 1993, c. 15

APPLICATIONS FOR REGISTRATION OF TRADE-MARKS

30. Contents of application—An applicant for the registration of a trade-mark shall file with the Registrar an application containing

(*a*)   a statement in ordinary commercial terms of the specific wares or services in association with which the mark has been or is proposed to be used;

(*b*)   in the case of a trade-mark that has been used in Canada, the date from which the applicant or his named predecessors in title, if any, have so used the trade-mark in association with each of the general classes of wares or services described in the application;

(*c*)   in the case of a trade-mark that has not been used in Canada but is made known in Canada, the name of a country of the Union in which it has been used by the applicant or his named predecessors in title, if any, and the date from and the manner in which the applicant or named predecessors in title have made it known in Canada in association with each of the general classes of wares or services described in the application;

(*d*) in the case of a trade-mark that is the subject in or for another country of the Union of a registration or an application for registration by the applicant or the applicant's named predecessor-in-title on which the applicant bases the applicant's right to registration, particulars of the application or registration and, if the trade-mark has neither been used in Canada nor made known in Canada, the name of a country in which the trade-mark has been used by the applicant or the applicant's named predecessor-in-title, if any, in association with each of the general classes of wares or services described in the application; [1994, c. 47, s. 198.]

(*e*) in the case of a proposed trade-mark, a statement that the applicant, by itself or through a licensee, or by itself and through a licensee, intends to use the trade-mark in Canada; [1993, c. 15, s. 64; 1993, c. 44, ss. 230, 236(1)(h).]

(*f*) in the case of a certification mark, particulars of the defined standard that the use of the mark is intended to indicate and a statement that the applicant is not engaged in the manufacture, sale, leasing or hiring of wares or the performance of services such as those in association with which the certification mark is used;

(*g*) the address of the applicant's principal office or place of business in Canada, if any, and if the applicant has no office or place of business in Canada, the address of his principal office or place of business abroad and the name and address in Canada of a person or firm to whom any notice in respect of the application or registration may be sent, and on whom service of any proceedings in respect of the application or registration may be given or served with the same effect as if they had been given to or served on the applicant or registrant himself;

(*h*) unless the application is for the registration only of a word or words not depicted in a special form, a drawing of the trade-mark and such number of accurate representations of the trade-mark as may be prescribed; and

(*i*) a statement that the applicant is satisfied that he is entitled to use the trade-mark in Canada in association with the wares or services described in the application.

31. Applications based on registration abroad—(1) An applicant whose right to registration of a trade-mark is based on a registration of the trade-mark in another country of the Union shall, before the date of advertisement of his application in accordance with section 37, furnish a copy of the registration certified by the office in which it was made, together with a translation thereof into English or French if it is in any other language, and such other evidence as the Registrar may require to establish fully his right to registration under this Act.

(2) *Evidence required in certain cases*—An applicant whose trade-mark has been duly registered in his country of origin and who claims that the trade-mark is registrable under paragraph 14(1)(*b*) shall furnish such evidence as the Registrar may require by way of affidavit or statutory declaration establishing the circumstances on which he relies, including the length of time during which the trade-mark has been used in any country.

32. Further information in certain cases—(1) An applicant who claims that his trade-mark is registrable under subsection 12(2) or section 13 shall furnish the Registrar with evidence by way of affidavit or statutory declaration establishing the extent to which and the time during which the trade-mark has been used in Canada and with any other evidence that the Registrar may require in support of the claim.

(2) *Registration to be restricted*—The Registrar shall, having regard to the evidence adduced, restrict the registration to the wares or services in association with which the trade-mark is shown to have been so used as to have become distinctive and to the defined territorial area in Canada in which the trade-mark is shown to have become distinctive.

33. Applications by trade unions, etc.—Every trade union or commercial association that applies for the registration of a trade-mark may be required to furnish satisfactory evidence that its existence is not contrary to the laws of the country in which its headquarters are situated.

34. Date of application abroad deemed date of application in Canada—(1) When an application for the registration of a trade-mark has been made in or for any country of the Union other than Canada and an application is subsequently made in Canada for the registration for use in association with the same kind of wares or services of the same or substantially the same trade-mark by the same applicant or the applicant's successor in title, the date of filing of the application in or for the other country is deemed to be the date of filing of the application in Canada, and the applicant is entitled to priority in Canada accordingly notwithstanding any intervening use in Canada or making known in Canada or any intervening application or registration if

(*a*) the application in Canada, including or accompanied by a declaration setting out the date on which and the country of the Union in or for which the earliest application was filed for the registration of the same or substantially the same trade-mark for use in association with the same kind of wares or services, is filed within a period of six months after that date, which period shall not be extended;

(*b*)   the applicant or, if the applicant is a transferee, the applicant's predecessor-in-title by whom any earlier application was filed in or for any country of the Union was at the date of the application a citizen or national of or domiciled in that country or had therein a real and effective industrial or commercial establishment; and

(*c*)   the applicant furnishes, in accordance with any request under subsections (2) and (3), evidence necessary to establish fully the applicant's right to priority. [1992, c. 1, s. 133; 1993, c. 15, s. 65; 1994, c. 47, s. 199.]

(2) *Evidence requests*—The Registrar may request the evidence before the day on which the application is allowed pursuant to section 39. [1993, c. 15, s. 65(4).]

(3) *How and when evidence must be furnished*—The Registrar may specify in the request the manner in which the evidence must be furnished and the period within which it must be furnished. [1993, c. 15, s. 65(4).]

35. Disclaimer—The Registrar may require an applicant for registration of a trade-mark to disclaim the right to the exclusive use apart from the trade-mark of such portion of the trade-mark as is not independently registrable, but the disclaimer does not prejudice or affect the applicant's rights then existing or thereafter arising in the disclaimed matter, nor does the disclaimer prejudice or affect the applicant's right to registration on a subsequent application if the disclaimed matter has then become distinctive of the applicant's wares or services.

36. Abandonment—Where, in the opinion of the Registrar, an applicant is in default in the prosecution of an application filed under this Act or any Act relating to trade-marks in force prior to July 1, 1954, the Registrar may, after giving notice to the applicant of the default, treat the application as abandoned unless the default is remedied within the time specified in the notice.

37. When applications to be refused—(1) The Registrar shall refuse an application for the registration of a trade-mark if he is satisfied that

(*a*)   the application does not conform to the requirements of section 30,

(*b*)   the trade-mark is not registrable, or

(*c*) the applicant is not the person entitled to registration of the trade-mark because it is confusing with another trade-mark for the registration of which an application is pending,

and where the Registrar is not so satisfied, he shall cause the application to be advertised in the manner prescribed.

(2) *Notice to applicant*—The Registrar shall not refuse any application without first notifying the applicant of his objections thereto and his reasons for those objections, and giving the applicant adequate opportunity to answer those objections.

(3) *Doubtful cases*—Where the Registrar, by reason of a registered trade-mark, is in doubt whether the trade-mark claimed in the application is registrable, he shall, by registered letter, notify the owner of the registered trade-mark of the advertisement of the application.

38. Statement of opposition—(1) Within two months after the advertisement of an application for the registration of a trade-mark, any person may, on payment of the prescribed fee, file a statement of opposition with the Registrar. [1992, c. 1, s. 134.]

(2) *Grounds*—A statement of opposition may be based on any of the following grounds:

(*a*) that the application does not conform to the requirements of section 30;

(*b*) that the trade-mark is not registrable;

(*c*) that the applicant is not the person entitled to registration of the trade-mark; or

(*d*) that the trade-mark is not distinctive.

(3) *Content*—A statement of opposition shall set out

(*a*) the grounds of opposition in sufficient detail to enable the applicant to reply thereto; and

(*b*) the address of the opponent's principal office or place of business in Canada, if any, and if the opponent has no office or place of business in Canada, the address of his principal office or place of business abroad and the name and address in Canada of a person or firm on whom service of any document in respect of the opposition may be made with the same effect as if it had been served upon the opponent himself.

(4) *Frivolous opposition*—If the Registrar considers that the opposition does not raise a substantial issue for decision, he shall reject it and shall give notice of his decision to the opponent.

(5) *Substantial issue*—If the Registrar considers that the opposition raises a substantial issue for decision, he shall forward a copy of the statement of opposition to the applicant.

(6) *Counter statement*—The applicant shall file a counter statement with the Registrar and serve a copy on the opponent in the prescribed manner and within the prescribed time after a copy of the statement of opposition has been served on the applicant. [1993, c. 15, s. 66(2).]

(7) *Evidence and hearing*—Both the opponent and the applicant shall be given an opportunity, in the prescribed manner, to submit evidence and to make representations to the Registrar unless

    (*a*)   the opposition is withdrawn or deemed under subsection (7.1) to have been withdrawn; or

    (*b*)   the application is abandoned or deemed under subsection (7.2) to have been abandoned. [1993, c. 15, s. 66(2).]

(7.1) *Withdrawal of opposition*—The opposition shall be deemed to have been withdrawn if, in the prescribed circumstances, the opponent does not submit either evidence under subsection (7) or a statement that the opponent does not wish to submit evidence. [1993, c. 15, s. 66(2).]

(7.2) *Abandonment of application*—The application shall be deemed to have been abandoned if the applicant does not file and serve a counter statement within the time referred to in subsection (6) or if, in the prescribed circumstances, the applicant does not submit either evidence under subsection (7) or a statement that the applicant does not wish to submit evidence. [1993, c. 15, s. 66(2).]

(8) *Decision*—After considering the evidence and representations of the opponent and the applicant, the Registrar shall refuse the application or reject the opposition and notify the parties of the decision and the reasons for the decision. [1993, c. 15, s. 66(2).]

39. When application to be allowed—(1) When an application for the registration of a trade-mark either has not been opposed and the time for the filing of a statement of opposition has expired or it has been opposed and the opposition has been decided in favour of the applicant, the Registrar shall allow the application or, if an appeal is taken, shall act in accordance with the final judgment given in the appeal.

(2) *No extension of time*—Subject to subsection (3), the Registrar shall not extend the time for filing a statement of opposition with respect to any application that has been allowed.

(3) *Exception*—Where the Registrar has allowed an application without considering a previously filed request for an extension of time to file a statement of opposition, the Registrar may withdraw the application from allowance at any time before issuing a certificate of registration and, in accordance with section 47, extend the time for filing a statement of opposition. [1993, c. 15, s. 67.]

REGISTRATION OF TRADE-MARKS

40. Registration of Trade-marks—(1) When an application for registration of a trade-mark, other than a proposed trade-mark, is allowed, the Registrar shall register the trade-mark and issue a certificate of its registration. [1993, c. 15, s. 68; 1993, c. 44, ss. 231(1), 236(1)(i).]

(2) *Proposed trade-mark*—When an application for registration of a proposed trade-mark is allowed, the Registrar shall give notice to the applicant accordingly and shall register the trade-mark and issue a certificate of registration on receipt of a declaration that the use of the trade-mark in Canada, in association with the wares or services specified in the application, has been commenced by

(*a*)   the applicant;

(*b*)   the applicant's successor in title; or

(*c*)   an entity that is licensed by or with the authority of the applicant to use the trade-mark, if the applicant has direct or indirect control of the character or quality of the wares or services. [1993, c. 15, s. 68; 1993, c. 44, ss. 231(1), 236(1)(i).]

(3) *Abandonment of application*—An application for registration of a proposed trade-mark shall be deemed to be abandoned if the Registrar has not received the declaration referred to in subsection (2) before the later of

(*a*)   six months after the notice by the Registrar referred to in subsection (2), and

(*b*)   three years after the date of filing of the application in Canada. [1993, c. 44, s. 231(2).]

(4) *Form and effect*—Registration of a trade-mark shall be made in the name of the applicant therefor or his transferee, and the day on which

registration is made shall be entered on the register, and the registration takes effect on that day. [1993, c. 15, s. 68.]

(5) *Section 34 does not apply*—For the purposes of subsection (3), section 34 does not apply in determining when an application for registration is filed. [1993, c. 44, s. 231(3).]

AMENDMENT OF THE REGISTER

41. Amendments to register—(1) The Registrar may, on application by the registered owner of a trade-mark made in the prescribed manner, make any of the following amendments to the register:

(*a*) correct any error or enter any change in the name, address or description of the registered owner or of his representative for service in Canada;

(*b*) cancel the registration of the trade-mark;

(*c*) amend the statement of the wares or services in respect of which the trade-mark is registered;

(*d*) amend the particulars of the defined standard that the use of a certification mark is intended to indicate; or

(*e*) enter a disclaimer that does not in any way extend the rights given by the existing registration of the trade-mark.

(2) *Conditions*—An application to extend the statement of wares or services in respect of which a trade-mark is registered has the effect of an application for registration of the trade-mark in respect of the wares or services specified in the application for amendment.

42. Representative for service—(1) The registered owner of a trade-mark who has no office or place of business in Canada shall name another representative for service in place of the latest recorded representative or supply a new and correct address of the latest recorded representative on notice from the Registrar that the latest recorded representative has died or that a letter addressed to him at the latest recorded address and sent by ordinary mail has been returned undelivered.

(2) *Change of address*—When, after the dispatch of the notice referred to in subsection (1) by the Registrar, no new nomination is made or no new and correct address is supplied by the registered owner within three months, the Registrar or the Federal Court may dispose of any proceedings under this Act without requiring service on the registered owner of any process therein.

43. Additional representations—The registered owner of any trade-mark shall furnish such additional representations thereof as the Registrar may by notice demand and, if he fails to comply with that notice, the Registrar may by a further notice, fix a reasonable time after which, if the representations are not furnished, he may expunge the registration of the trade-mark.

44. Notice for information—(1) The Registrar may at any time, and shall at the request of any person who pays the prescribed fee, by notice in writing require the registered owner of any trade-mark that was on the register on July 1, 1954 to furnish him within three months from the date of the notice with the information that would be required on an application for the registration of the trade-mark made at the date of the notice.

(2) *Amendments to register*—The Registrar may amend the registration of the trade-mark in accordance with the information furnished to him under subsection (1).

(3) *Failure to give information*—Where the information required by subsection (1) is not furnished, the Registrar shall by a further notice fix a reasonable time after which, if the information is not furnished, he may expunge the registration of the trade-mark.

45. Registrar may request evidence of user—(1) The Registrar may at any time and, at the written request made after three years from the date of the registration of a trade-mark by any person who pays the prescribed fee shall, unless the Registrar sees good reason to the contrary, give notice to the registered owner of the trade-mark requiring the registered owner to furnish within three months an affidavit or a statutory declaration showing, with respect to each of the wares or services specified in the registration, whether the trade-mark was in use in Canada at any time during the three year period immediately preceding the date of the notice and, if not, the date when it was last so in use and the reason for the absence of such use since that date. [1993, c. 44, s. 232(1); 1994, c. 47, s. 200(1).]

(2) *Form of evidence*—The Registrar shall not receive any evidence other than the affidavit or statutory declaration, but may hear representations made by or on behalf of the registered owner of the trade-mark or by or on behalf of the person at whose request the notice was given.

(3) *Effect of non-use*—Where, by reason of the evidence furnished to the Registrar or the failure to furnish any evidence, it appears to the Registrar that a trade-mark, either with respect to all of the wares or services specified in the registration or with respect to any of those wares or services, was not used in Canada at any time during the three year period immediately preceding the date of the notice and that the absence of use has not been

due to special circumstances that excuse the absence of use, the registration of the trade-mark is liable to be expunged or amended accordingly. [1993, c. 44, s. 232(2); 1994, c. 47, s. 200(2).]

(4) *Notice to owner*—When the Registrar reaches a decision whether or not the registration of a trade-mark ought to be expunged or amended, he shall give notice of his decision with the reasons therefor to the registered owner of the trade-mark and to the person at whose request the notice referred to in subsection (1) was given.

(5) *Action by Registrar*—The Registrar shall act in accordance with his decision if no appeal therefrom is taken within the time limited by this Act or, if an appeal is taken, shall act in accordance with the final judgment given in the appeal.

RENEWAL OF REGISTRATIONS

46. Renewal—(1) The registration of a trade-mark that is on the register by virtue of this Act is subject to renewal within a period of fifteen years from the day of the registration or last renewal.

(2) *Notice to renew*—If the registration of a trade-mark has been on the register without renewal for the period specified in subsection (1) the Registrar shall send a notice to the registered owner and to the registered owner's representative for service, if any, stating that if within six months after the date of the notice the prescribed renewal fee is not paid, the registration will be expunged. [1992, c. 1, s. 135(1).]

(3) *Failure to renew*—If within the period of six months specified in the notice, which period shall not be extended, the prescribed renewal fee is not paid, the Registrar shall expunge the registration. [1992, c. 1, s. 35(1).]

(4) *Effective date of renewal*—When the prescribed fee for a renewal of any trade-mark registration under this section is paid within the time limited for the payment thereof, the renewal takes effect as of the day next following the expiration of the period specified in subsection (1).

Transitional Provision

Where a notice was sent under subsection 46(2) of the said Act before the coming into force of subsection (1), the renewal of the registration of the trade-mark shall be dealt with and disposed of as if subsection (1) had not come into force. [1992, c. 1, s. 135(2).]

EXTENSIONS OF TIME

47. Extensions of Time—(1) If, in any case, the Registrar is satisfied that the circumstances justify an extension of the time fixed by this Act or prescribed by the regulations for the doing of any act, he may, except as in this Act otherwise provided, extend the time after such notice to other persons and on such terms as he may direct.

(2) *Conditions*—An extension applied for after the expiration of the time fixed for the doing of an act or the time extended by the Registrar under subsection (1) shall not be granted unless the prescribed fee is paid and the Registrar is satisfied that the failure to do the act or apply for the extension within that time or the extended time was not reasonably avoidable.

TRANSFER

48. Trade-mark transferable—(1) A trade-mark, whether registered or unregistered, is transferable, and deemed always to have been transferable, either in connection with or separately from the goodwill of the business and in respect of either all or some of the wares or services in association with which it has been used.

(2) *Where two or more persons interested*—Nothing in subsection (1) prevents a trade-mark from being held not to be distinctive if as a result of a transfer thereof there subsisted rights in two or more persons to the use of confusing trade-marks and the rights were exercised by those persons.

(3) *Registration of transfer*—The Registrar shall register the transfer of any registered trade-mark on being furnished with evidence satisfactory to him of the transfer and the information that would be required by paragraph 30(*g*) in an application by the transferee to register the trade-mark.

CHANGE OF PURPOSE IN USE OF MARK

49. Change of purpose—If a mark is used by a person as a trade-mark for any of the purposes or in any of the manners mentioned in the definition "certification mark" or "trade-mark" in section 2, it shall not be held invalid merely on the ground that the person or a predecessor in title uses it or has used it for any other of those purposes or in any other of those manners.

LICENCES

[1993, c. 15, s. 69]

50. Licence to use trade-mark—(1) For the purposes of this Act, if an entity is licensed by or with the authority of the owner of a trade-mark to use the trade-mark in a country and the owner has, under the licence, direct or indirect control of the character or quality of the wares or services, then the use, advertisement or display of the trade-mark in that country as or in a trade-mark, trade-name or otherwise by that entity has, and is deemed always to have had, the same effect as such a use, advertisement or display of the trade-mark in that country by the owner. [1993, c. 15, s. 69; 1993, c. 44, ss. 233, 236(1)(j).]

(2) *Idem*—For the purposes of this Act, to the extent that public notice is given of the fact that the use of a trade-mark is a licensed use and of the identity of the owner, it shall be presumed, unless the contrary is proven, that the use is licensed by the owner of the trade-mark and the character or quality of the wares or services is under the control of the owner. [1993, c. 15, s. 69; 1993, c. 44, ss. 233, 236(1)(j).]

(3) *Owner may be required to take proceedings*—Subject to any agreement subsisting between an owner of a trade-mark and a licensee of the trade-mark, the licensee may call on the owner to take proceedings for infringement thereof, and, if the owner refuses or neglects to do so within two months after being so called on, the licensee may institute proceedings for infringement in the licensee's own name as if the licensee were the owner, making the owner a defendant. [1993, c. 15, s. 69; 1993, c. 44, ss. 233, 236(1)(j).]

51. Use of trade-mark by related companies—(1) Where a company and the owner of a trade-mark that is used in Canada by that owner in association with a pharmaceutical preparation are related companies, the use by the company of the trade-mark, or a trade-mark confusing therewith, in association with a pharmaceutical preparation that at the time of that use or at any time thereafter,

> (*a*) is acquired by a person directly or indirectly from the company, and

> (*b*) is sold, distributed or advertised for sale in Canada in a package bearing the name of the company and the name of that person as the distributor thereof,

has the same effect, for all purposes of this Act, as a use of the trade-mark or the confusing trade-mark, as the case may be, by that owner.

(2) *Where difference in composition*—Subsection (1) does not apply to any use of a trade-mark or a confusing trade-mark by a company referred to in that subsection in association with a pharmaceutical preparation after such time, if any, as that pharmaceutical preparation is declared by the Minister of Health, by notice published in the *Canada Gazette*, to be sufficiently different in its composition from the pharmaceutical preparation in association with which the trade-mark is used in Canada by the owner referred to in subsection (1) as to be likely to result in a hazard to health. [1996, c. 8, s. 32.]

(3) *Definition of "Pharmaceutical preparation"*—In this section, "pharmaceutical preparation" includes

(*a*) any substance or mixture of substances manufactured, sold or represented for use in

(i) the diagnosis, treatment, mitigation or prevention of a disease, disorder or abnormal physical state, or the symptoms thereof, in humans or animals, or

(ii) restoring, correcting or modifying organic functions in humans or animals, and

(*b*) any substance to be used in the preparation or production of any substance or mixture of substances described in paragraph (*a*),

but does not include any such substance or mixture of substances that is the same or substantially the same as a substance or mixture of substances that is a proprietary medicine within the meaning from time to time assigned to that expression by regulations made pursuant to the *Food and Drugs Act*.*

---

* R.S.C. 1985, c. F-27

LEGAL PROCEEDINGS

52. Definitions—In sections 53 to 53.3,

"court" means the Federal Court or the superior court of a province;

"duties" has the same meaning as in the *Customs Act*;*

"Minister" means the Minister of Public Safety and Emergency Preparedness;

"release" has the same meaning as in the *Customs Act*.* [1993, c. 44, s. 234; 2005, c. 38, ss. 142(j), 145(2)(j).]

---

* *Customs Act*, R.S.C. 1985, c. 1 (2nd Supp.)

2. *Definitions*—(1)

. . .

"duties" means any duties or taxes levied or imposed on imported goods under the *Customs Tariff*, the *Excise Act, 2001*, the *Excise Tax Act*, the *Special Import Measures Act* or any other Act of Parliament, but, for the purposes of subsection 3(1), paragraphs 59(3)(*b*) and 65(1)(*b*), sections 69 and 73 and subsections 74(1), 75(2) and 76(1), does not include taxes imposed under Part IX of the *Excise Tax Act*; [1995, c. 41, s. 1; 1997, c. 36, s. 147(1); 2002, c. 22, s. 328(2).]

. . .

"release" means

(a) **in respect of goods, to authorize the removal of the goods from a customs office, sufferance warehouse, bonded warehouse or duty free shop for use in Canada, and**

(b) **in respect of goods to which paragraph 32(2)(b) applies, to receive the goods at the place of business of the importer, owner or consignee;** [2001, c. 25, s. 1.]

---

53. Proceedings for interim custody—(1) Where a court is satisfied, on application of any interested person, that any registered trade-mark or any trade-name has been applied to any wares that have been imported into Canada or are about to be distributed in Canada in such a manner that the distribution of the wares would be contrary to this Act, or that any indication of a place of origin has been unlawfully applied to any wares, the court may make an order for the interim custody of the wares, pending a final determination of the legality of their importation or distribution in an action commenced within such time as is prescribed by the order.

(2) *Security*—Before making an order under subsection (1), the court may require the applicant to furnish security, in an amount fixed by the court, to answer any damages that may by reason of the order be sustained by the owner, importer or consignee of the wares and for any amount that may become chargeable against the wares while they remain in custody under the order.

(3) *Lien for charges*—Where, by the judgment in any action under this section finally determining the legality of the importation or distribution of the wares, their importation or distribution is forbidden, either absolutely or on condition, any lien for charges against them that arose prior to the date of an order made under this section has effect only so far as may be consistent with the due execution of the judgment.

(4) *Prohibition of imports*—Where in any action under this section the court finds that the importation is or the distribution would be contrary to this Act, it may make an order prohibiting the future importation of wares to which the trade-mark, trade-name or indication of origin has been applied.

(5) *How application made*—An application referred to in subsection (1) may be made in an action or otherwise, and either on notice or *ex parte*.

(6) *Limitation*—No proceedings may be taken under subsection (1) for the interim custody of wares by the Minister if proceedings for the detention of the wares by the Minister may be taken under section 53.1. [1993, c. 44, s. 234.]

53.1. Proceedings for detention by minister—(1) Where a court is satisfied, on application by the owner of a registered trade-mark, that any wares to which the trade-mark has been applied are about to be imported into Canada or have been imported into Canada but have not yet been released, and that the distribution of the wares in Canada would be contrary to this Act, the court may make an order

   (*a*) directing the Minister to take reasonable measures, on the basis of information reasonably required by the Minister and provided by the applicant, to detain the wares;

   (*b*) directing the Minister to notify the applicant and the owner or importer of the wares, forthwith after detaining them, of the detention and the reasons therefor; and

   (*c*) providing for such other matters as the court considers appropriate.

(2) *How application made*—An application referred to in subsection (1) may be made in an action or otherwise, and either notice or ex parte, except that it must always be made on notice to the Minister.

(3) *Court may require security*—Before making an order under subsection (1), the court may require the applicant to furnish security, in an amount fixed by the court,

    (*a*)   to cover duties, storage and handling charges, and any other amount that may become chargeable against the wares; and

    (*b*)   to answer any damages that may by reason of the order be sustained by the owner, importer or consignee of the wares.

(4) *Application for directions*—The Minister may apply to the court for directions in implementing an order made under subsection (1).

(5) *Minister may allow inspection*—The Minister may give the applicant or the importer of the detained wares an opportunity to inspect them for the purpose of substantiating or refuting, as the case may be, the applicant's claim.

(6) *Where applicant fails to commence an action*—Unless an order made under subsection (1) provides otherwise, the Minister shall, subject to the *Customs Act** and to any other Act of Parliament that prohibits, controls or regulates the importation or exportation of goods, release the wares without further notice to the applicant if, two weeks after the applicant has been notified under paragraph (1)(*b*), the Minister has not been notified that an action has been commenced for a final determination by the court of the legality of the importation or distribution of the wares.

---

* R.S.C. 1985, c. 1 (2nd Supp.)

---

(7) *Where court finds in plaintiff's favour*—Where, in an action commenced under this section, the court finds that the importation is or the distribution would be contrary to this Act, the court may make any order that it considers appropriate in the circumstances, including an order that the wares be destroyed or exported, or that they be delivered up to the plaintiff as the plaintiff's property absolutely. [1993, c. 44, s. 234.]

53.2. Power of Court to grant relief—Where a court is satisfied, on application of any interested person, that any act has been done contrary to this Act, the court may make any order that it considers appropriate in the circumstances, including an order providing for relief by way of injunction and the recovery of damages or profits and for the destruction, exportation or other disposition of any offending wares, packages, labels and advertising material and of any dies used in connection therewith. [1993, c. 44, s. 234.]

53.3. Re-Exportation of Wares—Where in any proceeding under section 53.1 or 53.2 the court finds

(*a*) that wares bearing a registered trade-mark have been imported into Canada in such manner that the distribution of the wares in Canada would be contrary to this Act, and

(*b*) that the registered trade-mark has, without the consent of the owner, been applied to those wares with the intent of counterfeiting or imitating the trade-mark, or of deceiving the public and inducing them to believe that the wares were made with the consent of the owner,

the court may not, other than in exceptional circumstances, make an order under that section requiring or permitting the wares to be exported in an unaltered state. [1993, c. 44, s. 234.]

54. Evidence—(1) Evidence of any document in the official custody of the Registrar or of any extract therefrom may be given by the production of a copy thereof purporting to be certified to be true by the Registrar.

(2) *Idem*—A copy of any entry in the register purporting to be certified to be true by the Registrar is evidence of the facts set out therein.

(3) *Idem*—A copy of the record of the registration of a trade-mark purporting to be certified to be true by the Registrar is evidence of the facts set out therein and that the person named therein as owner is the registered owner of the trade-mark for the purposes and within the territorial area therein defined.

(4) *Idem*—A copy of any entry made or documents filed under the authority of any Act in force before July 1, 1954 relating to trade-marks, certified under the authority of that Act, is admissible in evidence and has the same probative force as a copy certified by the Registrar under this Act as provided in this section.

55. Jurisdiction of Federal Court—The Federal Court has jurisdiction to entertain any action or proceeding for the enforcement of any of the provisions of this Act or of any right or remedy conferred or defined thereby.

56. Appeal—(1) An appeal lies to the Federal Court from any decision of the Registrar under this Act within two months from the date on which notice of the decision was dispatched by the Registrar or within such further time as the Court may allow, either before or after the expiration of the two months.

(2) *Procedure*—An appeal under subsection (1) shall be made by way of notice of appeal filed with the Registrar and in the Federal Court.

(3) *Notice to owner*—The appellant shall, within the time limited or allowed by subsection (1), send a copy of the notice by registered mail to the registered owner of any trade-mark that has been referred to by the Registrar in the decision complained of and to every other person who was entitled to notice of the decision.

(4) *Public notice*—The Federal Court may direct that public notice of the hearing of an appeal under subsection (1) and of the matters at issue therein be given in such manner as it deems proper.

(5) *Additional evidence*—On an appeal under subsection (1), evidence in addition to that adduced before the Registrar may be adduced and the Federal Court may exercise any discretion vested in the Registrar.

57. Exclusive jurisdiction of Federal Court—(1) The Federal Court has exclusive original jurisdiction, on the application of the Registrar or of any person interested, to order that any entry in the register be struck out or amended on the ground that at the date of the application the entry as it appears on the register does not accurately express or define the existing rights of the person appearing to be the registered owner of the mark.

(2) *Restriction*—No person is entitled to institute under this section any proceeding calling into question any decision given by the Registrar of which that person had express notice and from which he had a right to appeal.

58. How proceedings instituted—An application under section 57 shall be made either by the filing of an originating notice of motion, by counter-claim in an action for the infringement of the trade-mark, or by statement of claim in an action claiming additional relief under this Act.

59. Notice to set out grounds—(1) Where an appeal is taken under section 56 by the filing of a notice of appeal, or an application is made under section 57 by the filing of an originating notice of motion, the notice shall set out full particulars of the grounds on which relief is sought.

(2) *Reply*—Any person on whom a copy of the notice described in subsection (1) has been served and who intends to contest the appeal or

application, as the case may be, shall file and serve within the prescribed time or such further time as the court may allow a reply setting out full particulars of the grounds on which he relies.

(3) *Hearing*—The proceedings of an appeal or application shall be heard and determined summarily on evidence adduced by affidavit unless the court otherwise directs, in which event it may order that any procedure permitted by its rules and practice be made available to the parties, including the introduction of oral evidence generally or in respect of one or more issues specified in the order.

60. Registrar to transmit documents—(1) Subject to subsection (2), when any appeal or application has been made to the Federal Court under any of the provisions of this Act, the Registrar shall, at the request of any of the parties to the proceedings and on the payment of the prescribed fee, transmit to the Court all documents on file in the Registrar's office relating to the matters in question in those proceedings, or copies of those documents certified by the Registrar.

(2) *Register of registered users*—The transmission of documents on which entries in the register required to be kept under paragraph 26(1)(*b*) are based is subject to the provisions of subsection 50(6) of the *Trademarks Act*, as it read immediately before section 69 of the *Intellectual Property Law Improvement Act** came into force. [1993, c. 44, ss. 235, 236(1)(j), 238(4).]

---

* S.C. 1993, c. 15

---

61. Judgments to be Filed—An officer of the Registry of the Federal Court shall file with the Registrar a certified copy of every judgment or order made by the Federal Court, the Federal Court of Appeal or by the Supreme Court of Canada relating to any trade-mark on the register. [2002, c. 8, s. 177.]

GENERAL

62. Administration—This Act shall be administered by the Minister of Industry. [1995, c. 1, s. 62(1)(x).]

63. Registrar—(1) There shall be a Registrar of Trade-marks, appointed by the Governor in Council, to hold office during pleasure, who shall be paid such annual salary as the Governor in Council determines and shall be responsible to the Deputy Minister of Industry. [1995, c.1, s. 62.]

(2) *Acting registrar*—When the Registrar is absent or unable to act or when the office of Registrar is vacant, his powers shall be exercised and his duties and functions performed in the capacity of acting registrar by such other officer as may be designated by the Minister of Industry. [1995, c. 1, s. 62(1)(x).]

(3) *Assistants*—The Registrar may, after consultation with the Minister, delegate to any person he deems qualified any of his powers, duties and functions under this Act, except the power to delegate under this subsection.

(4) *Appeal*—Any decision under this Act of a person authorized to make the decision pursuant to subsection (3) may be appealed in the like manner and subject to the like conditions as a decision of the Registrar under this Act.

64. Publication of registrations—The Registrar shall cause to be published periodically particulars of the registrations made and extended from time to time under this Act, and shall in such publication give particulars of any rulings made by him that are intended to serve as precedents for the determination of similar questions thereafter arising.

65. Regulations—The Governor in Council may make regulations for carrying into effect the purposes and provisions of this Act and, in particular, may make regulations with respect to the following matters:

(*a*)   the form of the register and of the indexes to be maintained pursuant to this Act, and of the entries to be made therein;

(*b*)   the form of applications to the Registrar;

(*c*)   the registration of transfers, licences, disclaimers, judgments or other documents relating to any trade-mark;

(*c*.1)   the maintenance of the list of trade-mark agents and the entry and removal of the names of persons and firms on the list, including the qualifications that must be met and the conditions that must be fulfilled to have a name entered on the list and to maintain the name on the list; [1993, c. 15, s. 70.]

(*d*)   the form and contents of certificates of registration;

(*d*.1)   the procedure by and form in which an application may be made to the Minister, as defined in section 11.11, requesting the Minister to publish a statement referred to in subsection 11.12(2); and [1994, c. 47, s. 201.]

(*e*) the payment of fees to the Registrar and the amount thereof.

66. Time Limit Deemed Extended—(1) Where any time limit or period of limitation specified under or pursuant to this Act expires on a day when the Office of the Registrar of Trade-marks is closed for business, the time limit or period of limitation shall be deemed to be extended to the next day when the Office is open for business.

(2) *When Trade-marks Office closed for business*—The Office of the Registrar of Trade-marks shall be closed for business on Saturdays and holidays and on such other days as the Minister by order declares that it shall be closed for business.

(3) *Publication*—Every order made by the Minister under subsection (2) shall be published in the *Trade-marks Journal* as soon as possible after the making thereof.

NEWFOUNDLAND

67. Registration of trade-mark before April 1, 1949—(1) The registration of a trade-mark under the laws of Newfoundland before April 1, 1949 has the same force and effect in the Province of Newfoundland as if Newfoundland had not become part of Canada, and all rights and privileges acquired under or by virtue of those laws may continue to be exercised or enjoyed in the Province of Newfoundland as if Newfoundland had not become part of Canada.

(2) *Applications for trade-marks pending April 1, 1949*—The laws of Newfoundland as they existed immediately before April 1, 1949 continue to apply in respect of applications for the registration of trade-marks under the laws of Newfoundland pending at that time and any trade-marks registered under those applications shall, for the purposes of this section, be deemed to have been registered under the laws of Newfoundland before April 1, 1949. [1993, c. 15, s. 71.]

68. Use of trade-mark or trade-name before April 1, 1949—For the purposes of this Act, the use or making known of a trade-mark or the use of a trade-name in Newfoundland before April 1, 1949 shall not be deemed to be a use or making known of such trade-mark or a use of such trade-name in Canada before that date. [1993, c. 15, s. 71.]

TRANSITIONAL PROVISION

69. Prior applications for registration—An application for the registration of a trade-mark filed before this section comes into force shall not be refused by reason only that subsection 50(1) deems the use, advertisement or display of the trade-mark by a licensed entity always to have had the same effect as a use, advertisement or display of the trade-mark by the owner. [1993, c. 15, s. 71.]

RELATED PROVISION OF S.C. 1992, c. 1

135.

. . .

(2) *Transitional*—Where a notice was sent under subsection 46(2) of the said Act before the coming into force of subsection (1), the renewal of the registration of the trade-mark shall be dealt with and disposed of as if subsection (1) had not come into force.

INDEX

A

Abandonment for lack of use, 28 – 29, 139
Abuses, 15 – 16
Actions
- domestic courts, for foreign infringement, in, 112 – 113
- foreign courts, in, 111 – 112
- passing-off action, 71 – 72, 138

Actual use in Canada, 68 – 70, 86 – 87
Adjective, 132
Advertisement of registration, 93
Advocacy, 148 – 149
Agent, 90, 125 – 126
Agreement on Trade-Related Aspects of Intellectual Property Rights, 110 – 111
Allowance, 94, 104, 107
Amendment
- application, of, 91 – 92
- name, of, 133
- wares and/or services, of, 133

Applicant, 79 – 80, 100
Application. *See* **Trade mark application**
Application process. *See* **Trade mark application**
Appointment of representative, 90
Assignment of license agreement, 189
Associated with the wares, 63
Authorized uses, 27 – 28

B

Bad faith, 91, 162 – 163
Basis of application
- actual use in Canada, 86 – 87
- foreign country application or registration and use abroad, 87 – 88
- making known in Canada, 87
- priority claim, 89
- proposed use in Canada, 88
- U.S. registration system, 101 – 102

Bequests, 27
Board members, 133 – 134
Brand
- *see also* Brand protection
- business asset, as, 11
- diluted brands, 178
- meaning of, 9
- proliferation, effect of, 12

Brand management, 21

Brand protection
- domain names. *See* **Domain name**
- licensing. *See* **Licensing of trade mark**
- registrability
- • confusingly similar, 120
- • descriptive or misdescriptive, 119
- • existing recognition as trade mark, 121
- • generally, 118 – 119
- • name in any language, 120
- • name or surname, 119
- • official marks, 120 – 121
- • prohibited marks, 120 – 121
- • public misconception, 122
- searches. *See* Trade mark searches
- selection of trade mark
- • compound word marks, 118
- • generally, 116
- • inherently strong marks, 117
- • inherently weak marks, 117
- • secondary meanings, 118
- • suggestive marks, 117 – 118
- trade mark monitoring
- • parallel registrations, 134
- • potential infringement, 134 – 135
- • registered trade mark, protection of, 138
- • stopping infringement, 135 – 137
- • trade mark use, ensuring, 139
- • unregistered trade mark, protection of, 137 – 138
- use of trade mark
- • amendment of name or change of name, 133
- • amendment of wares and/or services, 133
- • consistent use, 132 – 133
- • continual use, 104 – 105, 130
- • distinctive use, 132
- • education of staff and board members, 133 – 134
- • evidence of, 28, 102
- • identification of licenses, 131
- • proper marking, 130 – 131
- • use as adjective, 132
- • use with generic name, 132

Branding
- abuses, 15 – 16
- charitable and not-for-profit organizations
- • distinguishing the organization, 15 – 16
- • equity, creation of, 17 – 19